PRAISE FOR *JULIEN FÉDON*

"An intriguing, provocative, informative and well-overdue attempt to unravel the unknown about the valiant Grenadian and West Indian hero, Julien Fédon. As a storyteller, Hall unearths information about the brilliancy and gallantry of Fédon as he clarifies misinformation British administrators provided in 1795-1796 about this mulatto estate owner who sought civil rights for French speaking Grenadians. *Julien Fédon* is scrupulously researched and unbiased."

— Anne Janice Farray, writer and poet

"This work is a definitive biography of a Caribbean legend too often distorted in official histories. An incisive and illuminating account of a Caribbean revolutionary."

— Kirkus Reviews

"The theme and contents are going to add a little more to Caribbean historiography."

— Hollis U. Liverpool, Ph.D., O.R.T.T. (Calypsonian Chalkdust)

"I heard about the saga of Julien Fédon from my mother and other elders; later, I was brave enough to hike to Fédon's Camp with my classmates. We dug up a large cannon and brought it to our school on one occasion…. One of our teachers and hiking guide was the author. His first book stimulated interest in Julien Fédon and Belvedere Estate. This biography of Julien Fédon is massive, detailed and exciting."

— Denise Donaldson, A Grenada Patriot

"Herman Hall takes us deep into the world of Julien Fédon, the legendary Grenadian mulatto who, in 1795, led one of the earliest rebellions against British colonial rule in the Caribbean. Mining a rich trove of archival materials, Hall recounts the exploits of the French mulattos, African slaves, maroons, and a handful of French planters who banded together under Fédon's leadership to wrest control of Grenada for nearly 16 months before finally succumbing to an armada of British forces sent to restore order in the West Indies…Rich in detail, this work is a must read for anyone interested in history and the Caribbean's early struggles to confront the twin evils of colonialism and slavery."

— **Ray Allen,**
Professor Emeritus of
Music and American Studies,
Brooklyn College CUNY

"The writer has a particular penchant for storytelling, dogged pursuit of Grenadian history in general, and an understandable fascination with the life and deeds of Julien Fédon, in particular. His research and unbiased scholarship take us deep into the world of this Fédon….Hall has authored a definitive work of a Caribbean legend at a time when Caribbean legends have too often been suspiciously omitted from or distorted in official histories."

— **David Brizan, Life Empowerment Coach**

"Herman Hall, grew up on Belvedere Estate, St. John's, Grenada, home of the revolutionary leader and mixed-race coffee planter, Julien Fédon, who led the longest revolt against the British in the 18th century Caribbean. *Julien Fédon* is the account not just of Fédon but of hidden stories such as the naval battle during the American Revolutionary War between the British and French fleets off Grenada…The heroic story of a defeated, yet triumphant, general, who changed Grenada forever."

— **Jennifer Hosten, author and Miss World of 1974**

Also By
Herman G. Hall

Belvidere Estate – Fédon's House
Grenada
Voices from the Past

200 Years of
West Indian-American Contributions
1776-1976

A booklet

(Coming in 2024)

From Alexander Hamilton to Kamala Harris

JULIEN FÉDON

Revolutionary, Patriot and Insurrectionist
The Untold Story of a Mulatto Leader

Herman G. Hall

H.H. Digital
New York
2022

Names: Hall, Herman G., author.
Title: Julien Fédon - Revolutionary, Patriot and Insurrectionist: The Untold Story of a Mulatto Leader / Herman G. Hall.
Description: First edition, 2022. Includes bibliographical references and index.
Subjects: LCSH: Julien Fédon – Grenada - History, 18th century – Revolution - Biography. Revolutionaries – Slavery - Caribbean - West Indies and Americas.

Library of Congress Control Number: 2021907339

ISBN 978-0-9970190-4-9 (hardcover)
ISBN 978-0-9970190-5-6 (paperback)
ISBN 978-0-9970190-6-3 (ebook)

Books published by H.H. Digital, LLC are available at special discounts for bulk purchases by corporations, institutions, and other organizations. For more information, please contact H.H. Digital LLC: editor@everybodysmag.com or (718) 941-1879.

Cover illustrator: Lennox Robinson, Robinson Graphics.

Interior design and formatting: Vally Sharpe, United Writer Press.

Battlefield Sketch — Mount Saint John through Belvedere to Fédon's Camp: Herman G. Hall.

For

Telfor Bedeau
Grenada's legendary hiker…and my cousin

Father Raymund Devas (Britisher, 1887–1975)
Roman Catholic priest and historiographer

Father Bernard Kadlec (Czechoslovakia)
Roman Catholic priest and hiker

Illustration by Lennox Robinson.
The author's visualization of Julien Fédon and revolutionaries in 1795-1796. A Frenchman displaying the French flag and a maroon or self-emancipated slave protecting General Fédon.

Cover Image Derived from Photograph: Morne Qua Qua/Fédon's Camp/Morne Vauclain mountain range taken at Ferme Peschier or Madame Peschier at the bottom of 1st Camp on the Saint Andrew side, by author on June 17, 2015.

Lower Peak: 1st Camp/Camp Equality/Fédon's Military headquarters.

Highest Peak: 2nd Camp/Camp of Death/Morne Vauclain/Fédon's Camp/Morne Qua Qua (Grenada's second highest mountain peak.)

Contents

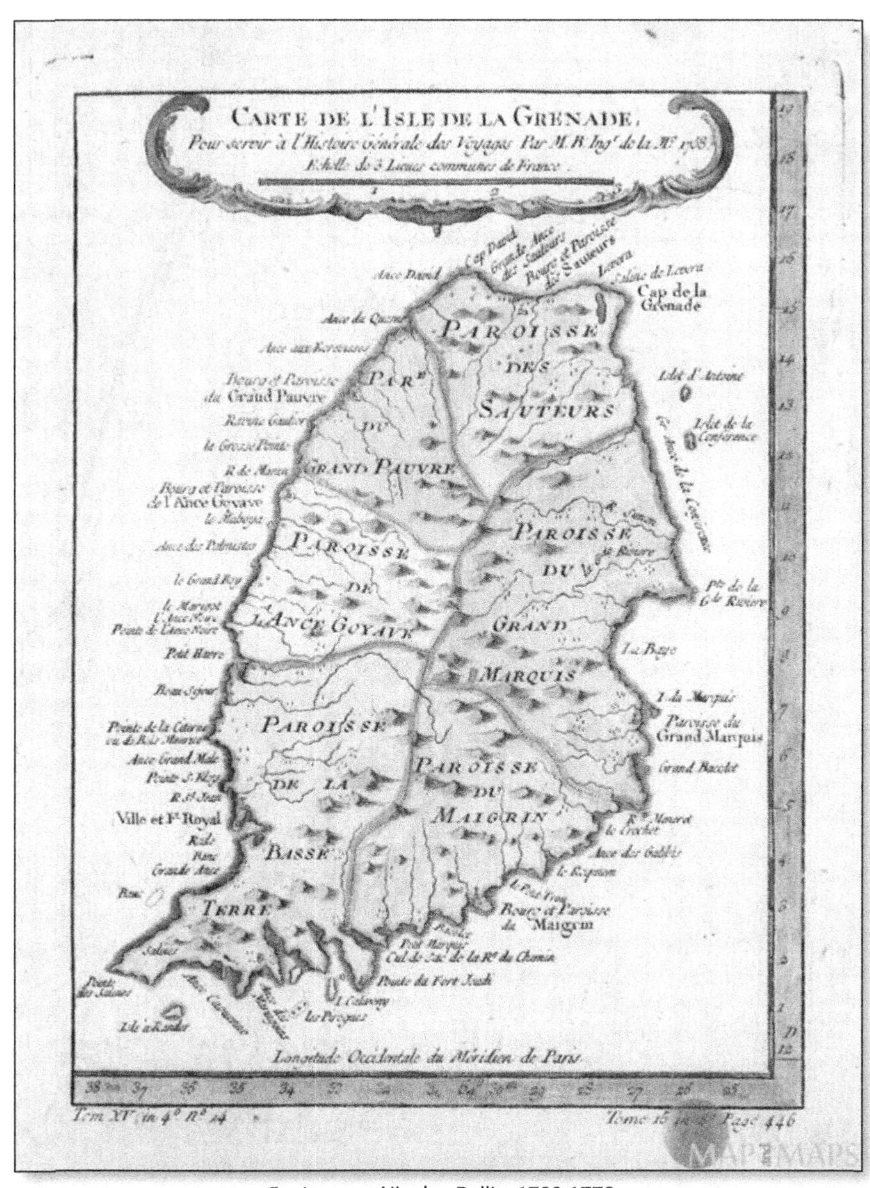

By Jacques Nicolas Bellin, 1703-1772
Courtesy Library of Congress, Geography and Map Division.

After England captured Grenada in 1762, Governor Robert Melvill commissioned Colonel Daniel Paterson, a cartographer, to survey the new English colony. Paterson accepted the 1763 French map and survey of Monsieur Jean-Baptiste Pinel, an updated version of Bellin's 1758 map. Paterson added more rivers, mountains and properties and he replaced French names of parishes and towns with English names. He released the map and survey in 1780.

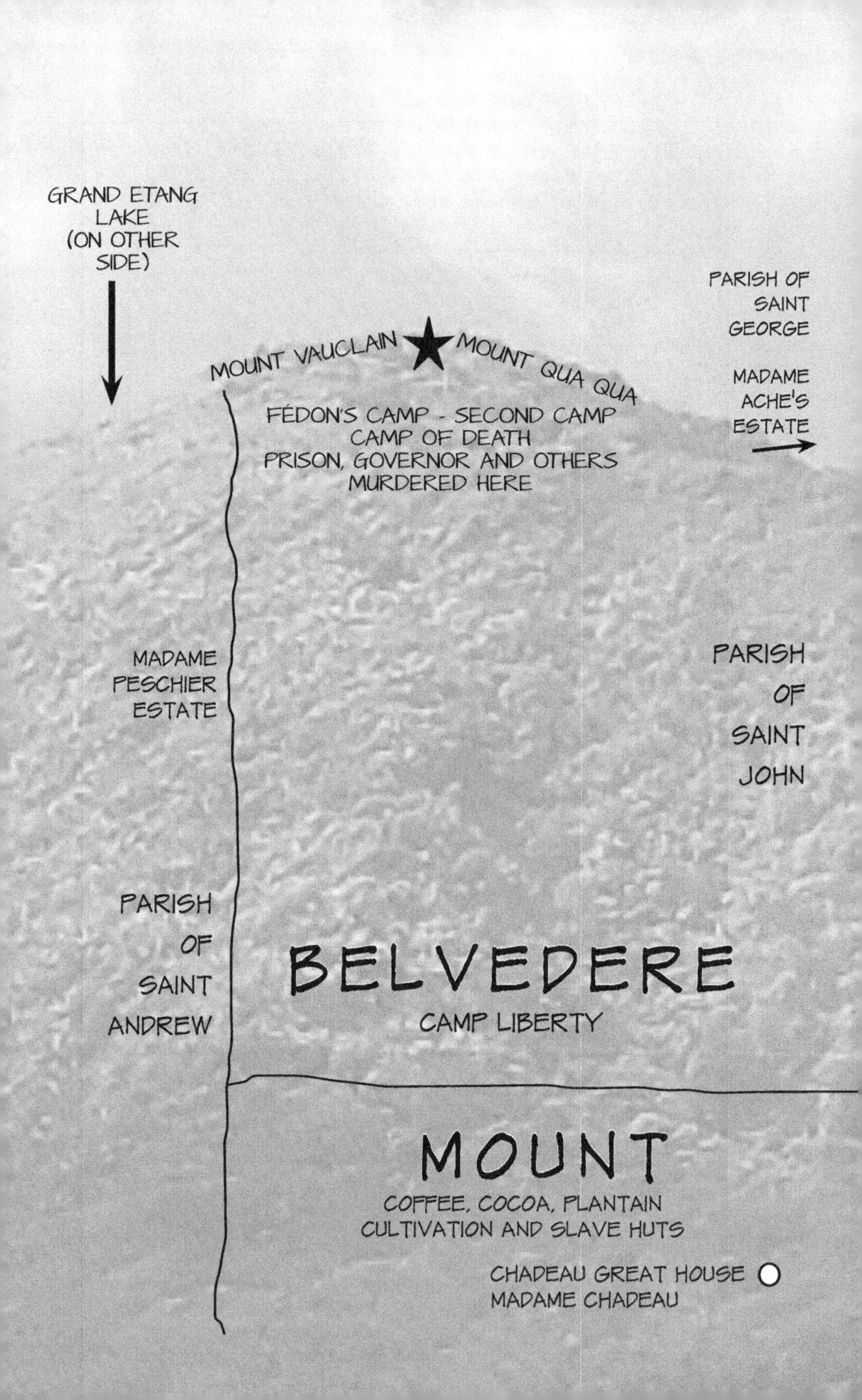

GRAND ETANG
LAKE
(ON OTHER
SIDE)

PARISH OF
SAINT
GEORGE

MADAME
ACHE'S
ESTATE

MOUNT VAUCLAIN ★ MOUNT QUA QUA
FÉDON'S CAMP - SECOND CAMP
CAMP OF DEATH
PRISON, GOVERNOR AND OTHERS
MURDERED HERE

MADAME
PESCHIER
ESTATE

PARISH
OF
SAINT
JOHN

PARISH
OF
SAINT
ANDREW

BELVEDERE
CAMP LIBERTY

MOUNT
COFFEE, COCOA, PLANTAIN
CULTIVATION AND SLAVE HUTS

CHADEAU GREAT HOUSE
MADAME CHADEAU

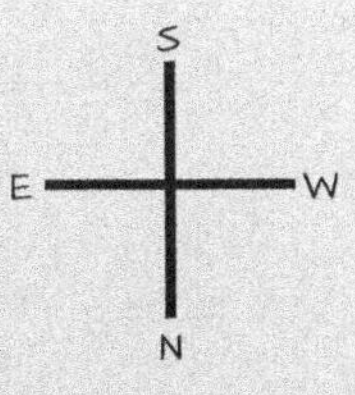

CAMP EQUALITY - FÉDON'S MILITARY HEADQUARTERS - FIRST CAMP
WHERE GOVERNOR HOME AND OTHER PRISONERS WERE HELD,
MARCH 17-22
FÉDON CANNONS MOUNTED ON STEEP RIDGES
OVERLOOKING BELVEDERE ESTATE

+JEAN-PIERRE FÉDON
KILLED IN THIS AREA

COFFEE, COCOA, PLANTAIN
CULTIVATION AND SLAVE HUTS

PARISH
OF
SAINT
JOHN

O BOUCAN WHERE GOVERNOR HOME AND OTHER
PRISONERS WERE HELD, MARCH 3-17

O FÉDON'S
HOUSE

ESTATE
CAMP LIBERTY

SAINT JOHN
COFFEE, COCOA, PLANTAIN
CULTIVATION AND SLAVE HUTS

LACROIFADE ESTATE
JEAN FÉDON HOUSE

O MORNE JALOUX
ESTATE

O CLOZIER

INTRODUCTION

During the 1980s, when asked to write "a life of Marie Antoinette of France," biographer Joan Haslip said she refused because, over the centuries, many books had been written about the reviled Queen Marie Antoinette (1755–1793). "But I was told," Haslip continued, "that in every generation there are certain characters who require reassessment." Haslip did relent; she reassessed the fabled queen in her best seller, *Marie Antoinette*, published in 1987.[1]

In 1990, when graciously autographing my copy of his classic work, *Free Coloreds in the Slave Societies of St. Kitts and Grenada, 1763–1833*, Professor Edward L. Cox opined, "Hoping that this could be a small contribution in the seemingly endless task of uncovering and reinterpreting the history and culture of our nation."[2]

With the unearthing of new information about the Fédon family, now is an opportune time to reassess and reinterpret Julien Fédon, an historic Grenadian revolutionary leader, and attempt to present his biography.

When referring to the decision by free French-speaking mulattos, the self-emancipated slaves (maroons) and French whites to rise violently against the injustice of British rule in 1795, I call it a "rebellion" or "Fédon's Rebellion." However, I refer to the sustained sixteen-month attack led by Julien Fédon between 1795 and 1796 as "Fédon's Revolution." This revolution led to the end of property ownership by the large, French-speaking mixed-race population, and Grenada's society changed forever. Fédon's Rebellion led to Fédon's Revolution.

The French, the first European nation to settle in Grenada, called the area that Julien Fédon would eventually make famous "Belvedere." The British later called it "Belvidere." In legal documents throughout the centuries, it was spelled both Belvedere and Belvidere. As a youngster living on the estate, I remember the laborers of the 1950s fondly teasing each other, especially when "rum talking," about the correct spelling of the estate's name. Although most laborers could not read and write, some said Belvidere (the British way) and others argued Belvedere (like the French). I follow the custom of Frederick Adams, my adopted father and uncle-in-law, who was born and lived on the estate, by spelling it either way. In this book, I've chosen to spell it "Belvedere" in contrast to my 2016 book, *Belvidere Estate – Fédon's House: Voices from the Past*, published in 2016.[3]

Lofty speeches have been given, papers presented, articles published, and scholars—as recently as 2021—earned their doctorates based on Fédon's Revolution or Fédon's Rebellion. The internet also has a profusion of writings, both scholarly and nonacademic, on the subject. Yet nobody, to my knowledge, has presented a book exclusively on Julien Fédon, the individual who led the rebellion and caused the revolution.

In *Belvidere Estate – Fédon's House: Voices from the Past*, I presented Julien Fédon mainly through oral stories passed down from generation to generation by laborers on Belvedere Estate and told to me while growing up there. Belvedere was the estate that Julien Fédon and his wife owned and which became the headquarters of the revolution.

I am now challenging myself to present a thorough biography of Julien Fédon. Though such a task is both challenging and thought-provoking, lacunas in Grenada's historiography should be plugged.

The difficulties facing a biographer of Julien Fédon are numerous. Other than the fact that he led a rebellion against the British, little more is known about Julien Fédon. As a result, scholars focus on the revolt that he led rather than on Fédon, the individual. Scholars should be excused, though, for not focusing on the man. The task is too tough when so little is known or has been recorded. As technology improves, I am optimistic that a future writer will locate documents that clarify unanswered questions and continuing speculation about Fédon.

I am not part of the academic world and am not a professional historian. I did not seek grants to research this book or fund the cost of travel and accommodation. History is my hobby. Therefore, I extend my gratitude to researchers who came before me and, while researching Fédon's Revolution for advanced scholastic degrees, visited the primary sources—including archives in England, Scotland, France, the United States, and elsewhere to retrieve correspondence between planters and officials in Grenada and their family and friends and with officials in Britain, France, and the United States.

One of my primary sources was the Grenada Registrar's Office. Seeing, for the first time 18th century documents that mention Belvedere Plantation and Julien and Marie Rose Fédon's names written on deeds made me feel like a kid opening gifts on Christmas morning.

As a youth living on Belvedere Estate, I always felt that additional information about Julien Fédon must be hidden away somewhere in Grenada—perhaps in the governor's and/or administrator's homes. Father Raymund Devas, the aging historian to whom this book is dedicated, became visibly angry whenever I, a rather undisciplined teenager at the time, argued that, in addition to the information in Father Devas's books, there must be more about Fédon buried somewhere in Grenada.

In 1966, when Sir Ian Turbott, the colonial governor of Grenada, twice visited the American-established St. John's Christian Secondary School to see my play, *A Day in West Indian History*—which was based on Fédon's Revolution—I begged him for a visit to Government House, as I was convinced that important documents were there. He acerbically turned me down. Nevertheless, I do pay tribute to New Zealand-born Sir Turbott, who sincerely appreciated my play. His visits actually inspired me to take even more interest in Grenada's history.

To Father Raymund Devas (1887-1975), the Roman Catholic priest who visited Belvedere, I owe enormous thanks. I can still recall a blurry image of his visits when I was just a toddler. And later, when I became of age and the old priest stopped by Belvedere, we would chat and argue about Fédon and identify the mountain peaks and valleys where fierce fighting between the British and revolutionaries occurred.

Father Devas did not see my play about Julien Fédon, although he endorsed the script. As a priest within the "establishment"—that is, the Roman Catholic and Anglican churches in Grenada of the 1960s—he did not want to step foot in an American evangelical school compound. The "establishment" resented the encroachment of the American missionaries' brand of theology and the introduction of what was considered the "inferior" American system of education in the British colony.

Nobody was more elated than Father Devas, however, when my first article on Julien Fédon was published in *The West Indian* newspaper of March 3, 1967, to celebrate Grenada's attainment of "statehood." The aging priest actually drove to the mountains of Belvedere to congratulate me.[4]

A few months later, May 1967, I arrived in New York, seeking a college education. I expected to spend only four years, but I'm still here! Father Devas and I corresponded. I recently found my 1967 *Collins Caribbean Diamond Diary*; in it was a note dated Thursday, July 20, where I wrote: "Received letter from Fr. Devas."

⸻⸶⸷⸸⸻

ON NOVEMBER 20, 2017, AFTER more than 62 years of hiking to Fedon's Camp, my first time, perhaps, 1953-54, I took what was likely my final hike to Fédon's Camp. Accompanying me was Brother John Wells, an 80-year-old planter, and Kenrick Harper, his 40-year-old son and my cousin. As we ascended and descended the mountains, often through torrential rain and mist, I was begging them to wait for me. I was breathless and fell frequently in the slippery mud and puddles. Flashbacks of numerous trips in my youth, up and down the mountains, overwhelmed me. I found myself, loudly and rather humorously, saying, "Forgive me, Father Bernard and Father Devas for running ahead of you, leaving you, although you pleaded with us tireless little boys to wait for you. I now know how you felt."

On the 2017 hike, when Brother John, Kenrick, and I reached the valley of a mountain peak below Fédon's Camp, also known as Camp of Death and Morne Vauclain, I stopped to reflect. It was here, on a hike in the early

1960s, where Father Devas explained to Father Bernard that this deep valley was where most cannon balls landed during the morning of April 8, 1795—both from Fédon's forces on Morne Vauclain (Fédon's Camp) and from the British who had nearly scaled another mountain peak, called First Camp. The two sides rained bullets on each other until Fédon ordered the execution of Lieutenant Governor Ninian Home and other British prisoners. It was there in the valley that we little boys frequently found cannon balls and unearthed parts of decaying 18th century cannons.

So, Belvedere, Fédon's Camp, Battle Hill, Pilot Hill, Chadeau, Gouyave Estate, Telescope, and other areas in Grenada were my primary sources for this book. Other sources were the narratives of Rev. Francis M'Mahon, Dr. John Hay, Colonel Gordon Turnbull, Thomas Turner Wise, Henry Thornhill, and Lieutenant Colonel William Dyott, all of whom experienced Fédon's Rebellion and Fédon's Revolution firsthand.

My secondary source was the research of scholars who earlier delved into European and American archives.

For the last 227 years, information about Fédon was obtained principally from British archives, with documents written by biased Englishmen who focused on Fédon's cruelty and anti-British sentiments. Professor Philippe Girard, author of several books on Haitian General Toussaint Louverture, is correct when he says, "History is written by winners." Or, as Nigerian novelist Chinua Achebe suggests, "Until the lions have their own historians, the history of the hunt will always glorify the hunter."[5]

The British won. The audacious Julien Fédon—who launched what was, perhaps, the first significant "war" on the mighty British Empire with his ragtag army of free mulattos, free Africans, maroons, enslaved, and liberal French whites aided by the French military—lost. Though losers are maligned and often written out of history, Fédon lives on in the minds and hearts of our native Grenadian and other Caribbean historians. They continue to glorify Fédon, the loser.

Over the centuries, laborers on Belvedere Estate, Fédon's home, and on surrounding estates proudly shared the stirring story of Julien Fédon. I was privileged to listen to those stories from the time I was a toddler, as I was born and raised on Belvedere Estate. For those laborers, Fédon was a freedom fighter—valiant and intelligent.

Julien Fédon is also part of Grenadian folklore. In the mid-20th century, children were told "to listen at night for the sound of Fédon's white stallion." They were told about Fédon's intelligence and magical powers; that he attached the horseshoes on his horse's hooves in the opposite direction to mislead the enemy; of his ability to swim from Grand Étang Lake, in the central part of the island, through a made-up subterranean river to Black Bay on the island's western coast.[6]

MOST BIOGRAPHERS KNOW THE BIRTHPLACE, year of birth and death, and final resting place of the person about whom they are writing. In preparing to narrate the life of Julien Fédon, I cannot say I visited the village, town, estate, or even the island where he was born. In fact, nobody knows Fédon's precise birthplace or birth year. My research has also not led me to his burial site or even the island where he took his last breath. When and how he died is unknown. Historians and "Fédonists" merely speculate about Fédon's place of birth, death, and age. They do not know if he was tall or short, big or small, handsome or ugly—because no portrait of him made during his lifetime has ever been found. The Fédon family was unassuming and not part of the social scene; therefore, and most likely, no portrait was ever made.

What is undeniable is that, for 16 months from March 1795 to June 1796, Julien Fédon controlled most of Grenada. He destroyed the flourishing sugar and coffee colony, murdered the governor, caused the death of thousands, but freed the slaves.

Indeed, mystery surrounds not only Julien Fédon, the individual, and the revolution that he led but, more importantly, the significance of the revolution and its historical impact. Interestingly, Fédon is not mentioned in any of the history textbooks used in high schools in the Caribbean. This curious omission, or silencing, of Fédon's Revolution is particularly egregious in light of Douglas J. Hamilton's assertion, "While none of the British islands experienced revolutions like that led by Toussaint Louverture in St. Domingue [Haiti], probably the most significant uprising took place in Grenada."[7]

My work cannot reveal much about Julien Fédon's early life. Records of his boyhood days and most of his entire adult life are yet to be found. Not even The Reverend Francis M'Mahon and Dr. John Hay, residents of Gouyave who knew Fédon very well and who would become his prisoners and then be reprieved, included information about Fédon's youth in their narratives.

Fédon is mostly known through that 16-month period when he held the colony ransom and led a revolt against King George III of Britain, to whom Fédon had earlier pledged his allegiance. It was this 16-month period that created the legendary Julien Fédon, an integral part of 18th century Caribbean history and an undeclared national hero of the nation of Grenada – Grenada, Carriacou, and Petite Martinique. Individuals from all three islands participated in the rebellion.

Marcus Mosiah Garvey visited Grenada in 1937 and once spoke of mental slavery. Garvey's words, "Emancipate yourself from mental slavery," later popularized by Robert Nesta Marley in his hit, *Redemption Song*, could be one reason why Julien Fédon was never declared a national hero of Grenada. In spite of its attempt in the postcolonial period to flirt with other political ideologies, Grenada continues to be embedded in the British way of life and has not completely emancipated itself from "mental slavery." When it does, the government of the day, backed by the will of the people, will officially name its national heroes, create a public holiday to honor them, erect monuments in their memory, and teach children about them.[8]

There may be no rush to name Grenada's national heroes, however, since many of those likely to be considered were actually thorns in the British backside—beginning with Julien Fédon.

From a constitutional perspective, Grenada has been linked to Britain since the reign of King George III, and that linkage has not been severed despite Grenada's independence in 1974. Queen Elizabeth II remains Queen of Grenada.

By supporting France, Britain's archrival, by leading a rebellion to eliminate British domination of Grenada, by accepting the title of "General of the French Republican Forces" and for his disloyalty to King George III, Fédon committed high treason.

More than 200 years later, the British have not forgiven Julien Fédon. But, should an 'independent' Grenada continue to dishonor Fédon rather than recognizing his noble actions? Had the British captured him alive, they would have executed him—perhaps tied his body from a large branch on a tree top to dangle near St. George's Market Square until vultures and other creatures had picked every bit of Fédon's flesh and bone. Based on what the British did to a Fédon conspirator, Jacques Chadeau, one can only imagine what they would have done to Fédon if he had been captured alive—or even dead.

In May 1808, a decade after the failed revolution, Jacques Chadeau was betrayed by a jealous lover, captured by "a detachment of the Loyal Black Rangers," and hanged. The Loyal Black Rangers were empowered by the British to ferret out maroons and revolutionaries. Hanged in the Market Place, Chadeau's body was then dragged to Point St. Eloi, about three miles away, where it hung from a tree for birds to feast.[9]

Three years before Chadeau was hanged, the British had made Joachim Philip an example of what would happen when revolutionaries were caught. In February, 1803, seven years after the rebellion ended, Joachim Philip was betrayed on Petite Martinique, the nearby island that his family owned. Slavery was restored in Grenada, and France had given up hope of ever recapturing the colony; the British were in full control. After learning of Philip's whereabouts and of others once the rebellion ended in 1796, the

British hastily executed Philip on February 25, 1803, only 10 days after his capture, in St. George's Market Place (Square.) The legislature paid 20 Joes to Alexander Murray, 10 Joes to James Tazwell, and 5 Joes to Joseph Barthelemy for aiding in the capture of Philip. (Joes refers to "Johannes," the Portuguese name for the coins used in Grenada at the time.)[10]

Descendants of the Philip family of Petite Martinique—such as poet, carnival band designer, and calypso promoter Dawad Wayne Philip of Trinidad & Tobago—are aware that one of their ancestors was a leader of Fédon's Rebellion.

Joachim Philip's father, a white Frenchman named Honoré Philip, owned most of Petite Martinique and other properties in Grenada. He married an African. After Honoré Philip's death, his mixed-race children inherited his wealth. Some siblings emigrated to Spanish Trinidad and England after the Fédon's Rebellion.

Joachim Philip, like several leaders of Fédon's Rebellion, was obviously well off. Yet, even well-off French-speaking mulattoes sacrificed their estates and their lives to end British hegemony and slavery in Grenada. In the 21st century, some people still say, "Dead wrong! Fédon, Philip, and others desired to return Grenada to France."[11]

Through the centuries, many believed that it was men with criminal minds and no principles who rebelled against the British. While this was not the case, what prompted those men of wealth and property to free the slaves and end British rule continues to be a subject of lively discussion.

The £500 sterling reward offered by Sir Ralph Abercromby, commander of British forces in the West Indies, to anyone who captured Fédon "dead or alive" was unclaimed. Nobody caught Fédon, and nobody collected the £500 sterling—not even Louis La Grenade, a Grenadian mulatto and notorious bounty hunter who made a fortune capturing runaway slaves.

Fédon was a wanted man for several reasons. He murdered Governor Ninian Home, who represented the King of England, and other prominent

Britishers; he emancipated the enslaved; and he destroyed the colony's flourishing economy, causing England to lose more than £2,500,000 sterling. That's billions of dollars in today's currency. The British itemized the destruction:

Sugar and rum works and other buildings destroyed on 65 estates @ £6,000 each	£390,000
Cattle, horses, and mules on do	£65,000
Works and other buildings on 35 coffee estates @ £1,000 each	£35,000
One-fourth of the Slaves killed, dead, or otherwise lost to their owners, 7000 @ £50 each	£350,000
Loss on the Crop of 1795, and on the Crop of the three following years, calculated at:	£1,500,000
	£2,340,000
Negro Houses, Plantation Utensils not in the above rough statement	£160,000
	£2,500,000 [12]

FÉDON LEFT NO SPEECHES, NO letters, no testimonials or other documents for historians to dissect. As a result, researchers speculate about the cause of Fédon's Rebellion and why its leaders committed such horrible crimes against the British.

Information about Fédon's wrath is mainly extracted from letters dispatched to family, friends, absentee estate owners, and public officials in England, Scotland, Ireland, and the United States of America. "Monsters or rather devils in human shapes," one observer described the revolutionaries.[13]

I have been searching feverishly for anything that Julien Fédon may have written or said. I have not found anything substantial other than his letter of March 4, 1795, from Belvedere House, his home, to Council President Kenneth Francis Mackenzie demanding that the British surrender Grenada to him. The letter, most likely, was not written by Fédon. It may have been drafted by French Republicans who arrived in Grenada from French Guadeloupe or by Fédon's aides. Rev. Francis M'Mahon, then a guest prisoner at Fédon's home, observed revolutionaries drafting documents. In the letter attributed to Fédon, no personal feelings were expressed; it was purely a threatening communique from the revolutionaries to Mackenzie, outlining the consequences if he did not surrender Grenada to them.

I was electrified when I eventually found a lengthy quotation from Fédon expressing his inner thoughts, but that lasted only a few minutes. I asked myself, "Why have I not seen this statement from Julien Fédon before? Something is not right here." Upon reading the footnotes and bibliography in Professor Selwyn R. Cudjoe book, *Beyond Boundaries: The Intellectual Tradition of Trinidad & Tobago in the Nineteenth Century*, I realized that the quotations attributed to Fédon were not true. They were taken from Edward Lanza Joseph's popular novel, *Warner Arundell: The Adventures of a Creole*. The novel is merely a historical fiction, and Cudjoe's quotations were "creative embellishment."[14]

Cudjoe was not misleading the reader; rather, he was demonstrating how momentous events in history are sometimes refashioned by novelists in order to dramatize the story in fiction thrillers. Most people are not excited by academic books, so novelists dramatize events in order to draw in readers. They spice up their novels, even though the facts may stretch the truth or be downright erroneous. Edward Lanza Joseph used Fédon as the "spice" in his novel.

Since no one knows Julien Fédon's whereabouts after July 27, 1796, when he was last seen at Mount Sinai, a mountain peak in the Parish of Saint Andrew, he has become a mythical character. Novelists were enticed to include him in their fiction, along with stories about his rebellion and his adversary Louis La Grenade, as Edward Lanza Joseph brilliantly did in the 19th century and novelist Dunbar Campbell did in *Blood of Belvidere* in the 21st century.[15]

Since almost no documents written by Fédon and his revolutionary cohorts have been found as yet, many academicians speculate about specific aspects of Fédon's Revolution. On the other hand, fiction writers create plots, use the revolutionary leaders' names, or create fictionalized characters in their novels about Fédon and his revolution. As a result, people can easily confuse the real Fédon with the fictionalized Fédon.

Edward Lanza Joseph (1792-1838) was an early fiction writer on West Indian life and times. The young and adventurous Englishman was on his way to join Simón Bolívar's army in South America, when his boat sailed into Trinidad. Joseph never left sweet Trinidad. He is acclaimed as one of Trinidad's foremost journalists, playwrights, actors, and authors. In 1838, Joseph released his three-volume novel, *Warner Arundell: The Adventures of a Creole*. Through his fictitious character Arundell, Joseph may have been the first to include Julien Fédon in a fictional account.

Edward Lanza Joseph and *Warner Arundell: The Adventures of a Creole* were given new life in 2001, when scholars Lise Winer and Bridget Brereton edited the novel and the University of the West Indies Press published it. Joseph's fiction is creative and witty. He provides a thin line between fiction and facts and the real Fédon from the invented one. Publishing houses are still reproducing this book as being "culturally important," thereby continuing to present a fictionalized Julien Fédon.

I agree with Professor Curtis Jacobs for believing that Joseph may have interviewed Fédon family members clandestinely living in Trinidad. Long before Julien Fédon dreamed of rebelling, his sister and brother-in-law were living in Spanish Trinidad. During and after the failed revolution, family members and other plotters escaped to Trinidad—most likely using false identities. Perhaps Julien did, too. Some passages in the novel about Fédon's movements seem logical and thereby accurate. Joseph did not live long enough to reveal his sources for the novel; he died in 1838, the year the novel was published.

While history from a British perspective has not treated Julien Fédon fairly, one cannot entirely fault the British. By losing the war, Fédon and his colleagues did not have an opportunity to explain why they did what they did. Beginning in the late 20ᵗʰ century, Caribbean researchers have begun to extract our suppressed histories and are finding bits of information about Fédon, his family, and the rebellion. This information is helping to rehabilitate Fédon's image and to challenge the distorted portrait of Fédon painted by the British.

Julien Fédon and his revolution failed. In spite of the apparent mischaracterization by the British, Fédon is a national hero in the mind of many of today's Grenadians—but not all.

Journalists occasionally asked Maurice Bishop, the revolutionary prime minister of Grenada (1979-1983), how he and his government could revere Fédon when Bishop was also a direct descendant of Louis La Grenade, Fédon's archenemy. Bishop would respond with a pause, a radiant smile, and say, "Times have changed, the circumstances are different."[16]

In order to make this book reader friendly to the general public, I chose to add notes numbers at the end of paragraphs in the main text. They are listed chapter by chapter in the back.

PART I

The Fédon Family

ONE

Pierre Fédon Departs France

On July 10, 1749, a pleasant summer day, the sailing vessel *L'Infante* departed the Port of Bordeaux, France, and inched its way out of harbor, bound for Martinique. Once at sea, the ship crossed the Atlantic Ocean, entered the Caribbean Sea, and headed for Martinique as fast (and as stealthily) as possible. Pierre Fédon—a young adventurer, fortune seeker, and goldsmith by trade—was on board.

> Fédon Pierre, orfèvre, a embarqué dans le port de Bordeaux,
> sur l'Infante, le 10 Juliet 1749, à destination de la Martinique.[1]

The captain, crew, and passengers were mostly Roman Catholics. Chances are, they prayed daily to Saint Peter, the Blessed Virgin Mary, and the Almighty, asking each to prevent one of those vicious summer storms, which often lashed the West Indies, from sinking *l'Infante*. Most likely, they also asked God to shield their vessel from the naval fleets of England, Spain, and all other enemies of France.

In all probability, *l'Infante*'s cargo included cases of Bordeaux wine and brandy. The wine and brandy were not gifts for those who provided the labor on sugar, coffee, and cotton plantations in the French West Indies. After all, those people were enslaved Africans, considered property or merely factors of production. The French spirits were for the enjoyment of French citizens residing in Martinique, along with their French Creole offspring.

Broadly speaking, a "Creole" was a white person born in the West Indies of European parents. A French Creole was someone born in the West Indies of a white French mother and a white French father. Centuries later,

"Creole" would evolve to include Caribbean people of different races who had a sip of African blood.

Also, among *l'Infante*'s cargo on its trip to Martinique were farming equipment, such as forks, cutlasses, lumber, spades, and axes; huge copper basins used for fermenting sugarcane juice into molasses and rum; and empty barrels that later would be filled with molasses and rum for *l'Infante* and other vessels to carry back to France.

Oh, yes, and ammunition! Bayonets, swords, guns, cannons, and cannonballs were certainly part of the cargo. The ammunition would be stored in the forts of Martinique or sent to other French islands, such as Isle de La Grenade (Grenada). France was quickly building forts on its West Indian colonies to defend those "possessions" from invasion by other European rivals. On Isle de La Grenade, for example, France had already built two forts to protect Port Louis, the island's French colonial capital.[2]

By 1649, Isle de La Grenade had been renamed several times—and would be renamed a few more times, as well. On August 15, 1498, for example, Christopher Columbus sailed north from Trinidad, which he had spotted the day before but hadn't landed. He saw a mountainous island and, based upon his two previous voyages to the Caribbean, knew that people lived there and that the island must have a name. Nevertheless, without even stopping, Columbus decided to rename the island "Conception" and claim it for Spain.

The aboriginal inhabitants, the Kalinago, called their beautiful island Camerhogne. Two years after Columbus sailed by, Italian mapmaker Amerigo Vespucci (for whom "America" is named) called the island "Mayo" when creating his map of the "New World" in 1500. Portuguese mapmaker Diogo Ribeiro ignored all previous designations by naming the island "La Granada" on his 1529 map. Then, for almost a century, the native Kalinago people valiantly prevented Europeans from conquering their beloved Camerhogne until they were outwitted by the French. The French changed the Portuguese-Spanish spelling of La Granada to "La Grenade."

SOME WOMEN ABOARD *L'INFANTE* WERE on their way to join their husbands and loved ones. Others, taken against their will from various towns in France, were being transported to Martinique, La Grenade, and other French possessions to serve the social and sexual needs of lonely white French planters and merchants.

Most passengers, though, were men—and they likely represented various classes of French society. Perhaps a few were aristocrats with investments in the West Indies. Some might have been relatives of King Louis XV, visiting the islands to assess their two principal properties: plantations and slaves. But the majority were lower-class French males on their way to the New World to begin a new life. Some would become managers and overseers of sugar and coffee plantations. Others would become merchants, agents, and craftsmen. They all aspired to make a fortune in the booming French West Indies.

Aristocrats and the Court of King Louis XV flaunted their wealth. They lived opulent lifestyles in Versailles, thanks to the monies earned from their West Indian estates. That indirectly encouraged French lower-class men to sail to the West Indies and, with luck, get a piece of the action. Vessels such as *l'Infante* transported them across the Atlantic.[3]

Men of noble birth and family members of French monarchs had invested in the New World about a century before. Islands such as Guadeloupe, Saint Lucia, Isle de La Grenade, Saint Vincent, Dominica, and Martinique had been conquered and the native population annihilated in the name of the French monarchy…and Christianity. Villages in many of those islands, 500-600 years later, still carry the names of early French investors. For example, Soubise, Mirabeau, and Marquis in today's Grenada were named for Prince de Soubise, Marquis de Mirabeau, and Earl of Marquis—each of whom seized large parcels of land and developed them into estates.

The handful of aristocrats aboard *l'Infante* may have been heirs or offspring of the early investors/invaders. At the time, two industries—sugar and the Atlantic slave trade—were rapidly approaching their zenith, causing France to become a world power (along with Spain, Holland, and England).

But the French aristocrats, whether living in France or in the West Indies, needed the help of other Frenchmen to develop their estates and sustain the production of sugar. They depended on French skilled labor to manage the estates, design great houses and sugar mills, construct roads and bridges, create towns, and establish commercial businesses.[4]

A separate unpaid labor force provided the manual labor on the sugar estates. France and other European nations obtained this labor from West Africa, where Africans were seized, chained, and forced to board vessels bound for the West Indies and the Americas.

❧

PIERRE FÉDON WAS NOT THE poorest of the poor aboard *l'Infante*. While he had no royal blood and was not a titled aristocrat, he unquestionably belonged to the "upper" lower class of France. He was skilled. He had a trade. He was listed on the ship's passenger list as an *"orfèvre"* (goldsmith).

Young Pierre Fédon was likely both melancholy and excited as he stood on deck, watching the city of Bordeaux and the coastline of France gradually disappear and pondering these obvious questions:

Will I make a fortune in the West Indies? Will I be successful? So successful that, upon my return, a baronage will be bestowed upon me? Will I even survive and return to my family? Will I raise a family in the West Indies? Or will *l'Infante* be captured, and I will become a prisoner of the English?

In that era, men traveled to the New World at an early age. Pierre, then in his late teens or early 20s, would certainly be excited about joining the thousands of Frenchmen experiencing a new beginning in the French West Indies or in other French colonies such as Louisiana or Quebec in North America. If the weather remained good and the wind blew in *l'Infante*'s favor, the vessel would arrive in Martinique within four to seven weeks— mid to late August or early September, at the latest.[5]

Few women were aboard the ship; few French women were on the island, as well. And most women who were already on Martinique were married. Pierre, however, soon fell in love with a free mulatto from Martinique named Brigitte Joachim Philip.

Brigitte was the apple of Pierre Fédon's eye. They likely married shortly after meeting, although there is no official record of their marriage. There are, in fact, no documents about Pierre's entire sojourn on Martinique—not even the precise month or day of his arrival.

Brigitte already had a son, Machaud, and Pierre apparently accepted the toddler as his own son. Machaud grew up to become a bounty hunter for the British, locating runaway slaves and maroons in Grenada, but later took a leadership role in his brother's rebellion. In 1796, the British sought Machaud for high treason.

The scanty information about Pierre and Brigitte Fédon is extracted mainly from documents discovered in Grenada in the first decade of the 21st century, more than 226 years after their existence, and from the passenger list of *l'Infante*. There are no certificates indicating whether Pierre and Brigitte's children were born on Martinique, but they were definitely born free and not into slavery: their father was white; their mother, a free mulatto or person of color.

Only one of Pierre and Brigitte's sons carved his name in Grenadian and world history: Julien Fédon.

TWO

Pierre & Brigitte Fédon in Grenada

On December 13, 1764, General Robert Melvill, a Scottish soldier and Grenada's first civilian British governor, arrived in the colony. Governor Melvill promptly audited local businesses and organized the collection of taxes from business owners, mainly French people and free French people of color, retroactive to the 1763 tax year. The French, the original European settlers in Grenada, represented the majority of the colony's population and owned virtually all of the island property. Melvill simply followed the French custom of collecting taxes, but he also targeted poor French farmers who were not accustomed to paying any taxes on their small properties.[1]

An old tax record confirms Pierre Fédon's 18th-century residency in Grenada, along with the parish in which he and Brigitte, his wife, resided. Pierre Fédon was listed as a taxpayer. He paid the newly established British government 18 livres in taxes for three slaves that he owned in Grand Pauvre (Saint Mark). The audit indicates that none of the "three negroes" was younger than 14 years of age and that Pierre Fédon had no "horned cattle…horses…sheep…mules." Having no animals indicates that Pierre was, indeed, poor and could not afford to purchase stock.[2]

Governor Melvill's taxation records are included in British historical records. Under the Peace of Paris 1763 accords, however, the defeated French were allowed to take with them all documents relevant to their rule of Grenada. Most of those documents have not been found. As a result, it is unknown whether Pierre Fédon paid taxes to the previous French administration.

In the 17th and 18th centuries, British, French, Spanish, Portuguese, and Dutch investors developed estates in both North America and the West Indies. Many of those developers had royal blood; others were aristocrats. In France, Pierre Fédon—an *orfèvre* (goldsmith)—was unlikely to have enough money to purchase a large property when he arrived in Martinique. Whatever money he had then or accumulated later, he apparently invested it on the Isle de la Grenade. Land was easily available there and less expensive than on Martinique. Perhaps that is why Pierre and his wife eventually settled on Isle de la Grenade.

Upon Pierre Fédon's death, his children inherited just 6.5 acres of land (two French quarreys) and a few enslaved people. Again, the small acreage indicates that he was, at best, a *petit bourgeois* with, as Governor Melvill's audit reveals, no livestock (horned cattle, horses, sheep, or mules)—which was even more valuable than slaves.

PIERRE FÉDON'S WHEREABOUTS IS UNKNOWN for the period between September 1749, when he arrived in Martinique, and 1763, when he paid taxes in Grenada. As historical documents become available or easier to retrieve, a researcher may one day find evidence of those missing 14 years. Sometime during that 14-year period, however, Pierre Fédon apparently gave up his craft as a jeweler and became a planter, the principal source of earning a decent living in the West Indies at the time.

The acrimonious 18th-century rivalry between France and England does shed some light on Pierre Fédon's whereabouts during that missing part of his history.

During the first week of February 1762, England captured Isle de la Grenade without a shot being fired. French Governor Pierre-Claude Bonvoust d'Aulnay de Prulay realized that his small militia was no match for the mighty British naval force, and he wisely surrendered. One year later, according to Article IX of the Treaty of Paris (signed on February 10, 1763), France formally relinquished Isle de la Grenade to England. The British renamed the island "Grenada," created its own British style of government, and promptly curtailed the French population's religious and political freedoms and the French way of life.

Since the tax record shows that Pierre and Brigitte Fédon were residents of Grand Pauvre in 1763, chances are that they lived on the island prior to that. And if that is, in fact, the case, Pierre and Brigitte may have viewed British warships, under Commodore Robert Swanton, sailing off the coast near Sauteurs, Grand Pauvre, and Gouyave en route from Martinique to capture Port Louis, capital of Isle de la Grenade, where the French governor ultimately capitulated.

The Fédons were likely perturbed in 1763 and 1764, when their new homeland—renamed Grenada—officially became British, and French citizens such as themselves were branded "new or adopted subjects."[3]

Julien Fédon, one of Pierre and Brigitte's sons, was about 10 years old at the time and likely watched the mighty British armada sailing by, as well. He may have been mesmerized—as the hills between Grand Pauvre and Gouyave would have provided a magnificent view of the blue Caribbean Sea and the flotilla of ships of all sizes, their white sails fluttering in the ocean breeze.

Was young Julien aware that control of his island home changed from France to Britain? If so, what was his attitude toward the British? And did that play a role in his eventual attempt to take back Grenada from British hegemony in 1795? While intriguing, it is unlikely that we will ever know the answers to those questions.

Until February 1762, Isle de la Grenade was rapidly developing and providing opportunities for French investors and the French working class. But no wise-thinking French person would emigrate from Martinique to Grenada once it became a British colony governed by the British military. Given those tense times, it is unlikely that Pierre Fédon, a Frenchman, and his French-speaking mulatto wife would head for British Grenada after February 1762. British Grenada became an enemy of France, and a French person wishing to emigrate to Grenada would have been perceived to be disloyal to the French monarchy.

At the same time, and for many reasons (security, economic, political, and religious), British Grenada didn't want French citizens moving in. And for Grenada's resident French nationals or French-speaking people, many actually born in Grenada, the British were making their lives miserable. As a result, some French estate owners fled with their most valuable possessions (their slaves) to neighboring Spanish Trinidad—where, like France, the population was Roman Catholic. That hasty departure, beginning in 1762-1763, was just the first exodus of Grenadians fleeing to nearby Trinidad.[4]

While it's possible, it's also unlikely that Pierre and Brigitte Fédon sailed from Martinique to Grenada immediately after their marriage in late 1749. Energetic, adventurous, restless young people often make bold moves. It's more likely that the young Fédons settled in Grenada in the 1750s, either remaining in Martinique for a couple of years or living on other French islands—perhaps Sainte Lucie (Saint Lucia), Dominica, Guadeloupe, or St. Vincent—before making Grenada their home. And if that were the case, Julien Fédon and some of his siblings may have been born on an island other than Martinique or Grenada.

The British captured Guadeloupe in 1759—one of the first islands that the British snatched from France during the Seven Years War (1756-1763)—but Guadeloupe was returned to France in 1763 as part of the Treaty of Paris. If Pierre and Brigitte were residents of Guadeloupe in 1759 or earlier and did not desire to be English subjects, for example, they and their children may have emigrated to French Grenada between 1759 and February 1762. If so, they would certainly become frustrated when, shortly after their arrival, French Grenada became British Grenada.

Again, it is pure conjecture as to where Pierre and Brigitte and some or all of the children resided or what they were experiencing in the 1750s. What is known, though, is that, by 1763, Pierre had established himself as a small planter in the "Pariosse du Grand Pauvre" in Grenada and was obligated to pay taxes to the newly installed British administration for his land and three slaves.[5]

In accordance with Article XXII of the Treaty of Paris, the French brought to Martinique records of land purchases, birth and death certificates, and other documents pertaining to the French in Grenada. Those historical documents may have been lost or destroyed during fires, hurricanes, shipwrecks, invasions, and/or simple sloppiness—or actually taken to

France, where they remain buried in an archive. Then again, Martinique passed into the hands of England for a few years, 1762-1763, 1804, 1809-1814, and during the French Revolution, 1794-1802. So, we may never know what the British did with French public documents in "Martinco," as the British referred to Martinique.

For all those reasons, the exact year of Pierre and Brigitte Fédon's arrival in Grenada and the years and places of birth of their children, including Julien Fédon, are simply assumptions. The only documented fact is that Grenada's Governor Robert Melvill's 1763 tax records confirm Pierre Fédon's residency in Grenada during that year.

On the other hand, the marriage certificates of some of Pierre and Brigitte Fédon's children and the birth certificates of some of the couple's grandchildren do provide a glimpse into the timing of the family's residence in Grenada. The couple were blessed with eight children and many grandchildren; however, the precise island and birth year of the couple's four boys and four girls—Etienne, Jean, Julien, Jean-Pierre, Marianne, Marie-Louise, Escolastique, and Marie—is unknown. Some of the children may have been born in Grenada, but all eight—along with Machud, Brigitte's son from her previous relationship—very likely grew up in the Parish of Grand Pauvre (also called Parish of Sainte Rose).

⚬⚬⚬

PIERRE FÉDON AND HIS DESCENDANTS have been carved into Caribbean history—despite appearing with various spellings. That was not unusual in the 18th century. Words, including family names, were often spelled phonetically and influenced by the language spoken by the person doing the spelling. French, English, and Spanish were spoken in Grenada. And even though the Britishers—Scots, Irish, and English—all spoke English, they pronounced and spelled words differently.

On the *l'Infante* manifest, for example, Pierre's last name appears as "Fédon." Early records of the Fédon family in Grenada, though, show spellings that include Foedon, Feydon, and Fidon. Based on signatures on receipts, deeds and manumission certificates, some Fédon siblings also placed a simple X as a substitute for their signature. Even Pierre Fédon's soon-to-be famous (or infamous) son Julien, apparently literate, sometimes signed his name as Feydon or Foedon.

At the 1780 baptism of "Margueritte Rose Marie Anne Foedon," daughter of Jean and Margueritte Cavelan Fédon, Grandma Brigitte became her granddaughter's godmother and Julien became his niece's godfather. Margueritte's baptismal certificate lists Brigitte as a widow. Then, in late 1780, Grandma Brigitte became godmother of another granddaughter—this time, a daughter of Julien and Marie Rose Cavelan Fédon. That baptismal certificate also mentioned that Brigitte was a widow.

Pierre Fédon, therefore, died in early 1780 or before. The exact year of his death, and where he died, is unknown. Most likely, Pierre died and was buried on his small property in Grand Pauvre, which his eight children inherited. We know that because, in 1788, the children—and, in some cases, their spouses—deeded the property to their mother, Brigitte. That deed reaffirmed Brigitte as being a widow.[6]

The son who demonstrated the most responsibility and leadership was Julien. The family held him in high esteem by making him the godfather of several nephews and nieces. He paid the marriage registration fee when his younger sister, Marie, wed Michel Beleran on November 12, 1788.

It is unknown whether Julien was the first of the Fédon siblings to marry, but details of his marriage to Marie Rose Cavelan are certainly fascinating—as we'll now find out.

THREE

Julien Fédon — Son of Grenada

For French Grenadians—French nationals, children of French parentage born in Grenada or other French West Indian colonies, French-speaking mulattos, and even French-speaking enslaved people—the new year gives them hope. The French population is overjoyed, because the political and social climate of Grenada has changed to their advantage. Once again, Grenada is a French colony. Rights and privileges denied to them during the brief years of pernicious British rule, 1762-1779, have been restored. French-speaking Grenadians—the majority of the colony's population—are no longer labeled "new subjects" or "adopted subjects."

It is Monday, January 31, 1780. Julien Foedon and Marie Rose Cavelan have been married in French Grenada: "Acte de mariage de Julien Foedon et de Marie Rose Cavelan," according to their marriage certificate.[1]

And a week later: "Revalidé le mariage, selon les Rites de l'église Catholique Romaine le sept février"—Revalidated marriage, according to the Rites of the Roman Catholic Church on February 7, 1780.[2]

January 31, 1780, was likely a blissful day when the marriage of Julien and Marie Rose Fédon took place in the town of De L'Ance Goyave—and again, when it was revalidated by their church. The reason for two dates is revealed in the archives.

Most Grenadian residents at the time were Roman Catholics, the island's first Christian religion. During British governance (1762-1779), Anglicanism was introduced and became the authorized religion. Only marriages and baptisms performed in Anglican churches were considered legitimate. In 1780, the Roman Catholic faith once again became the official religion of the colony, and marriages performed in its church became legal.

The Roman Catholic church was established in Grenada as early as 1674 to convert the native Kalinago people to Christianity. Since it was the long-standing policy of France to have a Roman Catholic Church in each town, the church owned a sizable amount of prime property in each of the island's towns—all sanctioned by the French government. Between 1763 and 1779, the British confiscated some Roman Catholic churches and portions of church property to establish the Church of England (Anglican), much to the chagrin of the large French-speaking population that included mulattos and free Africans. The current site of the Anglican church in Grenada's capital city of St. George's, for example, was originally the site of a Roman Catholic church.

The person (perhaps the Roman Catholic priest) officiating and revalidating the marriage of Julien and Marie Rose on January 31 and February 7, 1780, was meticulous. He wrote, *"avons Realisé le marriage de Julien foedon; et de Rose cavelan, maries depuis Six ans per le ministre anglois …"* ["we have recognized the marriage of Julien Foedon; and Rose Cavelan, married six years ago by the English minister"]—indicating that the couple were first married in 1774 by an Anglican priest.[3]

For business, legal, political, and social reasons, it made sense for a couple that married in an Anglican Church in 1774—when the British controlled Grenada and did not recognize marriages in non-Anglican churches—to remarry in the Roman Catholic church once that became "legal" again under French rule.

The priest who mentioned the Fédon's 1774 marriage on the 1780 marriage certificate actually did historians a favor. Until the 21st-century, many European and Caribbean historians, including Grenadian scholars, asserted that Julien Fédon might have arrived in Grenada (from Martinique) in the late 1770s, during the 1780s, or in the early 1790s.

Grenadian historian Edward Cox, for example, in *Free Coloreds in the Slave Societies of St. Kitts and Grenada 1763-1833*, his doctorate thesis published in 1984, describes Fédon: "A mulatto of French extraction, he may not have been resident on Grenada in 1772 and certainly does not appear as a property holder that year." Cox continues, "With the exception of Joachim Philip, Fédon and his associates all came to public attention, suddenly, about 1790. There is a strong likelihood that none were born in Grenada and that all immigrated to the island either during the period of French occupancy between 1779 and 1784 or thereafter."[4]

The discovery of centuries-old documents about the Fédon family, found decaying in Grenada's Registrar's Office—mainly by historians Beverely A. Steele and Curtis Jacobs in the 21st century—shed new light on Julien Fédon's presence in Grenada. Referencing those documents, writers can now claim that Julien Fédon resided in Grenada as early as 1774 and actually may have grown up on the island in the 1750s—or even been born there.

A "Certificate of Freedom" issued to Marie Rose, Julien's wife, in 1787 by Dr. John Hay and Walter Carew, "two of His Majesty's Justices of the Peace for the said island of Grenada," helps pin down Julien's birth year.[5]

Alarmed by the large and growing number of free, French-speaking mulattos and free Africans in Grenada—and distrustful of them—the conservatives and Scots in control of Grenada's government required free people of color to show their Certificate of Freedom, manumission papers, and arrival documents (for the newly arrived). A person who failed to show a Certificate of Freedom was imprisoned until that proof was presented. Failing to show that proof ultimately placed the person in slavery.

Marie Rose, Julien Fédon's wife, was questioned and given a deadline to prove that she was not a slave. [Some writers claim that Marie Rose was jailed, but I have not stumbled on that evidence.] In any event, British officials ignored the fact that Marie Rose and her husband were owners of Lancer Estate, including the estate's estimated 10 slaves, and extend neither courtesy nor respect to the Fédons in their capacity as property owners and law-abiding subjects. That embarrassing episode for Julien's wife may very well be reflected in her husband's "rebellious" activities in 1795.

Eventually, Marie Rose Fédon was issued a Certificate of Freedom:

> By John Hay and Walter Carew, Esquires … Be it remembered
> on the fourth day of March in the year of our Lord 1787, Joseph
> Verdet and Francois Philip, Esquires … personally came and

> appeared before us & declared solemnly under Oath, that they
> … have known a certain Mestive Woman named Marie Rose
> Cavelan, of the age of Thirty four Years, or thereabouts, the
> Wife of Julien Fédon, a Mulatto and a Planter … the said Marie
> Rose Cavelan was regarded and reputed to be, to all intents and
> purposes whatever free from Slavery.[6]

Since Marie Rose was 34 years old in March 1787, she was born in 1752 or 1753. Customarily at the time, wives were two or three years younger than their husbands. Julien's year of birth, then, was likely 1750 or 1751, making him 37 or 38 years old in 1787. His father, Pierre, arrived in the Caribbean between late August and September 1749, when he met and married Julien's mother. Therefore, Julien could not have been born before 1750.

Rev. Francis M'Mahon, the Anglican priest in Gouyave, and John Hay, the medical doctor there, provided information about Julien Fédon and his family in their exhaustive narratives about Fédon's Revolution but did not mention Julien Fédon's birthplace. If they knew that Grenada was not his birthplace, they would probably have made that significant observation. If Julien arrived in Grenada in the 1780s, Hay and M'Mahon probably would have mentioned that, too.

Those two loyal British subjects, M'Mahon and Hay, were residents of Gouyave for a long time: M'Mahon since 1784; Hay, even longer. As dutiful British gentlemen, M'Mahon and Hay called Gouyave by its British name, Charlotte Town. Dr. Hay and Rev. M'Mahon served the parishes of Saint John, Saint Mark, and Saint Patrick in various capacities. In addition to his priestly duties, M'Mahon was a magistrate in the three parishes; Dr. Hay was leader of the Saint John militia and a justice of the peace. Both men were acquainted with the Fédon family, as Julien Fédon was an established planter active in Grand Pauvre and Gouyave. In their writings, Hay and M'Mahon presume Julien Fédon was born and raised in the Paroisse de Grand Pauvre. Chances are, they are correct—but a document proving the point is yet to be found.

Given the charged political and religious climate in the 1780s, Dr. Hay and Rev. M'Mahon were neither friends nor enemies of Julien Fédon, the French-speaking mulatto. They came from starkly different backgrounds, had a different religious faith, spoke different languages, and were loyal to different and competing European powers.

With the British in control of Grenada, the French citizenry and resident mulattos were clearly subservient to British subjects. British laws prevailed, and the Grenada legislature was comprised mainly of British men, mostly Scots. Tension and a lack of trust existed between the two groups, and revenge was in the air. Oppressed during the first British rule, 1762-1779, the French returned the favor when they regained control, 1779-1783. That period of French domination lasted only four years, however, crushing the spirit of French Grenadians. When the British regained control in late 1783, they swiftly created harsh legislation to avenge the French.

So, given those conditions, Hay, M'Mahon, and Fédon were acquaintances, not friends. They were merely polite to one another. Who would have thought that Dr. Hay and Rev. M'Mahon would become Julien Fédon's prisoners in just a few short years?

In his account of "the insurrection," Rev. M'Mahon wrote of his thoughts when he was told, on the first day of the rebellion, March 3, 1795, that Fédon was the commander-in-chief. M'Mahon noted:

> "I thought I had nothing to fear from Fédon, who, as one of my parishioners, had conducted himself with much civility toward me and had only a few days before sent a present of beads from the mountains to my children."[7]

Those "beads from the mountains" that were sent to Rev. M'Mahon's children were hard, multicolored, and about the size of a peanut. As late as the 1960s, for Grenadians living in towns such as Gouyave, "the mountains" meant the interior of the island, where people have farmed for centuries. Fédon collected the beads on his Belvedere Estate.[8]

The Fédon family had the highest respect for the two Britishers and likely depended on Dr. Hay, the medical doctor for the two parishes, for their medical needs. Hay was also a "Guardian of the Slaves," meaning he had to ensure that enslaved people were not abused by their masters. And when the local British administration claimed that Julien Fédon's wife, Marie Rose, might be a slave, it was Dr. Hay who removed the cloud hanging over her status by swiftly issuing Marie Rose's Certificate of Freedom.

Further, Julien Fédon, despite being a staunch Roman Catholic, actually had a cordial relationship with the Anglican priest. On the second morning of the revolution, a rebel in Gouyave named Olinger—believing that drunken rebels may murder Rev. M'Mahon—escorted the priest to Belvedere so Julien Fédon could protect him. General Fédon, heading for Gouyave, met M'Mahon en route. And according to M'Mahon's writings, "Fédon directed some of his attendants to take me to his house, and desire his wife and daughter to keep me with them and take care of me."[9]

It is obvious, therefore, that the Fédon family and Rev. M'Mahon and Dr. Hay all had a high regard for each other and that Julien was not simply the coldhearted "monster" tagged by the British.

FOUR

The Fédon Siblings

Julien Fédon orders and supervises the massacre of Governor Home and 48 other British elites but spares the lives of M'Mahon, Hay, and Kerr. The three survivors, barefoot and nearly naked, descend from the mountaintop (Morne Qua Qua, or Fédon's Camp) and the scene of the barbarism to the middle camp [First Camp] and then to neighboring Madame Peschier Estate.

"Mr. M'Mahon, Mr. Kerr, and myself, were then ordered down to the middle camp…we halted under a shade at the battery…Jean Pierre Fédon was stretched out there. His wife, observing that I lost most of my clothes, pressed me to accept a shirt and pair of stockings, which I did," writes Dr. Hay.[1]

Margueritte Fédon, wife of Julien Fédon's slain brother Jean Pierre, does not forget the magnanimous services rendered to her by Dr. Hay and Rev. M'Mahon. She willingly helps them, along with Mr. William Kerr, on the dreadful afternoon of April 8, 1795, despite the death of her husband by British forces early that morning on the battlefield.

⸺ CΘC ⸺

To Belvedere laborers in the 19th and 20th centuries, "First Camp" was Fédon's military headquarters, and "Second Camp" was Morne Qua Qua, or Fedon's Camp. In the 21st century, a popular site where two oversized volcanic stones magically perch on a mountain peak is also called Morne Qua Qua. While the name is the same, that is not the site of the April 8, 1795 massacre.

Although Hay and M'Mahon confirmed the kindness of Fédon women in their narratives, inadequate information about the Fédon family has allowed history, in many ways, to be prejudiced against them. Most historians have primarily focused on Fédon's Revolution and not on the Fédon family itself or the kind deeds of some family members. Writers may be unaware of those kind deeds, as well, because they mainly search "unfriendly" British archives. Evidence of any compassionate deeds by Fédon family members is found mostly in documents from 1780 and 1788 that were tucked away in the Grenada Registrar's Office vault. It is in those documents that the actions and activities of Julien and his siblings—and Marie Rose and her siblings—are partially revealed.

⸺◈⸺

For the Fédon family of Grand Pauvre and Gouyave, 1780 was a wonderful time. The January 31/February 7 renewal of Julien and Marie Rose marriage vows, this time in a Roman Catholic Church, was the first of three marriage ceremonies for three Fédon brothers.

On July 24, 1780, Jean Pierre Fédon gave notice to marry Margueritte from Gouyave: *"24 juillet 1780: Contrat de pierre Feydon et Margueritte Libre."*[2]

"Libre" after her name validates Margueritte as a free woman. She has no surname, indicating that she may have once been enslaved and now refuses to keep her former master's surname. Or perhaps she has no known family…or simply considers herself independent.

Jean Pierre and Margueritte Fédon's marriage certificate, dated August 2, 1780, reads:

> Mariage de jean pierre foedon et de margueritte mulatres libres
> … jean pierre Foedon nê en legitime marriage de pierre foedon
> êuropéén, et de Brigitte Joachim Philip Negresse libre creole
> de l'isle martinique … et margueritte libre native de la Gouyave.[3]

In translation, the document reveals that Jean Pierre Fédon—born in the legitimate marriage of Pierre Fédon, a European, and Brigitte, a free Negro woman from Martinique—married Margueritte, a native of Gouyave.

Jean Pierre and Margueritte Fédon's July 24, 1780, marriage contract and marriage certificate provide another interesting glimpse into the Fédon family. That contract spells the last name as "Feydon," while the August 2 marriage certificate spells it "Foedon." And with three Fédon brothers—Julien, Jean, and Etienne—all courting, marrying, or engaged to marry the three daughters of Michael Cavelan, Jean Pierre found Margueritte three miles away in the lively town of Gouyave.[4]

One more wedding was scheduled for August 1780. On August 22, Julien's brother Jean, (not Jean Pierre) married Margueritte Cavelan, sister of Julien's wife, Marie Rose:

> Contract de Mariage de Jean feydon & margueritte Cavelan ... de la paroisse Sainte Rose de cette isle de la Grenada ... Et Marguerite Cavelan fille legitime de ... Michel Cavelan et ... Marianne Lemico ...[5]

Translation:

> Marriage Contract of Jean Feydon & Marguerite Cavelan ... of the parish of St. Rose of this island of Grenada ... And Margueritte Cavelan legitimate daughter of ... Michel Cavelan and ... Marianne Lemico ...

NOTE: The 18th-century Parish of Sainte Rose-Grand Pauvre is the Parish of Saint Mark. The 18th-century Town of Grand Pauvre is Victoria.

Like Jean Pierre Fédon and Margueritte Fédon's marriage certificate, that of Jean Fédon and Margueritte Cavelan validated the backgrounds of the Fédon parents, Pierre and Brigitte: *"le nommé Jean foedon, né en fil legitime marriage de Pierre foedon européén, et de Brigitte negresse libre creole de l'isle martinique."* The certificate reaffirmed that Pierre Fédon was European and that Brigitte was a free Creole woman from Martinique.[6]

Etienne Fédon then married Elisabeth, the third Cavelan sister, but the precise year is unknown.

In 1790, ten years after their marriages, Julien and Marie Rose Fédon purchased a property in Gouyave from his brother Jean and sister-in-law Margueritte. The Fédon siblings and their Cavelan spouses frequently bought and sold property from each other, including their slaves, reflecting the tight bond within the two families.

—⦾⦾⦾—

MICHEL CAVELAN, FATHER OF THE three Cavelan sisters, and Pierre and Brigitte Fédon, parents of the Fédon siblings, may have been friends in Martinique, immigrating to Grenada about the same time and settling in Grand Pauvre. The children would have grown up together, so three brothers marrying three sisters could have been preordained by their parents—or maybe matches made in heaven!

The 1763 tax records for Grand Pauvre listed Jacques Cavelan as the owner of nine adult slaves and two slaves younger than 14 years. Pierre Cavelan owned one adult slave and two child slaves. Like the Fédon family, the Cavelan family also purchased property in neighboring Gouyave. In 1772, F. M. Cavelan, a free mulatto, owned a 28-acre coffee estate and 10 slaves near Gouyave. Since F. M. Cavelan was mixed-race, the Cavelans who came from France married women of color. The archive shows that some Cavelans owned property in neighboring French Carriacou, just north of Grenada, having settled there from Martinique and then invested in the poorest parish of Grenada, Grand Pauvre.

—⦾⦾⦾—

THE YEAR 1780 WAS NOT only a busy year of marriages for the Fédons and Cavelans but for baptisms too. Two baby girls were born into the family in 1780. Jean Fédon and Margueritte Cavelan, with her mixture of Kalinago, African, and European blood, apparently were young lovers who couldn't wait until their wedding night, August 22, 1780, to share a bed; their daughter came into the world on April 15, 1780—four months before their wedding day.

As a result, Jean Fédon and Margueritte Cavelan Fédon and their family members had a double celebration on August 22. In addition to the wedding, the baby girl was baptized:

jourd'hui vingt deux du mois d'août, mil sept cent quatre vingt
… avons donna le Baptisme a petite fille a laquelle on a donna
pour nom Rose marie anne …[7]

Translated from 18th century French:

"This day twenty-two of the month of August, one thousand
seven hundred and eighty…we have given baptism to a little
girl, to whom we have given the name of Margueritte Rose
Marie Anne …"

And it continues: (born) "the 15th of April of the same year; of Foedon
Jean and Margueritte Cavelan the father and mother…."

At the *"Bapteme de margueritte Rose Anne foedon mestive,"* the baby's
uncle, Julien Fédon, became godfather; grandma Brigitte, godmother.
Other brothers were not named as godfathers of their nieces—only Julien—
signifying that the siblings recognized the status of their brother and
honored him by naming him godfather of their children.[8]

The baby's birth certificate states that Brigitte was a widow, confirming
Pierre Fédon's death in the 1770s. And stating that the baby is "mestive"
indicates that the child's grandmother, Marianne Lemico, was of Kalinago
extraction. The few Kalinago Indians who survived more than a century of
European annihilation dwelled mainly in Saint Mark (Paroisse Du Grand
Pauvre) and Saint Patrick (Paroisse Des Sauteurs).[9]

December 25, 1779 was a jovial day for Julien and Marie Rose Fédon.
They baptized their baby girl, Marie Rose, in the Anglican Church in
Gouyave. Evidently, the Fédons were still abiding by British law. Since
France once again ruled Grenada in 1779, they could have sidestepped
British decree by baptizing Marie Rose in the Roman Catholic church.
Perhaps, though, the young Fédons were being cautious, as Grenada had
returned to French control only a few months prior. Whether or not friends
and family, the Roman Catholic church, or the local French government
pressured Julien and Marie Rose to remarry and re-baptize their baby, both
ceremonies occurred in the Roman Catholic church in early 1780: *revalidé le
mariage, selon les Rites de l'église Catholique Romaine le sept février.*[10]

And on March 12, 1780—just 10 weeks after baptizing their baby on December 25, 1779, in the Anglican Church:

> Nous soussigné Miss. Apost. De l'ordre de St. Dominique et curé de la paroisse Sainte Rose St. Pierre de l'ance la Goyave certifion avoir baptisé le 25 decembre dernier une petite fille, née de Marie Rose Cablant [Cavelan], épouse de Julien Fédon selon la Sainte Rose Sainte Rose coutume Angloise au tems du baptême de la dite enfant mais à présent épouse légitime, ayant revalidé le mariage, selon les rites de l'église Catholique Romaine le 7 février dernier et légitimé la dite fille elle a été nommée Marie Rose par Michel Aubrang et Marie Fédon les parrain et marraine.[11]

Translation:

> We, the undersigned Miss. Apost. From the order of St. Dominic and parish priest of St. Pierre de l'ance la Goyave certify having baptized on 25 December last a little girl, born of Marie Rose Cablant [Cavelan], wife of Julien Fédon according to the custom Angloise at the time of the baptism of the said child but now a legitimate wife, having revalidated the marriage, according to the rites of the Roman Catholic church on February 7 and legitimized the said daughter she was named Marie Rose by Michel Aubrang and Marie Fédon the godfather and godmother.

Remarrying and re-baptizing their baby in the Roman Catholic church demonstrate how devoted the Fédons and other French-speaking mulattos were to their religion.

All that said, a sad moment for the Fédon and Cavelan families also occurred in 1780. The three Fédon brothers (Etienne, Jean, and Julien) who married the three Cavelan sisters (Elisabeth, Margueritte, and Marie Rose, respectively) lost their father-in-law, Michel Cavelan, *"agé aux environs de soixante ans natif de l'isle Martinique"* (age about 60 years born on the isle of Martinique.) He was laid to rest on May 14, 1780, most likely on his property in Grand Pauvre.[12]

Three of Pierre and Brigitte four daughters also found husbands. Marie married Michel Beleran, Marie Louise wedded Charles Nogues, and

Escolastique married Charles Forgerie. There are no documents revealing if Marianne found a beau.

WITH THE VARIOUS GOVERNMENTS OF Grenada having only nominal interest in preserving the nation's historical documents, the 18th-century Fédon documents stored in the Grenada Registrar's Office continue to disintegrate upon the slightest touch. The handwriting of those who wrote the deeds, other business transactions, and marriage and baptismal certificates are readable, but the crumbling paper has destroyed entire lines. We do, however, know the following: Upon their arrival on Isle de la Grenade, Pierre and Brigitte Fédon, patriarch and matriarch of the Fédon family, chose the small, western Paroisse of Grand Pauvre, the poorest parish in the colony (as indicated by its name), to purchase a small acreage, settle, and raise a family. Some or all of their eight children may have been born there. In all, nine children were in the household.[13]

There is no archival evidence that reveals the year of Pierre Fédon's death, but it appears from the grandchildren's baptismal records that Pierre died in the 1770s or in the first three months of 1780.

Pierre and Brigitte's children inherited their father's property, including the few slaves. On December 9, 1788, the eight children and the husbands of three sisters deeded the property to Brigitte. Although Grenada was under British rule in 1788, the deed was written in French and recorded at the Grenada Supreme Court by Benjamin Webster, Assistance Justice.

Only Julien signed his name. The other brothers, sisters, and brothers-in-law signed with an "X," indicating they were illiterate. Interestingly, Julien signed his name with an "X" on an earlier document; so, apparently, he did learn to read and write at some point. But the centuries-old belief that Pierre Fédon sent his son Julien to England for an education is obviously untrue. Pierre Fédon had little or no money.

The deed transferring the late Pierre Fedon's land to his widow, Brigitte, was witnessed by three other French-speaking persons: Paul Batarel, Jean Aguiton, and Julien Lussan. The three were likely family friends. One of those "friends," Julien Lussan, would later betray Pierre Alexandre, a leader of the rebellion in 1795, to the Spanish governor in Trinidad. Lussan then sailed to Grenada to do likewise there. Based on Lussan's testimony, the British captured Alexandre and instantly hanged him in St. George's market square in March 1795.

Through all those historic deeds, along with the various marriage and birth certificates, 21st-century writers are able to glean a few fascinating facts about the Fédon family and their friends. During his lifetime, for example, Pierre Fédon did not possess much land—a mere 6.5 acres. Whatever other property his children acquired was purchased with their own resources.

Deeds and other transactions also reveal the tight bond of French-speaking mulatto families. Michel Belleran and his wife Marie signed Brigitte's deed. That couple would eventually emigrate to the Spanish colony of Trinidad but not before selling their property in Gouyave to Julien and his wife, Marie Rose. Julien and Michel continued to remain close, as evidenced by Michel Belleran becoming the chief purchaser of arms in Trinidad for Fédon's Revolution in 1795-96.

Charles Nogues, who married Marie Louise, another of Julien's sisters, was secretly commissioned as an officer in the French Revolutionary Army and became aide-de-camp to his brother-in-law. During the early weeks of the rebellion, Nogues and Julien had a falling out. Nogues developed a friendship with Jean-Baptiste Victor Hugues, who sent Nogues to work in French-occupied Saint Lucia.

⸺ ∞ ⸺

APART FROM LOVE, THERE MAY have been a rather shrewd reason for the three Fédon weddings in 1780: France controlled Grenada for a second time; French whites, free mulattos, and free Africans were enjoying civil liberties made possible by French Admiral Comte d'Estaing's invasion; and the American War of Independence was well underway.

As a consequence of the American Revolution, d'Estaing was able to recapture Grenada in 1779, and Scots—such as Ninian Home, Alexander Campbell, and other British elites—became powerless. White French and French-speaking free coloreds, including the Fédons, were obviously delighted. The good times returned. Once again, Grenada was under the control of the French Crown, represented by Governor Comte de Durant.

An immediate upshot of the renewed French rule was that marriages and baptisms performed in Roman Catholic churches were again legal. In 1780, amid rumors about a British invasion and retaliation, three Fédon brothers, other French-speaking mulattos, and white French people hastened to marry or remarry within their preferred religion.

Four and a half years later, on September 3, 1783, and much to the irritation of the island's French and French mulatto population, France handed Grenada back to England through the Treaties of Versailles, a component of the Peace of Paris through which England officially lost its 13 North American colonies but retrieved the island of Grenada.

French Grenadians—white French and free French mulattos—became dispirited, despite having taken advantage of the opportunity between 1779 and 1783 to exercise their civil rights, including practicing their preferred faith.

On July 2, 1779, Governor Macartney surrendered Grenada at Hospital Hill (today's part of St. George's Cemetery) after thousands of French soldiers from Count D'Estaing navy invaded. Paintings of the French recapture of L'Isle de la Grenade were made by several artists. This engraving, with caption in French, is by Nicolas Ponce (1746-1831). Published by N Ponce and Godefory, Paris, 1783.

— Courtesy of the Library of Congress and National Army Museum, London.

FIVE

Battle off St. George's

There is no evidence that Julien Fédon, about 27 years old at the time, was in Grenada to witness the land battle for Grenada during the first week of July 1779 or, a few days later, the naval battle off St. George's.[1]

Even if Julien were not in Grenada, though, he would certainly learn about the violent restoration of Grenada to France and that fierce naval battle between the powerful French and English fleets. Those two events were actually extensions of the American War of Independence. France, the most important foreign supporter of the American Revolution, was simultaneously waging war against England and attacking British forces in the West Indies, as well as in and off the coast of the 13 American colonies.

Virtually ignored in U.S. history is the fact that the West Indies region (or individual Caribbean islands) was a war zone during the American War of Independence. Naval battles between French and British fleets took place off Saint Lucia, Saint Vincent, Saint Kitts, and other islands. Most likely, Grenadians (including Julien Fédon and other landowning French-speaking mulattos) understood why the American rebels declared their independence from England in 1776 and sought French support. Nineteen years later, in 1795, Fédon would take a page or two from that effort in order to stage his own rebellion.

ON THE AFTERNOON OF JULY 2, 1779, French General and Vice Admiral Charles Henri Jean-Baptiste, Comte d'Estaing arrived in Grenada with a large naval fleet after harassing, seven or eight months earlier, the British forces in New York and in Newport, Rhode Island. Although the battles of Lexington and Concord, in Massachusetts, occurred on April 19, 1775, the American rebels waited until July 4, 1776, to declare their independence from England. Two years later, in 1778, France would declare war on England—with the result that the West Indies or Caribbean also became a theater of war. French forces attacked British colonies such as Saint Vincent, Saint Lucia, and Grenada, thereby keeping British armadas in the region and diluting the British naval presence farther north in America.[2]

Comte d'Estaing ordered most of the 10,000 troops aboard his 25 warships to land at Molinere Bay, about three miles north of Grenada's capital, St. George's. Realizing that his miniscule British force could not defend Grenada against the mighty French force, Governor Lord George Macartney offered to surrender. D'Estaing promptly rejected the proposal, forcing Macartney and his core military to defend the colony. The battle occurred mainly at Hospital Hill (today, St. George's Cemetery and Presentation College) in the late afternoon of July 3, 1779.

After capturing Fort George, which the French built decades before and where Prime Minister Maurice Bishop would be assassinated more than 200 years later (1983), d'Estaing finally accepted Governor Macartney's surrender and sent him to France as a prisoner of war. Still not satisfied with his easy victory, Comte d'Estaing encouraged his soldiers and sailors to plunder St. George's and destroy all British ships in the harbor.

After the battle, d'Estaing and his men relaxed in Grenada, enjoying the spoils of war, but were stunned at sunrise on July 6, 1779 when Admiral John Byron appeared with a large British convoy. Admiral Byron was too late to save the colony but not too late to attack d'Estaing and the French fleet. Comte d'Estaing, however, remained victorious.[3]

The clash of those two world powers off St. George's, Grenada, is memorable in terms of British–French naval warfare during the American War of Independence. European and American tabloids published colorful articles about the battle. Paintings depicting the event are still displayed in museums or owned by private collectors around the world.

On July 6, 1779, the French fleet under Count d'Estaing was still anchored in and outside St. George's harbor was alarmed when a large British armada under Admiral John Byron appeared at 4 A.M. The battle off St. George's is known as the Battle of Grenada. Civilians on Grenada's west coast, including Sarah Cary at her Mount Pleasant Estate in Saint Mark, glimpsed the naval battle. *Image: Artist Jean-François Hue (1751-1823.) Combat naval de l'île de la Grenade, 6 juillet 1779. Date 1789 Medium oil. Courtesy Musée national de la Marine, Paris.*

People living on the island's western side—from Sauteurs, Grand Pauvre, and Gouyave in the north and central regions to St. George's in the south—may have seen vessels on fire, heard the thunder of cannons, and watched bodies wash ashore.

The possibility of the French recapturing Grenada was dreaded among British and American families on Grenada but eagerly welcomed by French Grenadians. Writing to a family member in Chelsea, Massachusetts, Sarah Cary explained, "We have various reports here of fleets and armies being sent to capture the islands and also of the English being sent for their defense...It is the subject of general conversation here."[4]

Mrs. Cary was pregnant in July 1779 and spent her months of pregnancy at her husband's Mount Pleasant Estate in Grand Pauvre, where a view of the sea was picture-perfect, rather than at Simon (Seamoon) Estate in Saint Andrew, where they lived during the dry season. Years later, her daughter Margaret, born in Grenada and at six years of age sent to school in England, found letters that her mother sent to friends in Chelsea. Margaret described memories of her parents and others on those violent days in July 1779:

> The French war brought inconveniences to their own door.
> The English families were obliged to take refuge with their French friends. For the English fleet—which had been eagerly looked for, and they saw it coming toward the harbor with great joy, hoping for speedy relief—was fallen in by Count d'Estaing, who cut off their hopes by sailing faster and driving first into the harbor.[5]

Like the Cary family, the Fédon family and others who resided on the western coast may have viewed the two fleets chasing each other—and Lord Byron's damaged fleet fleeing Grenada. The colonists may have observed the triumphant flotilla of Comte d'Estaing sailing to Saint Domingue (Haiti), where d'Estaing would refit his fleet and bring hundreds of enslaved people and mulattos to Savannah, Georgia, to attack the British in September, 1779.[6]

⸻⸻

IN 2017, WHEN U.S. PRESIDENT Donald Trump ridiculed Haiti, Caribbean historians and the Haitian-American community hastened to inform him about Haitian participation in the invasion of Savannah during the American Revolution. A teenaged daredevil named Henri Christophe, who would later become a founding father of Haiti, may have been aboard one of d'Estaing's warships that sailed from Grenada on July 6, 1779. The engraving on Christophe's statue in Haiti states that he was born in Grenada. Grenadians further claim that the self-appointed King of Haiti (Saint Domingue), Henri I, was born a free mulatto on Sans Souci Estate in Grenada's Saint George Parish. Others say that he was born enslaved on Sans Souci—and was a first cousin of Julien Fédon. King Henri I named his palace in Haiti "Sans Souci."[7]

Long before he dreamed of freeing Haiti, Toussaint Louverture knew Henri Christophe, a free person whose nickname was "Sans Souci." If Christophe were not actually born free in Grenada, he may have gained his freedom by participating in the attack on Savannah, Georgia, with d'Estaing's troops. Many enslaved people and free blacks from Saint Domingue (Haiti) who stormed Savannah would later lead the fight to abolish slavery in Saint Domingue and, in the process, gain Haiti's independence.

White French Grenadians and free French-speaking mulattos such as Julien Fédon and his family were motivated when France recaptured Grenada in 1779. But the French re-occupation of the island was short-lived.

SIX

Fédon Family Manumits Slaves

It's 1783. Only four years after the Battle off St. George's and the French defeat of the British, the island once again becomes a British colony. This time, though, Grenada was handed over by treaty. The Treaties of Versailles signed by France, England, Spain, and The Netherlands, along with the Peace of Paris, formally ends the American Revolutionary War. England recognizes America's independence, and most British Caribbean colonies captured by France since 1775 are returned to England.

White French and French-speaking people of color in Grenada are not happy becoming, once more, subservient to the British but reluctantly adhere to British rule. Thoughts of removing the British by force, however, are not on anyone's mind. The Fédon family members continue to earn a livelihood as small planters and petty slave owners. Family members, including Fédon's mother, sometimes free an enslaved person. Julien Fédon is in his late 20s or early 30s.

On February 18, 1784, Julien Fédon manumitted an enslaved individual called Isaac Marseile, a 21-month-old baby. Isaac's mother was not mentioned in the manumission certificate. Perhaps she was deceased, or perhaps she was a slave. Some slave masters manumitted the child but kept the mother in slavery. Once the free child became an adult, he or she could manumit the mother.[1]

Alternatively, Julien Fédon could have been baby Isaac Marseile's father, since it was customary for slave masters, whether white or mulatto, to have sexual liaisons with young female slaves. Julien Fédon had two girls, so perhaps he craved a son. If Isaac were Fédon's son, Fédon would want to remove the toddler from the bondage of slavery as soon as possible.

Manumission, or giving enslaved people perpetual freedom, was cumbersome in Grenada and other British West Indian colonies. The law stated, "Persons manumitting slaves must pay £100 sterling per slave to the public treasury, who must certify such payment on the back of manumission … Certified manumission must be recorded in the Registrar's Office."[2]

Further, the slave owner must assure the authorities that the enslaved person, when freed, would not be a burden to society. The person manumitting the enslaved must present three witnesses of good standing to two Britishers, known as "Guardians of Slaves," who would issue the Certificate of Freedom. The process took weeks to finalize.[3]

Julien Fédon may have taken immediate action to manumit toddler Isaac Marseile, ensuring his future freedom, in fear that the triumphant British would curtail manumission altogether. But why else might Fédon want to free little Isaac? Was he afraid that his darling wife, Marie Rose, might find out? And what was the hurry?

Julien Fédon did not present the three persons required to witness the manumission transaction; only one Britisher, Benjamin Webster (a justice of the peace), was present to issue the certificate. Unlike other manumission deeds, Isaac Marseile's was drafted, signed, and logged into the court record in a single day. By a twist of fate, Webster—who was also Registrar of the Grenada Supreme Court—supervised all legal documents, from marriage and birth certificates to estate sales and manumission deeds, that were accepted and stored by the Supreme Court. Acting together, Fédon and Webster discreetly freed young Isaac Marseile.

A slave master granting freedom to an enslaved person did not necessarily signify the munificence and godliness of the master. Manumission was also a business. Sometimes, the slave master made the decision for economic reasons; for example, to absolve the slave master from maintaining an aging or sick slave—although the law states that the slave must be in good health to qualify for manumission.

Some slave owners manumitted the enslaved for religious, ethical, or bloodline reasons. A dying slave master looking for forgiveness or seeking atonement or a clear conscience may have granted manumission to his enslaved children and their mother. Occasionally, it was a slave master's way of thanking an enslaved person for years of loyalty.

Now and then, too, the master would manumit his lover:

> *I, Louis Petit Monlauban, in the parish of Saint John…do fully, freely and absolutely enfranchise manumit and make free my Negro Woman Slave commonly called or known by the name of Rosalie… about thirty years old… from all manner of servitude and slavery… and granting unto the said Rosalie…all the privileges and advantages of a free born subject of Great Britain.*[4]

That manumission transaction was dated September 21, 1791. After being scrutinized by the British authorities, it was logged in at the Grenada Registrar's Office on October 4, 1791. Based on his name, Louis Petit Monlauban could be either a white Frenchman or a French-speaking person of color. Since he smugly described Rosalie as his "Negro Woman Slave… about thirty years old," she could have been the apple of his eye whom he planned to marry.[5]

Brewing tensions between the despotic British and the disparaged French dominated the early 1790s in Grenada, which was likely why Louis Petit Monlauban decided that Rosalie ought to have "all the privileges and advantages of a free-born subject of Great Britain…" It was a safety net for Rosalie.[6]

Although Fédon family members were small landowners, with each sibling and spouse owning from one to 39 acres of land but not enough acreage to classify them as wealthy or prestigious estate owners, the family nonetheless practiced chattel slavery. Like their land, livestock, and tools, the Fédons owned human beings as property—purchasing, selling, inheriting, exchanging, and occasionally manumitting them. The Fédons had no compunction about investing in slaves. It was a way of making ends meet. For that matter, even former slaves purchased slaves.

Sometimes, enslaved persons who gained freedom by buying themselves out of bondage or by being manumitted for any of myriad reasons might, within a short time, purchase a slave or two as an investment. That former (freed) slave would ensure that his or her own slave was well-fed and in good health in order to rent that slave to estate owners for a high sum.

So, a sizeable number of persons of color and a handful of free Africans owned slaves in the late 18th century, with a higher proportion in Grenada than in other British colonies. Most landowning mulattos were descendants of early French settlers. Born free, they inherited their father's property and became successful planters or merchants, earning enough money to purchase more land and more slaves.

Pierre and Brigitte Fédon's children and grandchildren were born free. Neither white nor British—and, as a result, unwelcome in the British colony's society—the Fédons and other free mixed-race families fostered closer relationships with free Africans and the enslaved. Perhaps those relationships were why the Fédon family frequently manumitted their slaves.

Manumitting notwithstanding, the Fédons continued to acquire other slaves as part of their land acquisitions—although archival documents showing that the Fédons purchased slaves directly from slave ships, slave brokers, or slave auctions have yet to be found. Rather, the archives show only that the Fédon family had and/or freed slaves.

On one occasion while living in Grand Pauvre, Julien and Marie Rose manumitted their slave, Louis. The three witnesses at the manumission were Paul Laurensy, Pierre Boudon, and Batarel—all friends of Julien and his wife. Certifying the deed and issuing the Certificate of Freedom were two Guardians of Slaves, Francis C. M. Clozier and William Bell.[7]

That same day, Julien's mother Brigitte, perhaps in her 60s, manumitted a slave named Anne and her six children: Jean-Louis, Matiale, Adelaide, Clotide, Jeanette, and Alexis. In keeping with strict British rule, three witnesses were at the manumission: John Adams Parker, Pierre Valie, and Etienne Ventour. Ventour would later become a ringleader of Fédon's Rebellion. Issuing the Certificates of Freedom were Guardians of the Slaves

Simon Bond, Francois Philip, and Patrick Fotheringham. Fédon later sold his Lancer property to Philip.[8]

Julien Fédon also granted freedom to Guillaume La Grange, another of his slaves. Fédon's three witnesses at that manumission proceeding were his close friends Antoine Roy, Etienne Ventour, and John Adams Parker. As the Guardians of Slaves, Dr. John Hay, Ventour's neighbor, and Baptiste Ollivier certified that Guillaume La Grange was "not likely to become burdensome to the Public and apparently healthy."[9]

And on July 10, 1791, after the Fédon's purchased Belvedere, Julien and Marie Rose manumitted a woman named Mary Jeanne and her three children: Francois Louis, Edward, and Rose. Legitimizing the manumission were Dr. John Hay and Jean Baptiste Ollivier, Guardians of Slaves.[10]

The year 1791 was quite eventful for Julien and Marie Rose. In addition to relocating to Belvedere in Saint John from Lancer in Grand Pauvre, they were liberating enslaved people while, at the same time, acquiring and selling slaves through property transactions. Eighty slaves were included in Julien and Marie Rose Fédon's purchase of Belvedere Estate, for example.[11]

On June 13, 1791, Julien and Marie Rose sold their Lancer property for £3,150 to Francois Philip, a Guardian of Slaves with property in boundary with Lancer. The sale included the land, the couple's former home, and "those ten negroes and other slaves whose name hereinafter particularly mentioned, that is to say, Ianvier, Modeste, Neptune, Bayonne, Elizabeth, Giles, Adeladie, Jeannette, Mannett, and Mary Rose."[12]

The deed stated that if a slave were pregnant, the baby in the mother's womb would become the property of Lancer's new owner, Francois Philip, and not of the Fédons. It was the custom in slave transactions across the West Indies for the baby, when born, to become the property of the owner at the time of the baby's birth.

Not all of Julien Fédon's slaves worked and lived on his property. Like many small property owners, he rented his slaves to large estate owners. Even before buying Belvedere, Julien rented some of his slaves to the large coffee estate, as implied in the deed.

SEVEN

Julien & Marie Rose Purchase Belvedere

When the Honorable James Campbell, a popular lawyer and planter, sold his 450-acre Belvedere Estate, he may have conducted the transaction unobtrusively to avoid alarming conservative Scots in the Grenada Assembly. Campbell, a senior member of the Assembly and acting governor (1788-1789), knew that the law inhibited the sale of large estates to people of color and French nationals. Nevertheless, the sale was executed to Julien and Marie Rose Fédon, an obscure French mulatto couple who subsequently became the owners of Belvedere Estate. And with that ownership came the prestige of being the only persons of color to own a large estate at the time.

On the seller's side of the transaction were four prominent Britishers: James Campbell (seller), witnesses Neil Campbell and Benjamin Webster, and Alexander Campbell—James Campbell's brother and also a lawyer. Alexander Campbell may have been in England and not present during the closing. He may have reviewed the deed on his return and kept a copy, but he made sure that a copy never got to Lushington & Law, the London-based finance company despite Alexander Campbell being Lushington & Law's agent in Grenada.[1]

Benjamin Webster, assistant justice of His Majesty's Court of Common Pleas, was acquainted with Julien and Marie Rose Fédon. As registrar of the Grenada Supreme Court, Webster ratified property sales, property acquisitions, and manumissions for the Fédons in order for those documents to be legal and kept in the Registrar's Office. And it was Webster who processed the manumission of 21-month Isaac Marseile for Julien Fédon in a single day in 1784, even though it ordinarily took weeks for investigations and court proceedings to complete a manumission. Webster knew the Fédons were semi-literate, not versed in English, and spoke mainly French.[2]

On the buyers' side at closing, only Julien Fédon and his wife were present. They had no legal representation, which was unusual for such a large purchase if evaluated by 21st century standards. In the 18th century, however, it wasn't uncommon for the same lawyers to represent both seller and buyer. Perhaps the Fédons simply trusted James Campbell, Neil Campbell, and especially Benjamin Webster. The seller and his two witnesses were among the *crème de la crème* of Grenada's legal fraternity. As a result, other lawyers—for political or business reasons—may have been uninterested (or even dreaded) questioning a legal document drafted or recommended by James Campbell, Neil Campbell, and Benjamin Webster and endorsed by the renowned Alexander Campbell.

When Isle de la Grenada officially became a British colony in 1763 and renamed Grenada, Alexander Campbell was one of the first Scots to arrive and purchase large properties. And in 1774, he won a tax case in the Privy Council in London on behalf of West Indian planters, making him highly esteemed in the British West Indies and in the 13 British Colonies in North America.

The notable foursome—James Campbell, Alexander Campbell, Neil Campbell, and Benjamin Webster—may have convinced each other that Julien Fédon, an industrious planter who verified his allegiance to the British monarch by signing the Public Declaration of Loyalty in 1790, should be given the opportunity to purchase Belvedere, a coffee-cultivated estate that was not particularly lucrative when compared to the island's sugarcane plantations.

There could also be a more furtive reason why the large Belvedere Estate was quietly sold to someone who was not permitted, by law, to purchase a large plantation. The sale could have been part of a grand act of thievery that was not uncommon during that time period.

Beginning with the first British rule of Grenada (1762-1779) and also during the second British rule (1784 onwards), British merchants and investors from England, Scotland, and Ireland—in collaboration with the

British ruling class in Grenada—muscled French plantation owners to sell or mortgage their estates. That was also when the colony's French planters hurriedly sailed to Spanish Trinidad and other French Caribbean islands, often in the middle of the night, bringing their most valuable possessions— the enslaved—to begin a new life and practice their preferred Roman Catholic religion.

The mortgages and other moneylending arrangements for those transactions were often controversial and perceived as a British scheme to grab plantations owned by Grenada's French residents. Mortgagors and mortgagees frequently accused each other of fraud. Unable to pay their exorbitant mortgages or ship equivalent amounts of produce, especially sugar, to British merchants in England and Scotland—and suspecting that the mortgagor would seize the mortgagee's land and slaves—the mortgagee, a French planter dubbed a "new subject" by the British, would flee to a friendly island (such as Saint Lucia) where the British were unwelcome.

Case in point: Incapable of paying back a £4,070 mortgage extended to him by London-based Bosanquet & Fatio, French planter Andrew Philippe, on April 13, 1773, sailed to French Saint Lucia with his 47 slaves. Bosanquet & Fatio requested that Saint Lucia's governor return the 47 slaves to Grenada, but the governor advised Bosanquet & Fatio to make the request directly to the Court of France.[3]

Also, British investors gave Madame Jacques—who may have been born or had resided in Grenada before the British captured the colony and then became a "new or adopted subject"—a £1,970 mortgage for her 153 acres and 50 slaves. The investors demurred upon hearing that her children were entitled to inherit the estate. Afraid that the investors would demand the £1,970 or claim her acreage and slaves if she were unable to make regular payments, Madame Jacques, a widow, vanished to a French colony with her slaves.[4]

These types of land grab, which began in the 1760s between the British in both Europe and Grenada against the French and free French-speaking mulattos in Grenada, would play out for decades. By the 1790s, though, the French and free mulattos, along with their slaves, were no longer disappearing from Grenada and headed to other islands. So, the British simply found better ways to play the game. Britisher James Campbell, owner of estates in both Grenada and Tobago, sold an estate he "acquired" to a free French-speaking mulatto, Julien Fédon. Was there anything sinister about that transaction? We may never know. Julien and Marie Rose might have been satisfied because one year later, August, 1792, they purchased a property in Gouyave from "the Honorable James Campbell." The Fédons paid James Campbell, Jr., who handled the transaction on behalf of his father then in England, a down payment of £800.

The house and land were "partly on Saint Dominique Street and partly on Saint Pierre Street in Charlotte Town ... bounded ... on the South by Saint Pierre Street, On the West by Saint Dominique Street, On the North by a lot of Land of the said James Campbell and on the East by Lands belonging to the French Church." The price including interest was £2,966. 2s. 6d. Like the Belvedere deal, the Fédon's were require to pay Campbell a yearly amount ending in June 1805.[5]

For archaeologist, the "French Church" is the old Roman Catholic Church and School building. Fédon's property was located in the area where Fish Friday is held (Back Street) and the library is located. What is now Saint Francis Street was probably Saint Pierre Street.

—⟨⟩—

JAMES CAMPBELL ADVOCATED IN THE Grenada Legislature that the French and mulatto planters residing in Grenada ought to convert from Roman Catholicism to Anglicanism to enjoy the largesse of British rule. At the same time, Campbell sold one of his largest estates to Julien Fédon, a staunch Roman Catholic, who refused to join the Anglican faith. Was the sale of Belvedere Estate to the Fédons, a couple with limited civil rights, part of a grand swindle by the three Campbells and Benjamin Webster?

By the early 1790s, Britishers (especially Scots) owned the sugarcane plantations, which were the most valuable, most profitable land in Grenada. Sugar, molasses, and rum (principal byproducts of sugarcane) were the products in most demand in the 18th-century global market. Former French-owned plantations—such as Grand Anse, Baillies Bacolet, L'Anse Aux Épines, Calivigny, Pointe Salines, Paraclete, Waltham, Tivoli, Dunfermline, Belmont, Petit Baccaye, Baccaye (now Westerhall), and La Sagesse—were all located in prime areas around the colony and were perfect for growing sugarcane.

As Britishers acquired the prime acreage in Grenada, French white and mulatto planters opted to purchase and cultivate land in the island's mountainous interior, such as Belvedere Estate, where frequent torrential rain was not conducive to growing sugarcane. Coffee, cocoa, and plantains flourished in the island's interior, but the demand in Europe was not great for those products.

James Campbell, Alexander Campbell, Neil Campbell, and Benjamin Webster—all astute businessmen with superb legal minds—owned estates and also managed, sold, and purchased other estates for absentee owners in Britain. Since Belvedere, a "coffee and cocoa plantation," was less valuable than a sugarcane estate, it would have made sense to James Campbell to sell the estate to Julian and Marie Rose Fédon.

With the signing of a "Memorandum of Agreement" on May 4, 1791, the ratification of the deed, and Julien Fédon's down payment to James Campbell on June 1, 1791, Julien and Marie Rose Fédon became owners of one of the largest estates in the colony during British reign. The deed, 32 pages long, details the purchase of the 450-acre Belvedere Estate. An excerpt:

> Julien Fédon of the Parish of Saint Mark in the Island of Grenada, a free Mulatto Planter, and Marie Rose Cavelan, his wife, of the one part and the Honourable James Campbell of the same parish and Island Esquire of the other part. Whereas in and by a certain Memorandum of Agreement bearing the date the fourth day of May last past ... between the above-named James Campbell ... and the above named Julien Fédon ... for conveying unto and to the use of the said Julien Fédon his Heirs and Assigns forever a certain coffee and cocoa plantation tract or parcel of land in the of Saint John called Belvidere.[6]

At the time, the Fédons owned more than 80 slaves:

> … with the buildings thereon … and also all those eighty negro and other slaves therein … and sixteen head horned cattle and five horses and other live and dead stock.[7]

There was an additional 20 enslaved:

> And also all those other twenty negro and other slaves of them, the said Julien Foden [sic] and Marie Rose Cavelan, his wife, since attached and now belonging to the same plantation.[8]

Clearly, several slaves that Julien and Marie Rose owned were toiling in Belvedere. Those 20 slaves were not listed as estate property, because James Campbell did not own them. The Fédons had previously rented those slaves to James Campbell. So, upon making Belvedere their home in June 1791, Julien and Marie Rose became the owners of 100 slaves—and subsequently continued the family custom of freeing slaves.

Every entry in the deed was meticulously explained. For example: The calves of pregnant "female cattle" and babies of pregnant slaves, when born, would be the property of Julien and Marie Rose Fédon. The names of slaves are also included in the lengthy document. And plantation tools and other estate properties are itemized, including:

> Dwelling houses and all outhouses, kitchens, stables, negro houses, mills, curing houses, and all other buildings edifices and erections of every sort … coffee and cocoa trees and all other growing things thereon … paths passages, waters, water-courses.[9]

The deed outlined the terms of the 14-year mortgage:

> He, the said Julien Fédon, did covenant with the said James Campbell not only that he would pay or cause to be paid to him the sum of fifteen thousand pounds of current money (the purchase money of the said plantation and premises) with interest at the rate of six Per Centum, per Annum.[10]

The Belvedere deed of sale between "Julien Fedon .... and Marie Rose Cavelan his wife .... and the Honourable James Campbell" was more than 30 pages.

Mortgage payments were due every June 1, beginning in 1792 and ending on June 1, 1805:

> The payment of one thousand seven hundred and fifty pounds of like current money (in first part of the said principal sum and interest) on or before the first day of June which will be the year of our Lord seventeen hundred and ninety two.[11]

The final payment was due in 1805:

> One thousand two hundred and twenty one pounds four shillings and six pence on the first day of June which will be in the year of our Lord one thousand eighteen hundred and five.[12]

After computing the annual six percent interest, the Fédons would pay James Campbell more than £20,000 for the £15,000 estate.

The Fédons paid 10 shillings to James Campbell for the indenture drafted in May 1791:

> Received the day of the date of the above written indenture of the above named Julien Fédon the sum of ten shillings current money of the said island being the consideration money above mentioned to be in hand paid by him to me.
> I say received, 10/Currency.
>
> Jas. Campbell
> Witness: Neill Campbell. Benjamin Webster.[13]

On June 1, Benjamin Webster observed the signing of the deed between the Fédons and James Campbell and evidently a down payment of 3,500. The next day, Webster in his capacity as assistant justice of His Majesty's Court of Common Pleas, officially accepted the deed when James Campbell "personally" brought it to him. There's no indication that the Fédons were present on June 2.[14]

The deed names properties in boundary with Belvedere:

> Towards the north with lands formerly belonging to Henry Louis Gailer deceased towards the south with lands late of Joseph Couston towards the east with lands belonging to the

heirs of John Harvey deceased and towards the west with lands belonging to the said James Campbell.[15]

The "lands belonging to the said James Campbell" is now the village of James Campbell.

The original copy of that deed of sale, seen by this writer in 2020 at the Grenada Registrar's Office, is readable. The paper is disintegrating and has to be handled tenderly; however, a few lines and words were pasted over with something similar to "Wite-Out," with writing over the paste. Hopefully, a forensic expert may one day determine if the deed was "doctored" in any way. The reference to the 10 shillings that Fédon paid to James Campbell is written over the paste and the 3,500 down payment is blurred.

The question, therefore, remains: Were those changes made between June 1, 1791, and June 2, 1791? Were the changes made after the rebellion or revolution, which ended in June 1796, by someone attempting to disparage Fédon and hide possible illicit activity by James Campbell? By then, Fédon was presumed dead and his wife and children had not been seen since April 8, 1795.

Belvedere Estate's borders in March 1795:

- To the north was La Croifade, a part of Mount Saint John. Fédon's brother, Jean, owned part of La Croifade; Chadeau Estate occupied another part; and the third section, Morne Jaloux, was probably owned by Louis La Grenade.
- To the southeast was Ferme Peschier Estate; above Ferme Peschier, a long mountain range stretches east to west, with Morne Vauclain its highest peak.
- To the east was Fraze Estate.
- And to the west was one of James Campbell's estates.

With the exception of James Campbell's property in the west, the other estates in boundary with Belvedere were all owned by mulattos of French ancestry and cultivated with coffee, plantains, and cocoa. The mulatto ownership of those neighboring estates would later become particularly advantageous to Julien Fédon and his revolutionaries.

⁕⁕⁕

FOR CENTURIES, EVERYONE ASSUMED THAT James Campbell owned Belvedere Estate when he sold it to Julien Fédon; however, research reveals that James Campbell no longer owned Belvedere when he mortgaged the plantation to the Fédons. Julien and Marie Rose, of course, certainly must have assumed that James Campbell had legal ownership.[16]

That said, June 1791 was when the couple and their girls relocated to their new home on Belvedere Estate: Belvedere House.

EIGHT

From Lancer to Belvedere

One wonders how Julien and Marie Rose Cavelan-Fédon's two daughters—Marie Rose, about 12 years old and her older sister, whose name is so far unknown, about 17—felt when, in June 1791, they moved from Lancer in the Parish of Grand Pauvre to their new home, Belvedere House, in the interior of Saint John. They traded a scenic view of the dazzling blue Caribbean Sea, which they could glimpse from the green hills of Lancer less than two miles away from the sea on the island's western side, for the picturesque rolling mountains of Belvedere in the middle of the flourishing sugar and coffee colony.

Perhaps the teenagers didn't care much about the move, since the only major change in scenery was being situated farther from the sea. To a certain extent, the western end of the Mount Saint Catherine Mountain range overshadows the interior of Grand Pauvre, so the girls were accustomed to the mountain peaks rising east and north of Lancer.

From Belvedere House looking south, Morne Vauclain's lush green peaks stretched east to west. Of course, it would not have been every day that the girls could see the pristine mountains whether near Lancer or Belvedere. Sometimes, the peaks were completely covered with pure white mist—especially in the early morning and on rainy days.

Since Lancer was not very far from the sea, the girls may have observed the annual whale migration heading north or watched vessels ferrying passengers and cargo to, from, and between Carriacou, La Baye, Sauteurs, Grand Pauvre, and St. George's. They may have viewed convoys of merchant vessels sailing to Europe laden with sugar, molasses, and rum.

June 18, 1791, Lancer deed: Julien and Marie Rose sold their Lancer house and property—35.5 acres or 12 quarries in Saint Mark—to Frenchman and neighbor Francois Philip for £3,550. The package included "those 10 negroes and other slaves ... plantation tools, utensils, dead stock and other things..." *(Courtesy Supreme Court Registry archives, Grenada.)*

They may have watched European naval fleets passing by. And they may have seen slave ships, packed with suffering enslaved Africans, as they approached the island.

To get a glimpse of the sea on the western side from Belvedere, the girls would have had to walk or ride on horseback to nearby Clozier Estate where the sea would appear in the far distance on a sunny day. Or they could have strolled to neighboring Fraze Estate where, near its great house, they could see the huge foamy waves of Granville Bay (Grenville Bay) on the eastern coast.[1]

Young Marie Rose and her older sister perhaps loved their new home, Belvedere Great House, with its large windows and elegant courtyard. They may have stood on the porch to see the seemingly endless hills and valleys of Morne Vauclain or Morne Qua Qua and the slave huts hidden in the flatlands among the coffee, cocoa, and plantain trees. The girls may have observed a two-floor coffee boucan near the slave huts, unaware that the boucan will one day become the prison of the colony's governor.

Perhaps the mixed-race teenagers preferred the cool breezes at Belvedere, the brilliant moonlight nights, the numerous hot and cold springs, the waterholes and ravines, the rivers filled with an abundance of crayfish and mullets, and the wildlife roaming and flying freely. A stroll down the hill from the elegant porch, following the rhythmic sound of moving water, would have brought them to the river where they would bathe and play on the large stones [as I did as a youth].

Chances are, the girls never dreamed that, a mere four years later, they would abandon their happy home; that Belvedere and its beautiful mountains would bring them misery by becoming a killing field and the execution site of the island's governor.

Until additional documents are found, a biographer can only envision the lives of Julien and Marie Rose's two daughters. Young Marie Rose's birth certificate, her presence at Morne Qua Qua on the morning of April 8, 1795, and the mention of an elder sister are all that is known about the girls.

Overthrowing the British was likely the last thing on Julien Fédon's mind when Belvedere House became his home. He had moved his family from the comparatively meager 38.5-acre Lancer to the 450-acre Belvedere Estate—

an extraordinary success for any mixed-race family. To have sacrificed that success, that wealth, by following the French Republic's doctrine of granting liberty to all people is a reflection of Fédon's character. Based on Dr. Hay and Rev. M'Mahon's writings, Fédon seems to have had no major issue with the British residents of Grenada when he purchased Belvedere Estate (from a white Britisher). But the harsh rule of Grenada's Lieutenant Governor Ninian Home and other Scots may have been what changed him.

THE LANCER DEED OF THE sale is still tucked away in the Grenada Registrar's Office. And although the deed is informative—mentioning the property's size as "twelve Quarries or thirty eight acres and a half of lands English measure"—it does not indicate when Julien and Marie Rose bought the property, from whom it was purchased, nor the price paid.[2]

Lancer's small size precluded it from Grenada's maps, but the deed does provide its location: "Bounded ... towards the North by Tufton Hall Estate and by lands ... of Pierre Veal deceased towards the east and south by lands of ... Francois Philip and towards the west by lands of the Honourable William Smith Esquire." Tufton Hall has retained its name throughout the centuries. Its 18th-century great house compound, owned by an international investor, has been renovated.[3]

It's significant to know that Lancer was bounded in "the west by lands of the Honourable William Smith Esquire," an ultraconservative protestant and member of the Assembly. Smith owned the large Revolution Hall Estate (renamed Brothers Estate in the 19th century). A road from his home and boucan, currently the site of St. John's Christian Secondary School, led to Smith's other property near Tufton Hall and Lancer. That road is still there and still used.[4]

As a child, walking with my family from Belvedere to Maran or Beau Plan, that road was our "shortcut" when we arrived at Brothers Estate great house and boucan. I was always terrified when, as a barefoot little boy, we reached the spot where the noisy river cut across the road and I had to step into the cold, rapidly moving water. Sometimes an adult lifted me up so I wouldn't slip on a stone and fall into the river and get wet. Today, a bridge spans the river at that point. The "shortcut" also leads to Victoria; William Smith co-owned Diamond Estate centuries ago. (Today, the ruins of Diamond Estate's great house and boucan are occupied by Jouvay Chocolate's factory.)

We know—again, by reviewing the deed—that Lancer was located between two large British-owned estates. But Fédon did not sell Lancer to William Smith; rather, he sold it to a Frenchman, Francois Philip of Gouyave. Did Smith want Fédon to sell Lancer to him? Were they friends or enemies? Perhaps the latter, as Smith was anti-French and against Roman Catholicism like his close friend and business associate Ninian Home.

William Smith died in 1794, a few months before Fédon's Rebellion commenced. Smith left Revolutionary Hall and his share of Diamond Estate to his estranged wife, who resided in England. He made sure, though, that his common-law wife in Grenada inherited part of his wealth: "To Sarah Dean now living with me in my house in Charlotte Town in Grenada, £100 immediately and an annuity of £150."[5]

Although Julien Fédon was in La Baye when the rebellion began, one of the first great houses and boucans that the Gouyave revolutionaries ransacked was Revolutionary Hall. Was it a revenge against the late William Smith? Joseph Barlow, Revolutionary Hall's overseer, was seized that night and on April 8, five weeks later, murdered with other Britishers at Morne Qua Qua. Due to the strategic location of Revolutionary Hall's boucan, it was occupied at various times during 1795-96 by Fédon's revolutionaries or by British forces. When traveling from Belvedere to plunder estates in Grand Pauvre, the revolutionaries also used the "shortcut" between Revolutionary Hall and Grand Pauvre.

Unlike the sale of Belvedere to the Fédons—where the deed was long and complicated—the deed for the sale of Lancer, from the Fédons to Francois Philip for £3,150, was transparent. The sale included Fédon's home and other buildings, livestock, and slaves. The indenture was made on June 2, 1791, when Philip paid "the sum of five shillings of current money" to the Fédons in the presence of Assistant Judge Ben Webster. On June 13, 1791, Francois Philip paid Julien and Marie Rose £3,150 witnessed by

Benjamin Webster. Webster officially accepted the deed and logged it into the Registrar's Office on June 18.[6]

What did Julien and Marie Rose do with the £3,150? The couple was not extravagant and it is unlikely that they intended to use it for a revolution, since that idea had not yet been conceived. Perhaps they gave the money to James Campbell as part of the deposit for Belvedere. Campbell, knowing he sold Fédon an estate that he no longer owned, may have made sure that Julien Fédon's payment was not recorded by Webster in the Court of Common Pleas.

NINE

Exploiting the Fédons

At midnight on March 2, 1795, the Fédon Revolution begins. Within weeks, Belvedere Estate becomes a household name. Newspapers in Europe and the United States such as Baltimore Federal Intelligencer, Oracle of the Day in Portsmouth, NH and Independent Gazetteer in Philadelphia, PA, describe the brutalities, and Americans who own estates and slaves in Grenada become alarmed about the destruction of their properties.

In London, Lushington & Law—the prestigious financial company that specializes in mortgaging estates in British colonies—is mortified. Belvedere Estate, which the firm owns, is the headquarters of the rebels. Moreover, Grenada's Governor Ninian Home, along with Lushington & Law's agent Alexander Campbell and other elite Britishers, have been executed by the rebels in the mountains above Belvedere.

Winston Lushington, an owner of Lushington & Law and a member of the British House of Commons, is embarrassed and also quite puzzled. How can the British government and the media say that the rebel leader, a French-speaking mulatto named Julien Fédon, owns Belvedere Estate when Lushington & Law is the owner? On the other hand, The Honorable Winston Lushington cannot show the media or Parliament a deed to verify his firm's ownership of the property. He has the deeds for other properties that his company owns in Grenada but not the deed for Belvedere.[1]

⸙

Many aristocrats and financial companies in Britain, including Lushington & Law, were absentee owners of estates in Grenada and other islands in the British West Indies. The companies extended mortgages to the owners of estates. Some purchased estates outright and created management teams in the colony or allowed the previous owner to manage the estate.

Belvedere and other estates owned by French whites and French-speaking mulattos were forfeited—other than, notably, properties that the free French-speaking mulatto Louis La Grenade owned. The government of Grenada and everyone in Britain—except, apparently, Lushington & Law—believed that Julien Fédon owned Belvedere Estate and, therefore, should be forfeited. James Campbell, however, declared that Belvedere Estate could not be forfeited, because he owned it. Campbell (the father or his son) claimed that Julien Fédon never made the annual mortgage payments for the years 1792 through 1795.

Knowing that Lushington & Law did not possess a deed for Belvedere Estate, James Campbell was shocked when the British firm claimed the property by presenting documents confirming that Alexander Campbell, its agent in Grenada, kept the mortgage deed for Belvedere Estate in the colony rather than sending it to England when James Campbell mortgaged Belvedere to Lushington & Law.

In December 1790, through its agent Alexander Campbell and his request, Lushington & Law made a "loan of £3,000 sterling to James Campbell Esquire upon Mortgage of a Plantation called Belvidere in Grenada." (Did the firm realize that Alexander Campbell and James Campbell were brothers?) A few months later, James Campbell mortgaged the same property to an unsuspecting Julien and Marie Rose Fédon for £15,000. And that was merely the beginning of what became a very big problem.[2]

Sometimes, Alexander Campbell represented both buyer and seller, mortgagor and mortgagee. On a visit to London in 1791, he received "fifty thousand pounds sterling money of Great Britain" from Lushington and Law for the Honorable Michael Scott, who lived and owned estates in Grenada. As Lushington and Law's representative in Grenada, Campbell then created the mortgage deed and sent a copy to London. Within the framework of the law, Scott appeared in the Grenada Court of Common Pleas to acknowledge that Lushington & Law was the mortgage holder of his estates and that Alexander Campbell was handling the transaction. The transaction was definitely above board, and the documents remain in good condition in the Grenada Registrar's Office.[3]

A shocked Winston Lushington was truthful when he explained that his office did not have a copy of the deed between his company and James Campbell pertaining to Belvedere Estate. A note in the deed states "Lushington and Law have no Title Deeds." Was it a ploy by the Campbell brothers to keep the deed in Grenada rather than sending it to England?[4]

FOLLOWING THE FÉDON'S REVOLUTION, PEOPLE claiming ownership of forfeited estates filed claims in European courts, as well as in Grenada's court. Sometimes the courts took years to render their verdict. For Belvedere Estate, it was 1820 when William Lushington was ultimately declared the owner of Belvedere Estate and his firm resumed control. At the time, Belvedere Estate slave population had decreased to 31 females and 38 males.

IN 1823, THOMAS DUNCAN, A resident of England, purchased Belvedere Estate, which—along with Gouyave Estate, Maran, and Morne Felix (all in Saint John) and Boulogne and Ferme Peschier in Saint Andrew—would remain in Duncan family ownership for almost 140 years. In the 1960s, some estates such as Maran were sold in small lots to ordinary Grenadians. Essie Campbell and some siblings bought Belvedere.[5]

The Duncan family took a keen interest in its Grenadian estates and lived in Gouyave when in Grenada. Sometimes, Gouyave was actually referred to as "Duncan Town," reflecting the family's contribution to the area. A plaque in Gouyave Anglican Church honors the memory of a Duncan family member who died in Gouyave. Growing up in Belvedere in the 1950s, we occasionally got clothing said to have been sent to us by the estate owners: "Some people name Duncan, living in England," the laborers said.[6]

Did James Campbell deliberately mislead the militias of Saint Patrick, Saint David, and Saint Andrew, as they assembled in La Baye on the second day of the rebellion? The day before, Fédon and his forces went to Belvedere from La Baye. The journey took about four hours, including stops at British-owned estates to seize both Britishers and their valuables.

Campbell, meanwhile, advised the militias to go to Belvedere from La Baye via Saint Patrick, Saint Mark, and Saint John in order to crush the rebellion. The militias arrived in Mount Saint John almost two days later, tired and too late. By that time, Fédon had consolidated his forces in Belvedere. While James Campbell knew the terrain of Belvedere and its surrounding areas, he remained in La Baye. In fact, during the bulk of the revolution, he stayed in St. George's, advising the government on ways to defeat Fédon.

James Campbell never visited Belvedere Estate while his brother, Alexander Campbell, and Governor Ninian Home were prisoners of Julien Fédon and made no attempt to plead with Fédon for their release. Was he afraid that Fédon would imprison and execute him, too? Was he afraid that Fédon had already discovered the questionable "sale" of Belvedere Estate—and that was why no further mortgage payments were purported to have been made after the initial down payment?

Once the Fédon Revolution ended, George Home (Governor Ninian Home's brother), who was living in Scotland, took over the ruined Paraclete and Waltham estates in Grenada and inherited their vast debts. It was then that George Home discovered that Alexander Campbell was co-owner of Paraclete. George Home mentioned the "shambolic handling of the estate's affairs by Campbell's brother James" and the fraud in which his brother, Ninian Home, was an integral part. George Home removed James Campbell from having anything to do with the estates, finding "fatal incorrectness" in legal documents created by Alexander Campbell regarding Paraclete, Waltham, and other estates.[7]

In Scotland today, Paxton House—the majestic house that Ninian Home built for his retirement—is a national landmark. Paintings of Paraclete and Waltham estates, along with Ninian Home's personal belongings and documents regarding his 30-year residency in Grenada and his horrible execution, are displayed in the museum and library.

The nefarious scam that the prominent Scots played on the Fédons is but one example of how the British exploited French-speaking mulattos in Grenada and a reason why, in 1795, most free, mixed-race Grenadians joined up with others to violently attempt to overthrow their British rulers.

Just three to four years after purchasing Belvedere Estate, Fédon discreetly planned the rebellion with other trustworthy people of color—and Belvedere House would become the revolutionary headquarters during the early weeks of the rebellion. Letters demanding that Council President Kenneth Francis Mackenzie surrender the island to the rebels would also be written at Belvedere House.

TEN

Julien & Marie Rose Liable to Pinel Family

Apart from being fascinated by their hero Julien Fédon, Belvedere laborers of the 1950s and before assumed he created the estate or bought an already developed coffee property. Sometimes when chatting about the origins of the names of cultivated areas, the older laborers, many born on the estate and lived their entire lives there, such as my Papa, Frederick Adams, mentioned a place in Belvedere or nearby they heard "long ago" people called Mount Saint Claire. The names of places changed every three or four decades, therefore, a cultivated area inherited the name of the last person who had a garden or lived in the area. By the 19th century, Mount Saint Claire may have lost its name. As a youngster with a keen ear, I vaguely heard of Mount Saint Claire but I thought it was uncultivated government land in Saint Andrew Parish near Belvedere. The laborers would have been surprised to learn that Mount Saint Claire was part of Belvedere; one can say, the original Belvedere Estate.

THE FRENCH WHO BROUGHT COFFEE and cocoa plants cultivated them across the colony but as sugar and molasses came into global demands, rich white French planters developed pristine areas nearer to coastlines into sugarcane estates such as Bonair and La Sagesse. Meanwhile, coffee and cocoa continued flourishing in the interior where the soil and climate were ideal. By the time the British arrived in 1762, free mixed-race planters and underprivileged French whites owned small coffee plantations in the mountains. Mount Saint Claire Estate was owned by the Saint Claire Lefebure family. Land surveyor Jean-Baptiste Pinel married Margaret Claire Lefebure.

Monsieur Jean-Baptiste Pinel's name is forever associated with Grenada maps. He created the last French map and released it in1763. Lieutenant Daniel Paterson copied Pinel's map to produce the first British map of Grenada released on February 1, 1780.[1]

The 1780 map shows that in 1763 Pinel owned lot 31, a 50-acre coffee and cocoa plantation. Based on Paterson's map, lot 31 is Mount Saint Claire. By the late 1760s, its size had increased to 160 acres probably the merger of Pinel and Lefebure lots.[2]

Jean-Baptiste Pinel died at an early age. In 1770, Pinel's widow, Margaret Claire Lefebure Pinel, on behalf of her five children, not yet of age, sold Mount Saint Claire "consisting of 160 Acres and 11 slaves" to Peter Nogues. Nogues died in 1772 and his family defaulted on mortgage payments.

Mount Saint Claire now back in the hands of the Pinels was sold in an auction in 1773 to William Lucas, owner of several estates, as a 249-acre coffee and cocoa plantation. (Lucas Street in St. George's leading to what were Lucas' estates near the forts at Richmond Hill still carries his name.)

Mount Saint Claire's expansion was the mergers of Moncton, a small acreage the Saint Claire Lefebure family owned, the property of Jean-Pierre Saulger (lot 23) and lands Nogues purchased from other planters. When Nogues added his other properties to lot 31, his estate totaled 249 acres.[3]

Lucas, a lawyer, politician and planter, realized that coffee estates in mountainous Grenada were, by far, less valuable than sugar estates in coastal areas. He sold the 249-acre estate in 1775 to John Porteous probably a Scott or Englishman. It was Porteous who named the merged properties Belvedere. Mostly likely Jean-Pierre Saulger had already named his property (lot 23), Belvedere and he may have started the construction of Belvedere House.[4]

Belvedere Estate, owned by John Porteous, was now a joining of several properties, lot 23 once owned by Saulger; lot 30 formerly owned by Peter

Nogues; lot 31 and Moncton previously owned by the Pinel-Lefebure family, and other undocumented lots. Its size, "four hundred and fifty six acres English statute."[5]

By 1777 John Porteous was encountering financial problems. One more time, Belvedere was placed in auction allowing James Campbell to purchase it for "five hundred pounds local currency" on May 21, 1779, less than two months before France conquered Grenada. A deed in the British archives details what Campbell purchased. "The said coffee and cocoa plantation called Mount Saint Claire and also upon other lands." The deal also included the "plantation slaves, stock and premises."[6]

It is understandable why Saulger and Porteous loved the name Belvedere or Belvidere. Belvedere, a French-Italian name and Belvidere, a Scottish name means the same thing, "beautiful to see." The panoramic view of Belvedere from Saulger home, the original Belvedere Great House, may have made Belvedere a beautiful place to see. As a four or five-year-old, I loved running to Belvedere House to learn my ABC and to enjoy the magnificent Belvedere valley and the tranquil mountain peaks of Fédon's Camp in the south.

Eleven years after his purchase of Belvedere, James Campbell either needed money or he was willing to make a hefty profit on his investment; perhaps the reason he secretly mortgaged Belvedere in late 1790 to Lushington and Law in London for £3,000 sterling and fraudulently sold it, a few months later, in 1791 to the Fédons for £15,000 local currency.

⸺⸙⸺

THE LAWYER WHO DRAFTED THE deed of sale of Mount Saint Claire to Peter Nogues was shrewd and clairvoyant. He made sure that regardless to how many times Belvedere was sold as long as the Pinel-Lefebure five children did not receive payment for the 160-acre Mount Saint Claire, the new owner was liable to them.

Although Belvedere was frequently auctioned, Monsieur Pinel children did not receive payment for the Mount Saint Claire-Moncton section. In 1792, they were adults living in French Martinique and French Tobago and represented in Grenada by William Smith prominent lawyer, politician and owner of Revolution Hall Estate and estates in Saint Mark.[7]

IT IS NOT KNOWN WHEN the Julien and Marie Rose Fédon purchased Belvedere in June 1791 if James Campbell and his lawyers told them that the Pinel children had to be paid for the Mount Saint Claire part. If they were not told, they may have been extremely frustrated in 1792 when informed they had to negotiate with each of the late Jean-Pierre Pinel children.

THINK OF THE TRANSACTION BETWEEN Sprint and T-Mobile in 2018 when "legions of lawyers from some top Am Law 100 firms" generated thousands of documents to close the megadeal. By 18th century standards, the 1792 transaction of the 160-acre Mount Saint Claire now part of Belvedere between the Pinels, James Campbell and Julien Fédon was exceedingly intricate. It will take a lawyer or professor of law versed in 18th century land transactions to clarify the deeds. Nevertheless, one can trace the origin of Belvedere and its owners due to details in the deeds.[8]

On June 5-6, 1792, numerous indentures and deeds were written. They were entered in the Court of Common pleas, St. George's on December 4, 1792. William Smith ensured that each of Monsieur Pinel five children was issued a deed. Deeds were created between James Campbell and the children, between Julien Fedon and the children and between James Campbell and Julien Fédon.

> This Indenture Tripartite made the Sixth Day of June in the year of our Lord One Thousand Seven Hundred and Ninety Two between Jean Baptiste Pinel of the island of Martinico (Martinique) Joseph Antoine Pinel of the said island of Martinico ... and Christopher William Irvine of the island of Tobago (representing his wife) ... All five acting herein by the Honorable William Smith ... their constituted attorney of the

first part; the Honorable James Campbell … at present in the City of London acting herein by James Campbell, Junior … his attorney of the second part, and Julien Fédon of the Parish of Saint John … a free mulatto planter of the third part.[9]

The deeds were created without a lawyer representing Julien Fédon although, it can be said, James Campbell, Jr. represented his father and the Fédons.

Each deed repeated the same information Jean-Pierre Pinel requested in his will that he wrote in French. He appointed his wife guardian of their five children who inherited their father's Mount Saint Claire and Moncton Estates. Each child upon reaching age 21 will get an equal share. On July 26, 1769, Margaret Claire Lefebure Pinel, now a widow, agreed to sell the properties including 11 slaves, cattle, one horse and a mule to Peter Nogues for £4,000. Nogues owned an adjacent property. The deed was sanctioned by the Grenada Court of Chancery in 1770.[10]

Beginning with Nogues, each time a purchaser defaulted on payment for Mount Saint Claire, the 160-acre estate reverted to the Pinel children. James Campbell owed the Pinels and since Julien and Marie Rose owned Belvedere in 1792, they too became liable to them for the Mount Saint Claire section of Belvedere.

> The Honorable William Smith of the Parish of Saint John … to execute for the said constituents all such deeds … as should be prepared for execution so as to rest in the said Julien Fedon his heirs and assigns, or in such as the said James Campbell should for that purpose the said plantation …. called Mount Saint Claire and the other premises mentioned in the indenture … now therefore this indenture …. and for and in consideration of the sum of 10 shillings sterling …. paid by the said Julien to each of them (five children).[11]

Julien Fédon paid 50 shillings sterling to the Pinels to own Mount Saint Claire. Evidently, James Campbell paid or negotiated with the Pinels through Smith what was owed on the Mount Saint Claire mortgage. Fédon now had to pay James Campbell the annual mortgage they negotiated in 1791 for the entire Belvedere Estate.

Overall, Julien and Marie Rose Fédon had to pay James Campbell two mortgages each year totaling thousands of pounds through 1805 for Belvedere and Gouyave properties.

ONE MAY NEVER KNOW WHETHER Julien and Marie Rose felt they were exploited. What is known is: Although William Smith died in 1794, the first estate the revolutionaries on the Gouyave side seized on March 2, 1795 was Smith's Revolution Hall Estate; the revolutionaries seized its overseer, Mr. Barlow, who was murdered with Home on others at Mount Qua Qua. It seems that Fédon had no mercy on Britishers he negotiated land deals with. James Campbell was smart enough to stay away from Fédon and Belvedere during the rebellion.

THE PURCHASE OF BELVEDERE ESTATE and a property in Gouyave from an eminent Scot by an ordinary, French-speaking mulatto couple may have made people think that things were all just dandy between the colony's British government and the French citizenry and free French-speaking mulattos—but it was quite the opposite. Ownership of Belvedere Estate and more than 100 slaves made Julien and Marie Rose Fédon one of the colony's wealthiest planters, yet the Fédons were not welcomed into Grenada's British social or ruling class. Ethnic, class and religious discord was rampant. And none of that escaped Julien Fédon.

PART II

Discontent in Isle de la Grenade

ELEVEN

Scots in Control

By the early 1790s, Grenada's contentious classes and its religious and ethnic groups were perceptible. The colony's societal structure resembled a pyramid, with the powerful, "natural-born" British citizens—actually born in Scotland, England, or Ireland—and their Grenada-born children, as long as both parents were British, at the pinnacle. As historian George Brizan observed, "By 1795, Grenada was divided into two communities, each hostile to the other—one Anglo-Saxon and the other Francophone."[1]

Upon capturing Isle de la Grenade on March 4, 1762, Britain may as well have renamed it "Little Scotland," as Scots dominated the island (except for 1779-1783, when France controlled it). The Scots chiefly administered the transition of Grenada from French to English rule; and in 1766, 13 of the 21 seats in Grenada's Assembly were held by Scots.[2]

By 1795, almost every governor—including Robert Melvill, Lord George Macartney, Ninian Home—and Council President Kenneth Francis Mackenzie were all Scots. And since governors appointed members of the council, the executive branch of government, they chose mainly Scots.[3]

So, the "natural" subjects were aristocrats from Scotland, along with a few wealthy people from England and Ireland. Money to purchase and develop estates came from family inheritances and wealthy investors, again mainly from Scotland. British planters owned the large estates, governed the colony, dictated religious policies, and controlled the civil liberty of French nationals and free mulattos either born or residing in Grenada.

Included in the elite group of Scots was Lieutenant Colonel Alexander Johnstone, son of Sir James Johnstone, Third Baronet of Westerhall near

Dumfries in Scotland, who bought Baccaye Estate in Saint David, Grenada, in 1766 for £23,500—likely from a fleeing French planter—and renamed it Westerhall. Only four years later, in 1770, the 1,000-acre Westerhall Estate was valued at £95,017.[4]

Other British nobles who purchased French-owned estates at bargain prices included James and Alexander Baillie of Inverness, Scotland, who purchased Hermitage Estate in 1765; Alexander Campbell, who purchased Tivoli Estate; and John Aitchison and Peter Gordon, who purchased Belmont Estate.[5]

Also, among the colony's British ruling class were middle- and working-class Scots and other Britishers: merchants, traders, small planters, overseers, bookkeepers, doctors, Protestant ministers, and poor whites. Loyal subjects such as Rev. Francis M'Mahon of Scotland and Dr. John Hay of England were also part of the middle class. While they did not make laws, they certainly enforced them.

When Fédon's Rebellion began in early 1795, Governor Ninian Home, Britain's head of government in the colony, stood at the very top of the social pyramid—safeguarding British interests while keeping a keen eye on the mistrusted French-speaking population. Ninian Home had been living in Grenada for almost 31 years. Upon his arrival in 1764, he would see French residents quietly practicing their religious faith, Roman Catholicism. Three decades later, as governor of the colony, Home would curtail the rights of those same French-speaking Grenadians while also exhibiting anti-Catholic sentiments.

Although Home owned numerous sugar cane plantations, including some 400 slaves, and managed others for absentee owners, history associates him mainly with Paraclete and Waltham estates. Paraclete is the resting place of his wife, Penelope. It is unclear who sold Paraclete Estate to Home, but he purchased the 631-acre Waltham Estate in 1776 for £34,000 from either the de Gannes family or a London investment company that may have held the mortgage.

Waltham is identified as Lot 20 in the 1780 British map of Grenada. Lieutenant Daniel Paterson, the British surveyor, copied the French survey of 1763 by Monsieur Pinel but changed the French names of parishes, towns, and rivers to English names; for example, Paroisse Du Grand Marquis became Saint Andrew, and Goyave River became Charlotte River.

———

OVER THE CENTURIES, EVEN IN the 21st, Waltham Estate carved its name into Grenada's history. The area was an enclave for the indigenous inhabitants who survived French annihilation. Julien Fédon and the wives of two of his brothers, who were of native ancestry, lived in the vicinity.

In 1722, Simon de Gannes de la Chancellerie, who descended from the ancient high *noblesse d'epte* of Britanny and Poitou in France, departed French Quebec and settled in Isle de la Grenade. It is unknown whether Waltham Estate in the Paroisse de Grand Pauvre existed before de Gannes arrived or whether he created Waltham from land lots that the government of France made available when it wrested the island from the indigenous people.[6]

Rosa de Gannes, a daughter of Simon de Gannes, was born at Waltham Estate in 1728 and, in 1742, married another French Creole (born in the West Indies of French parentage) named Philippe Roume de Saint Laurent. Philippe was in his late 30s when he married 14-year-old Rosa. He owned six estates: Paradise, Lataste, Trievia, St. Laurent, and Duquesne in Pariosse de Grand Pauvre and Belvedere in Pariosse des Sauteurs. When Philippe died in 1765, Rosa de Gannes Roume inherited his estates, as well as her parents' Waltham Estate, making her, at 37, one of the richest persons in Grenada.[7]

Rosa allowed her eldest son, 22-year-old Philippe-Rose Roume—born on October 13, 1743, and just 15 years younger than his mother—to manage her estates. Although Rosa and her children were born in Grenada, the British branded them "new subjects" (as they did other French people living on the island).[8]

"New subjects" lost their civil, religious, and political rights. Shrewd London speculators aggressively approached anxious French-speaking planters and persuaded them to sell or mortgage their estates. Young and rather naïve Philippe-Rose Roume and his mother were early victims of those ravenous British speculators. Ultimately, Bosanquet & Fatio, a London money-lending company, foreclosed on the estates for unpaid loans.

Embarrassed and deflated by losing the estates, Philippe-Rose Roume began a new life in Spanish Trinidad. He would eventually carve his name into the history of Trinidad, Haiti, and Tobago (Tobago was not yet part of Trinidad), as well as of France, Spain, and Grenada. Philippe-Rose Roume was an original West Indian nationalist.

After purchasing or otherwise acquiring lands in Maraval and Diego Martin in Trinidad and befriending Don Juan de Catilla, a Spanish officer and surveyor, Roume recommended that Trinidad accept French planters fleeing British Grenada with their slaves. In 1783, Spain accepted Roume's bold idea. Once emigrating to Spanish Trinidad became legal, the exodus of French Grenadians to Trinidad increased. Becoming a friend of both the Spanish and the French, Philippe-Rose Roume de St. Laurent went on to play significant roles in the French and Haitian revolutions.

Meanwhile, with the help of Francois Besson, Roume's mother, Rosa, valiantly attempted to recover her estates by taking her case to judicial courts in England and France. The Besson family, like the Roume and de Gannes families, were French nobility that owned large estates in Isle de la Grenade. By the early 1770s, Rosa had remarried and purchased Pointe Salines, a cotton and sugar plantation, from Francois Besson. In 1777, however, before she permanently emigrated to Spanish Trinidad, Rosa sold Pointe Salines back to Besson. (Today, Pointe Salines is the location of Grenada's Maurice Bishop International Airport.)[9]

As a youth in the 1750s and 1760s, Julien Fédon may have heard his parents and other French families complain about how the British were restricting the religious, political, and landowning rights of the French. As an adult and property owner, Fédon certainly observed the continuing British animosity toward the French—a situation that continued to deteriorate. Moreover, Britishers like Ninian Home and Alexander Campbell, who helped create tensions in the 1760s, still governed the colony.

Philippe Roume, Ninian Home, and Julien Fédon were all property owners in the Parish of Grand Pauvre, but there would have been little, if any, friendship among them. Roume and Fédon both spoke French and may have come across each other in Grand Pauvre. Perhaps Fédon saw Home, the British aristocrat, mounted on his horse going to and coming from his Waltham Estate. But did the French mulatto and the Scottish aristocrat ever greet each other? Probably not, due to their different language, race, and class.[10]

Roume and Home, however, were both white. And while Home was born in Scotland (1732) and Roume was born in Grenada (1743), both descended from European nobility and were educated men. Both were members of the Grenada Assembly but were loyal to opposite sides: Home, to Britain; Roume, to France.

Just 25 years old in 1768, Roume joined the Grenada Assembly when two seats were allocated to the French. He refused to take an oath against his Roman Catholic faith and declined to join the militia, much to the irritation of Home and other Scots. In 1776, Acting Lieutenant Governor William Young had enough of Roume's truculence and disqualified him from the Assembly.

Considering himself *persona non grata* in the island of his birth, Roume made his initial trip to Spanish Trinidad in 1777 and established himself there in 1781. He then created links to other West Indian colonies, including Saint Domingue (Haiti), and to the governments of Spain and France.

By 1792, Roume and Home were in different worlds, living on two different islands and moving forward in opposite directions. Home, after visiting Scotland and England for several months, returned to Grenada in November of that year as the island's Lieutenant Governor, appointed by British Secretary of State for War Henry Dundas. Dundas vehemently opposed the abolition of slavery and supported war against France; he advocated for the invasion of Saint Domingue, for the expansion of British colonies worldwide, and for curtailing the liberty of French-speaking Grenadians. With great alacrity, Ninian Home, a faithful British subject, enforced Dundas's philosophy by curbing French and mulatto freedoms even more.

Partly triggered by Home's conservative leadership, the reservoir of discontent that Roume had left behind in Grenada, two decades earlier, greatly intensified. By 1795, that reservoir was about to overflow—and Julien Fédon was ready to break the dam.

⸙

ALL WAS NOT WELL WITHIN the British ruling class of the early 1790s. Those aspiring to be lieutenant governor of Grenada and feeling deserving of the position were unhappy to learn that Henry Dundas bestowed the position upon Ninian Home without consulting anyone in Grenada. Perhaps Dundas's decision was based on Home's three decades of residency in the colony and his experience as a planter, lawyer, politician…and Protestant.

Ahh…not exactly. The Scottish old-boy network was definitely at play. Henry Dundas, Ninian Home's elder brother George Home, and Ninian Home's nephew Patrick Home were all close friends who had been influential in Scotland and in the British Parliament. In 1786, Ninian persuaded George to ask Dundas to appoint him governor of Dominica. Patrick Home, a regular guest at Denira, Dundas's home near Wimbledon in London, also lobbied Dundas on behalf of Uncle Ninian. In March 1792, George sent a note to Dundas: "I had the pleasure of seeing you at Denira and renewed the application for my brother in case of a vacancy in the Government of Grenada."[11]

There was a vacancy for the governorship of Grenada. Many expected Acting Governor Samuel Williams, who had been performing the duties since 1789, to be named governor in 1792. Moreover, Williams has also been acting governor in 1787-1788 and, therefore, was experienced.

Dundas discussed Ninian Home with British Prime Minister William Pitt; subsequently, in October 1792, Ninian Home was appointed Governor of Grenada. By sheer coincidence, Ninian and Penelope Home were vacationing in Scotland and England at the time and may have also met Dundas at social events.[12]

Upon returning to Grenada in December 1792 to assume the duties of governor, Ninian Home did not receive an enthusiastic welcome from his political rivals. Acting Governor James Campbell (1788–1789) and Acting Governor Samuel Williams had both been spurned on two occasions by Secretary of State Dundas, so a chilliness was definitely evident among the British ruling class in the colony.

Would James Campbell, Samuel Williams, and other Home adversaries rescue him if island-wide chaos erupted? Could Governor Home rely on the loyalty and support of the colony's small white French population? Or would that small white French population support Julien Fédon—or any other French-speaking mulatto—if a clash arose?

TWELVE

White French Roman Catholics

From a color, race, and Eurocentric perspective, white French people were considered just below the British subjects in terms of class in 18[th]century Grenada. From the 1760s through the 1780s, numerous French families, devoted Roman Catholics, along with their slaves had departed Grenada for neighboring Spanish Trinidad. Still hoping to amass a fortune in the West Indies, other French families relocated to French colonies such as Guadeloupe, Sainte Lucie (Saint Lucia), and Martinique. By March 1795, Grenada's white French population had decreased significantly; those that remained were powerless.[1]

Before the British conquest of Grenada in 1762, French citizens, free mulattos or free mixed-race people, and free Africans owned 100 percent of the estates. In a survey conducted 10 years later, in 1772 during the first British governance, the French (then called "new" or "adopted" subjects) owned just half of the estates. The British ("natural" subjects) owned about 42 percent, and free mulattos and free Africans owned about 8 percent.[2]

Just as the French ownership of plantations steadily declined, French political power was nearly obliterated. The British in Grenada abhorred the French for their nationality, their religion, and their allegiance toward France. French representation in the Grenada Assembly and Council was restricted, causing much discontent. Sometimes, however, the British elites—Scots, English, and Irish—were divided on the political rights bestowed upon the French.

On August 3, 1768, the British Government instructed Acting Governor Ulysses Fitzmaurice to have two Catholics sit in the Council and three in the Assembly and to appoint Catholics to administrative positions in the parishes. In this context, the British Government considered Catholics to be white Frenchmen—not French-speaking mulattos such as Julien Fédon and Louis la Grenade, who were also Catholic. Still, Scots and other Protestants in the legislature fervently opposed London's mandate. The few appointments made by Acting Lieutenant Governor Fitzmaurice were reversed when Robert Melvill, a Scot, became governor for a second time. The policy of Scots, such as Melvill and, later, Ninian Home, to exclude French Catholics from the legislature became law and was implemented.[3]

By early 1795, Britishers owned the prime sugarcane estates. White French people owned a few estates, such as Plaisance in Saint John, but the French population was miniscule. Yet, Governor Ninian Home and other Britishers expected the support of the French population during local calamities such as slave uprisings or invasions.

For someone who spent almost his entire adult life in Grenada, Home never appreciated French contributions toward developing the colony, such as creating the parishes, towns, forts, and ports and for importing the coffee and cocoa plants. Home ignored the fact that the French were in Grenada for 112 years, long before he arrived, and many French were descendants of early French settlers.

Ninian Home was distrustful of the island's white French population and did not discount the possibility of French whites and free French-speaking mulattos conniving together to create bedlam. Home was aware that white French planters seeking autonomy from France instigated the initial rebellion in French Saint Domingue (Haiti) in 1789. Though unsuccessful, those white French planters tried to imitate what revolutionaries had accomplished in 1776 in Britain's 13 colonies in North America.

In 1791, Saint Domingue's free mulattos revolted in order to gain the same liberties enjoyed by the colony's white population, but that revolt failed. Then it was the slaves turn. Saint Domingue's slaves followed the lead of the mulattos and the whites before them, and 1791 is recognized as the beginning of the successful Haitian Revolution. Also, in that year, a communiqué from Grenada to the British government informed the home country about the scale of the insurrection in Saint Domingue, where 68,640 slaves had already destroyed 1,126 estates.[4]

It is rather ironic that the warning to Britain about Saint Domingue came from Grenada. Would a similar scenario occur in Grenada? Would French whites, French-speaking mulattos, and enslaved people revolt against the British? If so, would they revolt as separate groups or as a single, united force?[5]

That concerned Governor Home and his colleagues. To complicate matters, renewed warfare between the two historic antagonists, Britain and France, forced Home in 1794 to proclaim martial law and place restrictions on French-speaking coloreds entering the colony.

⚭

Julien Fédon and other mulatto planters were not part of the British class nor the white French class but were certainly observing Home's drastic actions. By 1794, in remote Belvedere, Fédon and his trusted core group of free mulattos were preparing to end British governance of Grenada. For their own safety, the group included very few Frenchmen in their inner circle. A handful of French families who were opposed to various republican governments in France were living in Grenada and had pledged their allegiance to the British monarch. On Home's request, Julien Fédon and most other free people of color cleverly pledged allegiance to Britain's King George III, as well.

Did Julien Fédon and his cadre of French-speaking mulattos feel confident that they could end British rule by themselves? Did they know that they would need the support of the white French population? And was liberty for all people, including the enslaved, their motive? Perhaps Fédon knew that the combined support of free Africans, maroons, and the enslaved would be a powerful force against the British.

THIRTEEN

People of Color

Comprising the base of the social pyramid in 18th-century Grenada were people of color, with subgroups within that population. Free mulattos of French descent, such as the Fédons, Bessons, and La Grenades, constituted a large subgroup. The English-speaking mulatto population was not as large, and the free African landowning class was even smaller.[1]

The stealthy maroons were also part of that base. The maroons were recalcitrant and rejected bondage and did not fear Europeans. Also called "runaways" and "self-emancipated slaves," maroons lived elusively in the mountains since early 17th-century French rule. British planters, French planters, free people of color, and even some enslaved people were all afraid of the maroons.[2]

Like their counterparts in Saint Domingue (Haiti), where that island's innumerable factions and rebellion leaders bribed maroons for support, it was an open question as to whether Grenada's maroons would be asked to support whichever group spearheaded a rebellion.

The enslaved people who toiled in the fields or worked in the master's home represented the largest subgroup in terms of people of color. In the event that free people of color and French whites were to revolt against British oppression, would they exclude Grenada's enslaved population—as white organizers had during the initial stage of the Haitian Revolution?

People of color not only comprised the base of the social pyramid, they also comprised the majority of the population in the early 1790s—a trend that had been increasing since the mid-1760s. A 1763 survey revealed 455 free people of color and 12,000 enslaved and 1,225 white. A similar survey in 1783 indicated 1,125 free people of color and 24,620 enslaved.[3]

Was Julien Fédon aware that people of color comprised 80 percent or more of the colony's population? If he did know, could he unite the various segments despite their different languages, religions, shades of color, and status in order to end British domination?

Free French-speaking mulattos—including the Fédons, Louis La Grenade, and Joachim Philip—owned a considerable amount of acreage, both small and large properties. Many of the mulatto landowners were the descendants of 17th- and early 18th-century white French males and their young female slaves. Born free, Grenada was home. Other landowners in the people-of-color group were former slaves who inherited property through wills and manumissions; a few had purchased themselves out of slavery.

Upon seizing the island in 1762, the British were surprised to find significant numbers of people of color who were free and owned property—and the British were not pleased about it. To their further chagrin, most newly freed enslaved Africans were French-speaking people who supported anything French.

Between 1762 and 1795, through local legislation such as the 1767 law requesting £100 for each slave manumitted, the British slowed down the pace of coloreds becoming free and owning property. The premium that the British demanded for manumitting a slave made planters think twice before seeking manumission. Yet, during those three decades from 1762 through 1795, the Scots, English, and Irish unintentionally increased the colored population in the colony.

In 1763, there were 711 white British males in Grenada and 514 white British females, a "shortage" of 197 white females. The free colored population in that year included 236 males and 219 females, close to an even proportion.[4]

By 1777, Grenada's white male population was 1,034; the white female population, a mere 290. How did British males address the acute shortage of British women? Thousands of beautiful, young enslaved females had no choice but to yield to their master. The result! A dramatic increase in the free and unfree colored population was clearly visible by late 1794.[5]

A divide existed among the free coloreds, as well. French-speaking mulattos were biased toward France, accepted French values, and owned more property than English-speaking mulattos. In 1783, Grenada had 940 free French-speaking people of color and only 185 free English-speaking people of color—a disparity that continued throughout the 1780s. English-speaking mulattos tilted toward English values, and many threw in their lot with Britain.[6]

To make matters worse for the British around that time, French-speaking mulattos from other islands were rapidly arriving in Grenada. Governor Ninian Home was alarmed by the influx and, by early 1795, presented measures to curb the flow of new arrivals and monitor their movements. That influx, however, very likely pleased Julien Fédon.

In European colonies across the Americas, including Grenada, people of color were classified into various categories based on the percentage of African blood flowing in their veins. In French Saint Domingue and the British West Indies, a mulatto was defined as the offspring of a "pure" white European and a "pure" black African. The child of a mulatto woman and a white man was classified as a quarteron in Saint Domingue and a quadroon in Grenada.[7]

History describes Julien Fédon as a mulatto, and he is listed as a mulatto in property transactions. Actually, Julien Fédon was a quadroon, because he was the offspring of a mulatto woman and white European father. Marriage and birth certificates of the wives of the Fédon brothers, their daughters, and even their mother Brigitte record them as being *mustee* or *mestize*, indicating that they were of mixed race.

Those distinctions were important in Grenada and other islands, where mobility was determined by color. Some *mustees* and *mestizes* were, in fact, enslaved—which is why Marie Rose Cavelan Fedon, a *mestize*, had to prove her status. The more European blood one had and the lighter the pigmentation, the better chance that person had to progress.

Free Africans, or people with only African blood, did not own much property. And unlike free mulattos, they could not inherit property. In 1772, for example, free Africans owned five plantations, while mulattos owned 18; free Africans owned 148 acres and 100 slaves, while free mulattos owned 1,071 acres and 283 slaves. As a result of that wealth discrepancy, a chilliness existed between free Africans and the more prosperous free mulattos.[8]

In French Saint Domingue, Dutch Suriname, French Guiana (Guyana), Spanish Cuba, and the British West Indies, free mulattos and free Africans were encouraged by European planters to maintain the plantation system and slavery. That same strategy was implemented in Grenada. British whites actually included free Africans and free mulattos in some of their social events: "Symbolic reward and signals … such as special commissions in the militias, inclusion into white social events, and sharing worship in the same churches and finance to enable Free Coloured children to be educated in Britain."[9]

That directive may be why many writers, including Father Raymund Devas, erroneously assumed that Julien Fédon was educated in England. Father Devas quoted the introduction of Hay's book by a 'Military man' but Hay never wrote, "This man was educated in England." The 'Military man,' who lobbied for the continuation of slavery released Dr. Hay's manuscript in 1823. Hay died in Grenada in 1807.[10]

The divide-and-conquer tactic encouraged by European colonizers was played out in the Haitian Revolution, Fédon's Revolution, and other rebellions. Among free coloreds in Saint Domingue in 1793, for instance, "the mulatto army established their domination. But when the fighting was over, they chose some of the bravest slaves and offered them freedom if they would lead the rest back to slavery … The offer was accepted, and 100,000 slaves were led back to their plantations."[11]

It would take courageous leaders such as Toussaint (Breda) Louverture, Jean-Jacques Dessalines, and Grenada-born Henri Christophe in Saint Domingue, along with Julien Fédon in Grenada, to bridge the divide between free people of color, runaway slaves (maroons), and the enslaved.

Enslaved people, while together comprising the lowest rank on the huge base of Grenada's social pyramid, were not a homogenous group. House slaves felt they were better than field slaves, because they worked in the master's home and lived nearby. Field slaves had issues, too. Those born in Grenada or sent there from other colonies believed they were superior to the newly arrived from Africa, who could not understand a word of either English or French.

Furthermore, most slaves owned by British masters supported their British masters, while French-speaking slaves tended to support their French masters. In 1783, slaves owned by British planters totaled 16,240—and most spoke or understood English—while the 8,280 slaves belonging to French planters conversed in French. Would English-speaking slaves abandon their British owners if an opportunity to gain freedom appeared?[12]

It is likely that Julien Fédon was aware of the animosities in and among the enslaved population. In all probability, Fédon was also keeping abreast of developments in Saint Domingue, where white planters and merchants seeking autonomy from France rebelled violently but did not ask slaves to join them in their quest for independence. And, as a result, the white plantocracy of Saint Domingue failed. Perhaps Fédon and his plotters did not want to make that same mistake and were creating strategies to involve Grenada's enslaved people in the emerging insurrection against British exploitation.

TENSIONS HAD BEEN BREWING IN Grenada since the arrival of the British in 1762. And, by 1794-95, those tensions had grown. Internal problems were leading to outright violence, and external factors—such as violence in Saint Domingue and the revolution back in France—were adding fuel to the fire. Also, Carib leader Joseph Chatoyer in neighboring Saint Vincent and the maroons of Trelawny, Jamaica, were both about to lead their own rebellions against the British.[13]

Julien Fédon and his confidantes had a couple of important advantages. First, they were able to follow developments abroad, as communication was not too difficult. Americans who lived in the United States and owned estates in Grenada frequently corresponded with their managers, family members, and friends. Second, they were able to learn from the French and Haitian revolutions, both still in progress, and the successful American Revolution.

Although the American Revolution began in 1775 and ended in 1783, brisk trade between the former 13 colonies and Grenada continued—despite British opposition.

FOURTEEN

Julien Fédon and the Americans

It is July 4, 1776. Julien Fédon is in his early 20s and has been married for two years. The news about the North American colonies' unilateral declaration of independence and federating as one nation hasn't yet reached Grenada. Shortly, though, Julien, his father Pierre, and the rest of the Fédon clan will ponder developments in Britain's 13 colonies in North America and the deterioration of the relationship between England and the American patriots.

There's a shortage of food and lumber because England has prohibited its West Indian colonies from trading with the 13 rebellious colonies. Events unfolding in North America are also making discussions livelier among Grenada's legislators. Some are quite jittery. Although white French and French-speaking mulattos are excluded from election to Grenada's Assembly or appointment to the Scots-dominated Council, those populations are certainly aware that the North American issue is a source of contention among Grenada's politicians.

The 13 colonies on North America's Eastern Seaboard and the 26 British West Indian, or Caribbean, colonies (including Grenada) were spawned from the same mother country: England. And while all of those colonies were governed by England, sugar caused Britain to value its West Indian colonies more than its tobacco-growing North American ones. Barbados alone was worth more to England than its colonies in New England and the Carolinas—combined.

Long before July 4, 1776, the dissolving relationship between England and its American colonies, as well as the quest for independence, had become well known in Grenada and other British West Indian colonies. In 1775, for instance, Bermuda sent a delegate, Henry Tucker, to the First Continental Congress. Tucker connived with Benjamin Franklin to smuggle 3,150 tons of gunpowder from the British in Bermuda to George Washington troops in Boston. The Jamaica Assembly and the Grenada Assembly had passed resolutions supporting the independence movement in North America, despite the Grenada Assembly being bitterly divided over the issue. The conservative Scots, Irish, and Englishmen fought the liberal Scots, Irish, and Englishmen; nevertheless, legislators favoring the rebellion in Colonial America narrowly won the vote on the issue. A few days later, the losing side demanded another vote—and lost again. That time, the losing side accepted defeat; but with assistance from supporters in England, they cunningly arranged for the resolution to be dispatched "unofficially" to England in order to prevent its formal receipt by King George III.[1]

Importing codfish (saltfish), herring, lumber, and other products from North America and exporting sugar, molasses, rum, spices, and coffee to the 13 colonies were not the only reasons for the close relationship between Grenada and Colonial America. Several American colonists—such as Samuel Cary and Mather Byles of Massachusetts—lived, managed, and owned estates in Grenada.[2]

⟶⟡⟵

With France and England also at war, along with French support for the American patriots, the American War of Independence was not restricted to the American mainland. The British, Dutch, Spanish, and French West Indian islands and the surrounding Caribbean Sea saw battles between British and French naval forces. Julien Fédon, then in his mid-20s, was most likely living in Grenada in 1779 and gratified to witness the recapture of Grenada by the French.

⟶⟡⟵

THE YEARS 1779-1783 WERE SUSPENSEFUL for Grenada's French and French-speaking free mulattos, because Grenada was a French colony once more and a dismal place for English planters and politicians. They lost authority. Despite governing the island, however, many French people were afraid that the English would recapture the island.

Samuel and Sarah Cary apparently agreed with the goal of the North American patriots in the 13 colonies and with the actions of fellow Massachusetts native John Hancock, the first person to sign the Declaration of Independence (with the most flamboyant signature!), and his sloops traded in Grenada. To avoid offending conservative Scots and English, however, the Carys could not publicly gloat over the success of the American Revolution. In fact, Grenada's Governor Mathew mildly threatened to imprison Samuel, even though they were friends, and send him to England as a traitor.[3]

A few years later, in 1795, would the developments in North America inspire Julien Fédon to lead a revolt in Grenada against British domination and oppression? Did the American Founding Fathers have an impact on Fédon and other French-speaking mulattos, who were similarly unhappy with the British and with British rule?

In 1796, when Fédon's Revolution had ended, Julien Fédon and other rebel leaders had no time to pen their stories nor to reveal whether or how the American Revolution may have influenced them. The rebels were all either dead or living in secrecy. Also, no evidence has been found in the British, U.S., or French archives that indicate that the American experience contributed at all to Fédon's Revolution. Over the centuries, writers have conjectured that the American pursuit of liberty influenced Fédon, but that is impossible to confirm.

FIFTEEN

The Carys of Boston

The saga of Samuel Cary, his wife Sarah Gray Cary, and their son Samuel Cary, Jr.—residents of both New England and Grenada—is fascinating. Their ancestors and descendants are all deeply embedded in the colonial and postcolonial history of Massachusetts; their ancestral home is currently a museum and national landmark; and the Cary Family Letters are archived at the Massachusetts Historical Society and other institutions. Samuel and Sarah's granddaughter, Elizabeth Cary Agassiz (1822–1907), is celebrated as a founder and the first president of Radcliffe College in Cambridge, Massachusetts.[1]

Sarah Gray Cary's great uncle, John Gray, and her cousin, Samuel Gray, are both linked to the Boston Massacre—a street brawl that occurred on March 5, 1770, between colonists and a single British soldier that escalated into a bloody slaughter and energized the colonial crusade for independence from England. Samuel Gray, a ropemaker, was among the first three men shot by British soldiers on that memorable day and, mortally wounded, became known as one of the first casualties of the American Revolution.

Samuel Cary was born in Charlestown, Massachusetts, on September 20, 1742, and studied at Harvard College. Sarah Gray Cary, was born in Boston in 1753. Both trace their roots to 17th-century England. Cary's great grandfather, James Cary, sailed from Bristol, England, to the Massachusetts Bay Colony in 1639; Edward Gray sailed to Boston from Lancashire, England, in 1686. One of James Cary's sons, Captain Nathaniel Cary, Sr. (1645-1730), realized that a fortune could be made in the West Indies from the burgeoning, tobacco and cotton industries and the slave trade—

and he did, in fact, make a fortune by trading with England, the West Indies, and New England. Accused but found "not guilty" of practicing witchcraft during the controversial witchcraft trials (1692-1693) in Salem, Massachusetts, may have been the reason why Captain Nathaniel Cary, Sr. chose to live most of his life at sea.

The tradition of Carys and Grays working as traders, merchants, planters, slave owners, and preachers continued with Captain Samuel Cary, the son of Captain Nathaniel Cary, Sr. and father of Samuel Cary. The same year that his son was born, 1742, Captain Samuel Cary sailed into St. Kitts, established a business, and—like his ancestors—established trade with the rest of the British West Indies, Colonial America, and England. (Utterly confusing, but not particularly unusual at the time, four generations of sons born between 1683 and 1773 were named Samuel Cary.)[2]

Around 1764, Captain Samuel Cary recommended his 22-year-old son (the above-mentioned Samuel, born in 1742) to William Manning, a planter and merchant in Saint Kitts. Samuel began working for Manning but also befriended John Bourryau, who offered a challenging proposal: Bourryau would help the young man purchase his own estate in Grenada if Cary would emigrate to Grenada and manage Bourryau's 466-acre sugarcane estate, one of the island's largest, called Simon (Seamoon) in Saint Andrew. Cary visited Grenada with Bourryau in 1769 and accepted the offer. Bourryau later arranged for Cary to purchase Mount Pleasant, a 140-acre coffee estate in Grenada's Grand Pauvre area.

In addition to owning Mount Pleasant Estate and managing Simon Estate, Samuel Cary saw another opportunity. Asked to arrange for a ship to transport a cargo of lumber and other items from New England and return with sugar, Cary envisioned a lucrative import/export business. Eventually, he became a successful planter, estate manager, and merchant in Grenada and, as a result, enabled his descendants in Massachusetts to enjoy a rather affluent lifestyle.

After an absence of five and a half years, Samuel Cary returned to Massachusetts in July 1770 to mourn the death of his father, Captain Samuel Cary, who died on December 4, 1769, and to secure his share of his father's wealth. "I give my House and Land in Boston ... to my son

Samuel Cary and his heirs for ever," read the elder Cary's will. He left his son "£2200 Stl £1000 in money the other in House and land." In the five months back home, 28-year-old Samuel Cary fell in love with Sarah Gray, married her, and then sailed to Grenada *without her* on December 5, 1770, aboard *Captain Smithwick*—but not before arranging financing for Mount Pleasant Estate. Cary did return to Massachusetts to see Sarah on at least one occasion, because their child—known as Samuel Cary, Jr.—was born in late 1773.[3]

"In January 1774, Sarah Gray Cary made the heart-wrenching decision to leave her three-month-old son with her mother in Chelsea, Massachusetts, in order to be reunited with her husband, who had returned to Grenada." Sarah departed just as relations between England and the American colonies, especially Massachusetts, began to deteriorate. Boston Harbor was partially blocked by the British and otherwise frozen by the harsh winter, forcing Sarah to sail out of Portsmouth, New Hampshire.[4]

While residing in Grenada—21 years for Samuel and 18 years for Sarah—seven of their 13 children were born. Samuel and Sarah Cary returned to Massachusetts on July 2, 1791, to live a patrician lifestyle, using revenues generated from their Grenada investments. By then, Samuel Cary Jr.—the three-month-old son whom Sarah had left with her mother in 1774—was an adult living in Grenada and managing his parent's estate and their trading business.

⊶∞∞⊷

IN 1795, FÉDON'S REBELLION SHATTERED Samuel and Sarah Cary's dreams of a comfortable retirement, living off their estate and other businesses in Grenada. Fédon's forces had demolished nearly every estate in Grenada; as a consequence, the owners had nothing to export. The Cary's revenue pipeline was thereby destroyed.

Letters both to and from Cary family members provide vivid accounts of the Fédon Rebellion. Letters from Samuel Cary, Jr. to his parents in Massachusetts and to colleagues in England, for example, indicate that not all slaves joined Fédon's Rebellion. "The negroes are more in awe of the enemy than of us, so much so that they dare not venture amongst us, lest on their return to their estates they should be massacred," Cary, Jr. informs Joseph Marryat, living in England, in a letter dated May 6, 1795.[5]

After visiting Mount Pleasant a few days later, on May 12, 1795, Cary, Jr. again wrote to his parents and described the suffering of their slaves, their starvation, and their hiding in order to avoid being murdered by Fédon's forces for not joining the rebellion. "The negroes came running to us from different bushes and canepieces and informed us that the enemy had been there two days before and had killed four," he explained.[6]

Cary, Jr. rescued 70 enslaved people working at Mount Pleasant Estate and brought them to St. George's, but a few remained in hiding. Many enslaved by English-speaking planters, such as the Carys, also remained loyal to their masters. "My father's negroes proved all faithful," Cary, Jr. highlights in one of his letters.[7]

On the other hand, some slaves belonging to Britishers, including Governor Ninian Home's house slaves, accepted Fédon's decree that they were free and took pleasure policing their former masters when they became their prisoners.

Cary, Jr.'s life is in jeopardy. Educated in England and a proud British loyalist, despite being born in Chelsea, Massachusetts, he immediately joins the St. George's Regiment to fight Fédon's forces. He watches hopelessly as Simon Estate and other buildings owned by British planters—and by Americans supporting the British—are razed. "I went up the other day with McCarthy and a few negroes to Mount Pleasant to see if I could save anything. I found the dwelling house and negro houses burnt. They also burnt your papers," he informs his father.[8]

Writing to his parents on January 26, 1795, almost five weeks before the rebellion commences, Cary, Jr. warns them about a pending rebellion instigated by the French: "If we are taken and have our slaves liberated, we shall in our ruin involve many English merchants; to save themselves, therefore, they will naturally exert all their influence to secure us ... we have some disaffected

Frenchmen and a good number of the coloured race among us." Having themselves dwelled in Grenada for two decades, Samuel and Sarah Cary are not surprised about the looming crisis that their son describes or about the French influence.[9]

———⚮———

THE CARY, JR. LETTERS ALSO describe the interdependency of Grenada and Massachusetts, the impact of the American Revolution on Grenada, thoughts about philosophy and religion, the quandary of slavery, and the overall issue of Fédon's Rebellion; but the letters divulge no particular feelings about Julien Fédon—nor do they reveal whether Cary, Jr. ever met or chatted with Fédon or even heard of him before 1795.

———⚮———

SAMUEL CARY'S MOUNT PLEASANT ESTATE, located north of Waltham and south of Resource, and Julien Fédon's Lancer Estate were no more than two or three miles apart in Grand Pauvre, the colony's smallest and poorest parish. During Cary's 21-year residency in the colony, the family lived at Simon Estate, on the eastern side of the island, where Samuel Cary was manager, although Sarah and the children preferred to spend the rainy season at Mount Pleasant, in the west.

One of the Cary daughters, Margaret, revealed a little about their life at Mount Pleasant:

> There was very little society in the vicinity. Madame Lamellerie, a French widow, with her family, was the chief person; but as she did not speak English, and my parents did not speak French, there was never any intimacy.[10]

The Fédon, Cavelan, and other mixed-race families lived in the area, but language, class, and economic status hindered communications and socializing among the French-speaking and English-speaking families in Mount Pleasant and adjoining estates.

There was also an age difference between Samuel Cary and Julien Fédon. Cary was 26 when he purchased the 140-acre Mount Pleasant coffee estate in 1769 and cultivated it into a sugarcane estate. Fédon was approximately 16 to 18 years old at the time and, most likely, had not yet purchased Lancer, a 38.5 coffee plantation. Based on the length of time Cary spent in Grenada and his estate's location, he may have been aware of Julien Fédon.

By the time Samuel and Sarah Cary departed Grenada, "on June 1, 1791, with seven of their children, ages one to fifteen – Harriet, Edward, Ann, Henry, Lucius, Sarah and Margaret," the former North American colonies had become the United States of America. Samuel was then 52 years old; Julien Fédon was in his early 40s and had become successful. Fédon purchased Belvedere in May 1791 and sold Lancer a month later. It is hard to imagine that Samuel Cary—a former member of the Assembly and the Saint Andrew militia, owner of an estate, manager of Simon Estate, and trader who mingled with high-ranking British planters and governors— was unaware that Julien Fédon, a French mulatto, had purchased the large Belvedere Estate, since that kind of transaction was so unusual at the time.[11]

ENERGETIC, ARTICULATE, AND WELL VERSED in both Spanish and Italian, Samuel Cary, Jr. was 18 in 1791. It is inconceivable that he and Julien Fédon never crossed paths, although the letters of Sarah Cary, Samuel Cary, and Samuel Cary, Jr. seldom mention Julien Fédon. The letters describe the events of 1795 as, alternatively, "a negro insurrection," "the insurrection," "the coming of French negroes from other islands," and "a mulatto uprising."[12]

THE CARY LETTERS REMAIN VALUABLE to researchers—especially those written by Cary, Jr., because he provides an eyewitness account of the rebellion, the British strategy, the position of Fédon's forces, his own role in the militia, and the whereabouts of his parents' slaves. The letters, however, offer no personal view or views about Julien Fédon.

PART III

Battles

SIXTEEN

The Fédon Revolution Begins

It's close to 10 p.m. on Monday, March 2, 1795. Rev. Francis M'Mahon alights onto a Gouyave jetty from a boat that ferries passengers and cargo between Gouyave and St. George's. He is returning to his family after having attended the Garrison at Richmond Hill the day before, as Chaplain to the Troops. On the way to his home, called "The Parsonage House," Rev. M'Mahon greets Dr. John Hay, who is chatting with townsfolk on Front Street.[1]

Dr. Hay does not tell the Anglican priest—who is also a justice of the peace, magistrate, and Guardian of the Slaves in the parishes of Saint Patrick, Saint Mark, and Saint John—of the rumors that French-speaking mulattos are planning an insurrection against the British during the night. Like Dr. Hay, who hears about the pending insurrection around 9 p.m. and dismisses the rumors, Rev. M'Mahon will dismiss the gossip, too. He is returning from the colony's capital city and military headquarters, where everything is normal and there are no rumors of an imminent insurrection by Grenada's free people of color or a French invasion.

Dr. Hay observes that the residents of the boisterous town of Gouyave are "uncommonly quiet, and many of their doors are shut." No "adopted" subjects, as Dr. Hay and Rev. M'Mahon refer to white French people, are on the streets of Charlotte Town, the British name for Gouyave. People of color are not around, either. Yet, Dr. Hay does not suspect that something is just not right.[2]

⋙⋘

Dr. Hay had heard about a meeting of plotters that took place at Belvedere Estate. Did he think that the gossipers were referring to Belvedere Estate in Saint Patrick? Dr. Hay probably thought it unlikely that they were talking about Belvedere in Saint John, because he knew the owners, Julien Fédon and his wife, very well and doubted that they would sacrifice their large coffee estate and other wealth to lead an insurrection. Further, Fédon was not a political person or known to be a civil-rights advocate. He was not even a member of Saint John's Regiment. Furthermore, he took an oath swearing his loyalty to the British monarch, King George III.

It is already nighttime when Dr. Hay, commanding officer of Saint John's Regiment, is informed of the rumors. Apart from not taking the news seriously, he believes it is too late to contact regiment members living all over the parishes of Saint John and Saint Mark and order them to assemble in Gouyave before dawn. He plans to investigate the rumors the next day.

It is now midnight. The mountain peaks and valleys in thickly forested Belvedere are visible only by moonlight—although they are a sight to behold when descending from Belvedere to the town of La Baye on the coast between Soubise and Marquis in the parish of Saint Andrew.[3]

WHERE WAS JULIEN FÉDON ON the afternoon and evening of March 2? Perhaps he was in La Baye, spending a quiet afternoon and evening with fellow plotters from Saint Patrick and Saint Andrew. Or maybe he was laying low in Belvedere to avoid any suspicion. If in Belvedere, he left his home, Belvedere House, on horseback in the stillness of the clear, cloudless night and headed for La Baye, a distance of nearly seven miles. The dry season and moonlight would make that ride much easier.

Regardless of the route—via Chadeau or Mount Saint John through Windsor, via Fraze on the Belvedere Main Road, or through Ferme Pechier and Morne Longue—Fédon would get an occasional glimpse of the darkened sea and the rolling waves off La Baye, Soubise, and Marquis. He would arrive in La Baye close to midnight.

Unfortunately, there is no evidence of Fédon's precise movements or state of mind on the afternoon and evening of March 2, 1795. Had the British allowed conspirators to testify before hanging them without trial, their accounts might have been archived for posterity. Nevertheless, we can conjecture about some likely movements based on an interpretation of eventual results.

Belvedere is halfway between the towns of Gouyave in the west and La Baye (Grenville) in the east. From Belvedere, one would descend down the mountains to either La Baye or Gouyave. When universal suffrage was adopted in Grenada in the 1950s, laborers on the east side of Belvedere voted in the parish of Saint Andrew, and their children attended school in Birchgrove; laborers living on the west side of Belvedere voted in the parish of Saint John, and their children, including this writer, attended school in Gouyave.

Apart from the advantage of actually owning Belvedere Estate, the size and topography of the property and its remoteness from La Baye, Gouyave, and St. George's made it the perfect place for Julien Fédon and his followers to plan, prepare, and conduct their revolt.

By midnight on March 2, free French-speaking mulattos—Fédon's friends Antoine Roy, Sylvain Dragon, and Medar Chantimel; Fédon's brother Jean-Pierre; and a few trusted white Frenchmen residing in the parishes of Saint Mark and Saint John, including Pierre Labat, Joseph Le Blanc, and Roman Catholic priest Pascal Mardel—are all in Gouyave ready to start the rebellion to end British domination. Two other mulattos—Etienne Ventour, a planter, and Joachim Philip—lead the group. Philip's white French father and black mother own properties on the islands of Petite Martinique and Carriacou, just north of Grenada, and in the parishes of Saint Patrick and Saint John.

Dr. Hay and Rev. M'Mahon are both asleep. On the opposite side of the colony, trusted free mulattos from Saint Patrick, Saint David and Saint Andrew and a few reliable slaves are in La Baye with Fédon. The rebellion, led by Fédon and Jean Pierre Lavallee, a resident of Saint Patrick, begins around midnight. La

Baye's Britishers are violently awakened. "Out of fifteen English inhabitants then in the town, eleven are butchered" by Fédon's rebels.[4]

THOSE BARBAROUS ACTS GAVE FÉDON his bad reputation in history. He did not prevent the cruelty in La Baye; rather, he was said to have encouraged the slaughter. But the British provided that chilling account of the La Baye massacre. There is no historic verification, and no eyewitness accounts document the commencement of the rebellion. No one really knows whether Fédon encouraged or discouraged the massacre while his deputy, Jean Pierre Lavallée—"a strong, active, good looking young man, but turbulent and revengeful"—was said to have both performed and encouraged the vicious acts.[5]

In 1796, at the end of the rebellion, people of French origin were either banished or hanged and shot without a trial or an opportunity to tell their side of the story. In their respective books, however, eyewitnesses Dr. Hay and Rev. M'Mahon vividly explained each moment of their first hours of the rebellion in Gouyave.

On Tuesday morning, March 3, Julien Fédon and his rebels are in no hurry to get to Belvedere. Along the way, they plunder British-owned estates and seize the managers and overseers. A French priest, Abbot Peissonier, is arrested at Balthazar Estate, because he is a French Royalist. On their climb to Belvedere, the rebels execute Peissonier "at the side of a precipice, over which he fell into a ravine." Led by Jean-Pierre Lavallee, the rebels and their prisoners arrive in Belvedere around 7 a.m. from La Baye. A jubilant and confident Fédon arrives later.[6]

The revolutionaries from Gouyave are already at Belvedere, having arrived at dawn with their prisoners—including Dr. Hay. Unlike the revolutionaries from La Baye, the Gouyave rebels murder no one. The British, free mulattos, and white French people in Gouyave coexisted peacefully for years. Etienne Ventour and Dr. Hay are actually neighbors.

Upon waking Rev. M'Mahon to arrest and transport him to Belvedere, the priest is dumbfounded to see some of the rebels are men who sailed with him earlier in the evening aboard, "the passage canoe," from St. George's. He knows them, and they know him. Gentility prevails. Ventour commands a rebel to take M'Mahon back to Parsonage House.

WHEREAS LA BAYE WAS A killing field, with buildings destroyed and British residents—men, women, and children—hiding in the swamps, trenches, woods, and sugarcane fields, Gouyave was raucous but not bloody. British women in Gouyave such as Mrs. Agnes M'Mahon, although terrified, remained in their homes. On the other hand, French-speaking women in Gouyave were joyous.

Dr. Hay regretted not taking the rumors seriously. In his book on the subject, he indicates that he knew that most members of Saint John's Regiment would have made themselves intentionally unavailable for duty. Why? The regiment consisted of 177 persons, including "only thirty-two of His Majesty's natural-born subjects" and "thirteen commissioned officers." In other words, the Saint John's Regiment included a mere 45 British members. The other 132 soldiers— "forty-six adopted subjects [Frenchmen] and eighty-six free people of color, the two last privy to the plot"—were of French ancestry and supported Fédon; a few were his confidantes.[7]

A similar scenario existed in the parishes of Saint Patrick, Saint Andrew, and Megrin (Saint David), where most people in the regiments and militias were of French ancestry. They identified with French causes and supported Fédon.

Throughout his life, Dr. Hay—since buried in the Anglican churchyard in Gouyave—never realized the folly of Grenada's British ruling class disrespecting the colony's French subjects. The British denied French people and free French-speaking mulattos their civil rights even while the majority of people in the colony's militias and regiments shared the same French background that the British rulers suppressed. The attitude of Scots, including Governor Ninian Home, did nothing to help the British win the allegiance of French Grenadians, including that of Julien Fédon. Still, the British were shocked to see how readily the "adopted" subjects, whom they had trained, took up arms against them.

THE REST OF THE MONTH of March 1795 would define Julien Fédon's character and the rebellion that became known in history as Fédon's Revolution, although accounts of those days have surfaced chiefly from letters by Britishers and their reports to the British government and through accounts by absentee estate owners and family in either Britain or the United States. Those letters and accounts mainly focus on the destruction of property and the brutality of Julien Fédon and his followers. For centuries, writers would feast on those obviously biased details while ignoring any virtues of the French rebels or the British blunders that ultimately created an environment for rebellion.

IN THE HISTORY OF POLITICAL revolutions and the overthrowing of governments, the unexpected often happens. The leader of the revolution must quickly prove to supporters and foes who is in charge. The first 48 hours is, indeed, anarchy—and the leader must stabilize the mayhem in order to survive.

Julien Fédon faced that challenge and many more on March 3. The most satisfying time for him during the entire 16-month rebellion may have been his victory ride from La Baye to Belvedere that first morning. But any satisfaction he might have felt would last less than 10 hours.

Arriving in Belvedere about mid-morning, Fédon must immediately exhibit leadership. His orders must be obeyed, with death to any supporters or foes who disobeyed. Meanwhile, flocks of enslaved and maroons are arriving in Belvedere from all parts of the island, and Fédon must make a decision about them. Is he abolishing slavery?

Fédon expects low-ranking Britishers—overseers, managers, bookkeepers, and clerks—to be brought to Belvedere and imprisoned in the designated coffee boucan. He does not anticipate that the governor and other high-ranking Britishers will be so easily captured and brought there later that day.

Change of plans: The seizure of Governor Ninian Home, the famed Alexander Campbell, and other British elites would certainly energize British forces in Grenada and other islands to attack Fédon in Belvedere much sooner than he anticipates. He must first pacify supporters who are mummering about not seeing the French forces that arrived.

⸻ ∞ ⸻

JULIEN FÉDON AND HIS INNER circle misled the mulattos and French citizens into believing that French forces had landed and, as a result, all persons must pledge allegiance to France. Anyone failing to do that would be killed instantly and his estate forfeited. How long could they continue that expectation? Even some low-ranking revolutionaries were asking: "Where are the French forces?"

And with thousands of slaves, free people of color, maroons, and white French citizens arriving, uninvited, to Belvedere, how would Julien Fédon feed them? What responsibilities could he assign to them? How could he calm factions and ease the rivalry within the revolutionary group? Would he have the endurance to lead the revolutionaries into battle against British forces? These were some of the challenges facing Julien Fédon on March 3, 1795.

SEVENTEEN

Fédon's First Steps and British Missteps

By wearing French Republican military uniforms embossed with French epaulets, "roaring out" the French revolutionary slogan, "Vive la république," exhibiting the colors of the French Republic, and wearing "French cockades" in their hats, Julien Fédon and his revolutionaries made everyone—Britishers, French people, mulattos, and the enslaved—believe that the French had landed in Grenada or were about to come ashore. Thus, everyone obeyed directives from Fédon in order to avoid calamity.[1]

To further impress everyone, "Julien Fédon, General of the French Republican Forces," and "Besson, Officer of the Republic appointed at Guadeloupe," dispatched emissaries with the first written demands to the Council in St. George's along with stern warnings from France's commissioners in the Eastern Caribbean—Hugues, Goyrand, and Lebas— who had already recaptured British Guadeloupe.[2]

Appeals for help from government leaders in St. George's to neighboring colonies, along with reports to the British Government and letters from Britishers to family and friends abroad, claimed that France through Victor Hugues had incited an uprising of discontented French mulattos. The French men and even a few Britishers who joined Fédon were not mentioned in the reports and letters. The errors and stubbornness of Grenada's Council were also not mentioned. Meanwhile, Julien Fédon and his plotters waged an effective campaign that targeted white French residents. For example, Jean Pierre Lavallee's coldblooded murder of a Roman Catholic priest residing at Balthazar Estate on the morning of the rebellion—simply because the priest was a Royalist and an aristocrat—was a warning to all French whites that they had better support Julien Fédon or face death as traitors to the French Republic.

The white French people who lived in Grenada for decades, some born in the colony, were mostly estate owners enduring the truncated civil rights imposed by Governor Ninian Home and other Scots. So, it was fairly easy for Fédon to win them over. Others were plotters. In Gouyave, for example, Frenchmen such as "Joseph Le Blanc and Pierre Labat, whites" confidantes of Fédon joined French speaking mulattos, "Etienne Ventour, Pillage, Antoine Roy, Medar Chantimel and Sylvain Dragon," to arrest British men. They called their actions a "revolution" and not a rebellion. Rev. M'Mahon was shocked to see "Mr. Olivier, a French gentleman of good character," was a participant.[3]

By the second day of the revolt, Gordon Turnbull, a professional soldier from Scotland and a member of the St. George's Regiment, assembled with the Saint Andrew militia in Grenville/La Baye to crush the rebellion. He participated in several battles but, a few months later, left Grenada either frustrated or demoralized.

On November 9, 1795, in Edinburgh, Scotland, Gordon Turnbull released a military account of the early months of Fédon's Revolution. He pointed out military and political mistakes by the local British authority and by Council President Francis Kenneth Mackenzie and General Colin Lindsay.

With England and France at war in the early 1790s, France had no qualms about repossessing colonies such as Saint Vincent, Saint Lucia, and Grenada. One of Commissioner Victor Hugues goals, in fact, was to encourage strife in British colonies with French populations. Even before Hugues found the time to dispatch agents to Grenada, however, Julien Fédon clandestinely sent two trusted aides—his brother-in-law Charles

Nogues and Jean Pierre Lavallee of Sauteurs—to Guadeloupe to inform Hugues of their plans and to seek help.

The French role in Fédon's Revolution has been exaggerated over the centuries. It was the determination of dissatisfied French-speaking people—both whites and people of color—who spearheaded the rebellion; Victor Hugues did not thrust it upon them.

In 1776, 20 years earlier, news of the American Revolution was keenly followed in Grenada and its success well remembered. In 1789, news of the French Revolution arrived in Grenada even faster. The enslaved heard their masters talk about their displeasure with France for emancipating all slaves in French colonies. The French Revolution, following the success of the American Revolution, was inspiring to the revolutionaries and encouraged anti-British sentiment.

In Grenada—where the French culture, religion, and language continued despite the curbing of civil rights by Governor Home and previous governors—the French-speaking population was ready to overthrow the British. Julien Fédon and others may have revolted regardless of developments in France, but the French Revolution certainly must have been an impetus.

⸎

Little is known about Julien Fédon's activities in the early weeks of the rebellion or even its entire 16-month duration. Detailed eyewitness accounts by Gordon Turnbull, Rev. Francis M'Mahon, Henry Thornhill, Dr. John Hay, and Thomas Turner Wise—plus reports in letters and memos about Fédon—were all written by Britishers and were, as a result, most certainly biased. The writings relate "distressing scenes of murder, raping, and devastation."[4]

The principal objective of Julien Fédon and his revolutionaries, however, was their demand that the British government surrender the colony to them. It is unknown whether Fédon intended to make Grenada a French colony or whether he planned to declare it an independent nation, such as the 13 British colonies in North America had done two decades prior. Further, there is no evidence that Fédon sought to become governor or president of Grenada.

Some researchers are convinced that "Fédon was not seeking independence for Grenada but, rather, sought to rid Grenada of British colonial rule, abolish slavery, and then make the island part of the New French Republic." Other scholars argue that Fédon temporarily emancipated the enslaved with the intention of restoring slavery once he brought Grenada into the arms of France. There is no archival evidence verifying either of those allegations.[5]

Once the rebellion was working in his favor, though, Fédon expected Governor Home (whether captured or not captured) to accept his demand and hand over control of the colony. Meanwhile, Fédon would house British prisoners in a boucan in lower Belvedere perhaps using them to bargain with Home—an area that 20th-century Belvedere Estate laborers called "Old House."[6]

As of 2020, the "Old House" foundation was still there—covered by mud, trees, and vines. As a little boy in the 1950s, I sometimes helped laborers pick up nutmegs there. My friends and I loved to munch on the luscious ripe coffee berries and search for crayfish in the two ravines near "Old House."

Fédon's network of spies—mulattos, French whites and trusted former slaves—were functioning well. Oronoko, a house slave, reported to the Gouyave revolutionaries that Governor Home had arrived in Saint Patrick on Tuesday morning, March 3, 1795, and was planning to sail immediately to St. George's. The rebels in Gouyave, led by Jean Fédon, easily captured Governor Home and his friends—Alexander Campbell, Patrick Fotheringham, and Anthony Kerr—as they sailed by Gouyave.

Fédon did not anticipate having Governor Home as his prisoner less than 12 hours after the rebellion commenced. This rather amazing and rapid development became an added responsibility and made certain that the British would attack Belvedere sooner than expected in order to free Governor Home, capture Fédon, and restore law and order.

On Tuesday night—rather than devising a plan to seize the island's capital, St. George's, and create a government—Fédon and his revolutionaries focus on defending themselves against imminent British attacks as a result of their swift and easy capture of the governor. There is no time to communicate efficiently with Hugues in Guadeloupe.

Yet everything seems to be going in Fédon's favor. He orders Dr. Hay, his acquaintance and now his prisoner, to Gouyave for medical supplies "to dress the wound" of Fédon's close friend and Dr. Hay's neighbor, Etienne Ventour. Hay says that Ventour is "dangerously wounded in the arm by one of my pistols accidentally going off in his pocket." Ventour dies from the wounds before Hay arrives.[7]

Earlier that afternoon, Fédon observes enslaved people belonging to another estate owner in Belvedere and informs them that they are now free—a first step toward abolishing slavery in Grenada.

As the sun sets in Belvedere that Tuesday evening, Fédon visits Governor Home and the other prisoners in the boucan. He commands the guards to kill any prisoner who attempts to escape and, if the British attack, to execute all of the prisoners.

MARCH 3ʳᵈ ENDED ON A high note, despite the landing of French soldiers that was anticipated but never occurred. There is no evidence indicating that Victor Hugues made such a commitment. Were rumors of a French invasion a clever stunt concocted by Fédon?

On Wednesday, March 4, 24 hours after the rebellion began, Belvedere (now the revolutionary headquarters) was bustling and Julien Fédon was exerting his authority. He instructed people who had been enslaved only 24 hours before, along with mulattos and other supporters, to "set out in all directions to collect cattle, horses, and provisions of every kind." The plundering of estates owned by Britishers, as well as by Americans and French people who sided with the British, had begun.[8]

As news of the rebellion and capture of the governor spread, supporters scaled mountains, crossed rivers, and negotiated roads to get to Belvedere. At Belvedere House, the rebel ringleaders were drafting the document demanding the surrender of Grenada to present the next day to the British authorities in St. George's. Prisoners received two meals of boiled plantain and beef cooked by the women, led by Marie Rose Cavelan Fédon.

Meanwhile, a triumphant Julien Fédon departed Belvedere for Gouyave. En route, he came upon Rev. M'Mahon, now a prisoner, heading toward Belvedere. Fédon exhibited goodwill by ordering the guards to take Rev. M'Mahon directly to Belvedere House, where Fédon's wife and daughter would care for him. M'Mahon would stay at Belvedere House until the British arrived in Belvedere.

On Wednesday, March 4, Fédon sent two emissaries—his brother-in-law Charles Nogues and Joachim Philip of Petite Martinique—to St. George's with his two written demands: one to surrender the colony in two hours; the other the warning from Hugues in Guadeloupe. The two demands were rejected by Acting Governor Kenneth Francis Mackenzie, who disparaged Fédon and underestimated his abilities. Mackenzie issued a "Royal Proclamation, declaring a general pardon and amnesty to all persons ... excepting only those individuals who have committed the cruel and unmanly murders ... We do hereby offer a reward of Twenty Johannes [Portuguese gold coins generally used in the colonies] to any persons bringing in any of the said insurgents either dead or alive."[9]

Concerned that Fédon may seize the capital city, Mackenzie dispatched to Belvedere, via Gouyave, only 40 soldiers from a 190-member British regiment stationed at Richmond Hill Garrison in St. George's and merely 110 persons from the 280-member St. George's militia. The remaining 150 British soldiers and 170 militia men stayed to protect the capital. The acting governor ordered the Saint Patrick and Saint Andrew militias, already assembled in Grenville, to proceed to Belvedere, hoping that all of the forces would arrive in Belvedere around the same time, jointly attack Fédon, and rescue the prisoners. Since James Campbell misdirected the troops gathered in Grenville, the joint attack on Belvedere never occurred.[10]

Nevertheless, Mackenzie's reaction was unexpected by Fédon. Having the governor and other high-profile Britishers as prisoners did not force the government in St. George's to surrender Grenada. Frustrated and insulted, Fédon ordered the governor and other prisoners to draft and sign a letter informing Mackenzie that they would be killed if his soldiers attacked Belvedere.

The prisoners letter was delivered to Mackenzie on Friday, March 6, but he ignored it—and Fédon—once again. Fédon then realized that he had to prepare for battles across the colony. Fédon's leadership was tested, and his military genius was ultimately revealed. If Mackenzie believed he could scare or outfox Fédon, he was in for a rude awakening. At the same time, there were blunders by the British leaders in St. George's and by the military.

⎯⎯∞⎯⎯

Sailing to Palmiste Bay and then marching to Gouyave via Dougaldston Estate, the combined 150 soldiers from the St. George's militias and British regiments led by Captain Philip Gurdon, arrived in Gouyave on Thursday "about 4 o'clock, P.M." An astonished Captain Gurdon quickly realized that the revolutionaries had already abandoned Gouyave, leaving behind large quantities "of rum, wine, and porter" in the town's shops—to the delight of the men in Gurdon's militia. As Gurdon explained, "The negroes brought rum to the men from every house or hut." To add insult to injury, "the enemy … carried with them to the mountains two six pounders (cannons.)[11]

Gurdon reluctantly disobeyed the orders of Acting Governor Mackenzie by not immediately going to Belvedere. His fatigued force, now intoxicated, spent the night in Gouyave.

In the wee hours of Friday morning, Julien Fédon led an attack on Gurdon's troops, who were fast asleep and still half-drunk. Both sides suffered losses. Fédon, slightly wounded, retreated to Belvedere.

Gurdon's troops then headed for the boucan of Revolution Hall Estate, owned by the late Britisher William Smith, to spend Friday night (and avoid another night of drinking). They planned to head up to Belvedere, about six miles away, the following day. Meanwhile, in Grenville, the Saint Andrew and Saint Patrick militias were also delayed. Moreover, James Campbell had advised them to use a different route.

More and more Fédon supporters gathered in Belvedere, bringing with them provisions, cattle, sheep, mules, and horses that were stolen from nearby British estates. In spite of that support, however, Fédon had major problems. He had to defend Belvedere from imminent British attacks and retain his prized prisoners. He needed weapons, as those smuggled from Guadeloupe were insufficient. The boasting that French troops would soon arrive was also creating internal discord. Feeling deceived, some revolutionaries assembled in the courtyard of Belvedere House on Sunday afternoon, asking: "Where are the promised French troops?" Jean Pierre Lavallee, one of Fédon's principal ringleaders and considered his second in command, and other rebel leaders were cutlassed to death.[12]

Fédon narrowly escaped. Lavallee and Solie, a white Frenchman and also a trusted Fédon aide, were buried on a hillside below Belvedere House. [Belvedere laborers in the 20th century called the area "The Old Cemetery" and it was considered sacred ground by them.] A month later, on April 8, Julien Fédon's brother Jean would be buried there, too. Most likely he was buried with the same honors given to Lavallee, Solie and other revolutionaries. They sang the "Marseillois Hymn and burning some English flags over the grave."[13]

⁕

Sunday, March 8, 1795, is a day of "feasting, dancing and singing." Hundreds of the newly freed, maroons, French people, mulattos, and children all gather in Belvedere to celebrate. Displaying different colors, including the colors of the French Republic, Africans give thanks to African deities. They drum and chant songs in various West African languages and dance around the prison, mocking the prisoners. Fédon is aware that the enemy is in the vicinity.[14]

While the celebration proceeds in Belvedere, now called Camp Liberty, British Captain Gurdon finally arrives—three days late. The reconnaissance team that he leads reaches Mount Saint John, the boundary of Belvedere. Gurdon observes a boucan, Lacroifade, with men inside, which is protected by two "six pounders" (powerful field guns or mobile cannons).

⁕

Realizing that it would be foolhardy to attack, Captain Gurdon returned to Gouyave. Once reinforcements—soldiers and sailors aboard British naval ships deployed in the region—landed in Gouyave, Gurdon planned to return to Belvedere. To his shock, many of his men—who were members of the Saint George militia—abandoned him. Hearing rumors that the revolutionaries and the French were about to capture St. George's, the soldiers hurried home to protect their families and property.

Gurdon needed the local soldiers. They knew the ruggedness of the land, while the arriving British sailors had no local experience and, for many, this would be their first time in the tropics. "Seeing the state of the militia and thinking that, in all probability, the enemy would come down and attack me again [in Gouyave] in the night, I thought it prudent to embark the party than to hazard the lives of many," Gurdon reported. Dejected, he returned to St. George's around 9 p.m. on Sunday—much to the chagrin of Acting Governor Mackenzie.[15]

Gurdon not only failed to obey Mackenzie's command, the joint Saint Andrew–Saint Patrick militia did not follow orders to go to Belvedere. So, it was a double disappointment for Mackenzie, a civilian with no military experience who dispatched commands from the relative safety of St. George's. By comparison, Julien Fédon was also a civilian with no military or political experience but was leading his revolutionaries into battle.

British weakness afforded Fédon's revolutionaries the opportunity to control most of the island. Although inspired by the French Revolution, any backing of the revolutionaries by France or its colonies was negligible. The expected French troops never materialized. And from Guadeloupe, Hugues provided 100% percent moral support to the revolutionaries but inadequate weapons or military personnel. Instead, it was Fédon's federation of mulattos, maroons, the former enslaved, and Frenchmen—along with his network of contacts in St. George's and across the colony— that kept him abreast of British strategies and led to his success in early battles.

EIGHTEEN

Fédon Destroys Lindsay

A disconsolate Acting Governor Mackenzie, no longer confident that he can control the island, quell the rebellion, and rescue the governor, requests a British senior officer to assume military control in Grenada.

Four days later, on March 12, 1795, Brigadier General Colin Lindsay arrives in Grenada, having already ordered troops aboard British warships to meet him there. Lindsay is welcomed with great fanfare. Ten days later, in the wee hours of March 22, General Colin Lindsay is found dead—by suicide—in his tent erected on the boundary of Belvedere and Mount Saint John (Upper Chadeau).

B elvedere laborers of the 1950s frequently claimed seeing a ghost in a soldier's uniform in the area. "He cannot rest in peace, because he kill himself there during Fédon time," they chattered. As a teenager, I was frightened when walking to and from Belvedere and Chadeau—through dark thickly wooded areas and cultivated fields of coffee, cocoa, nutmegs, bananas, pigeon peas, dasheen, and yams. I never saw the ghost. Even if I had, I couldn't say it was General Lindsay's ghost, since several British officers were killed in the vicinity in 1795-96.[1]

Acting Governor Kenneth Francis Mackenzie wrote in his March 28, 1795 report to the colonial secretary in England, "[After Lindsay's] initial success in capturing the lower of the enemy's three Posts, had contracted fever and, in a fit of delusion, had committed suicide."[2]

Henry Thornhill added his own reasoning for Lindsay's suicide: "Exposing himself to, and going through all sorts of hardships and fatigues … must have operated in disordering the nervous system … which occasioned him to commit the melancholy act of violence he did, for on the 22th at four o'clock in the morning he shot himself."[3]

"The General once had a fall from his horse, and thereby fractured his scull which must, it is imagined, have proved an accelerating means of this malady" was another British pretext for Lindsay's death."[4]

Not all Britishers, however, were sympathetic. Writing from Scotland, George Home, brother of Governor Ninian Home, opined that Lindsay had been "a madman" for a long time.[5]

British reports disregarded the possibility that Fédon was a factor in the general's death. Had Lindsay given up after realizing that Julien Fédon was a foe whom he could not defeat? Had he taken Fédon too lightly?

Gossip that Fédon encouraged an African elder to cunningly place the potent herb *manchineel (mangineel)* in Lindsay's water "to drive him crazy" was also ignored. In fact, Julien Fédon and his revolutionaries had no opportunity to tell their side of the story at all. If they had, perhaps they would have taken at least some credit for Lindsay's suicide.[6]

Lindsay's untimely death by his own hand likely began with his appointment by Sir John Vaughan—commander of British Forces in the West Indies, veteran of several battles against the American colonists during the War of Independence, conqueror of French Martinique, and member of the House of Commons—to crush the rebellion in Grenada. "I confess I do not see how Sir John Vaughan could delegate such an Authority as 'Supreme Governor' of Grenada to General Lindsay," Thomas Turner Wise observed in his eyewitness account of the rebellion. Sir John Vaughan died in Martinique a few weeks after dispatching Lindsay.[7]

—∞—

LINDSAY BEGAN TO BLUNDER AS soon as he arrived from Martinique, with 20 artillery men, around 1 a.m. on March 12, 1795. As "Supreme Governor," he superseded Acting Governor Kenneth Francis Mackenzie's civilian authority and disregarded Mackenzie's strategy.[8]

Mackenzie preferred to prevent Fédon from getting ammunition by patrolling the island's coastline and to restrict Fédon's movement by strengthening bases such as Chadeau in Saint John, Pilot Hill in Saint Andrew and Madame Ache's in Saint George. Mackenzie no longer wanted to attack the revolutionaries, an action that had failed earlier. Instead, he advocated allowing the rebels to gradually break away from Fédon and surrender in their own time.

Lindsay, however, was anxious to defeat Fédon. And although he was a high-ranking general, he wished to personally lead the troops in battle. Further, his personality prevented him from fully evaluating or understanding the strength of Julien Fédon. "From the first Moment of his arrival he showed an anxious Impatience to go and invest the Rebel-Camp," according to Thomas Turner Wise's account. Lindsay also did not realize that Fédon had a web of spies.[9]

Lindsay's tactics included no element of surprise. With much pomp, he remained in St. George's from March 12-15, publicly preparing to march to Belvedere. Rather than allowing *The Beaulieu*, a warship that was transporting 150 soldiers, to anchor in St. George's on March 14, he ordered the ship to Gouyave to await him—and, as a consequence, alerted Fédon.

Around 4 a.m. on March 15th, Lindsay marched from St. George's to Gouyave with an estimated 400 troops, which included Captain Louis La Grenade's militia comprised of slaves and mulattos. By the time Lindsay's forces approached, around midday, Julien Fédon had already evacuated his men to Belvedere.

Lindsay considered the revolutionaries abandoning Gouyave as a sign of weakness—and then proceeded to make the same mistake that Captain Phillip Gurdon made in early March. Lindsay allowed his tired troops to spend the night in Gouyave and nearby Revolution Hall Estate.

On March 16th, Lindsay sent an unusual request from his location in Gouyave to Mackenzie in St. George's: "The Mules, every one, took themselves off, and the Negroes skulk out of the way. I have no money. I wrote you Yesterday to send me Mules and Money – thirty Joes in Silver."

["Joes" was an abbreviation of "Johannes," the Portuguese gold coins common in the colonies.][10]

Mackenzie yielded power to Lindsay yet was uncomfortable with him. Nevertheless, he sent the money and promised that the mules and "one hundred working Negroes" would be sent in the afternoon. He advised Lindsay to get "more Negroes and Mules" from British-owned estates around Gouyave, such as Beau Plan and Revolution Hall.[11]

⸻ ❧ ⸻

ON THE MORNING OF MARCH 17, Lindsay and an estimated 600 to 700 soldiers, marines, sailors, local militiamen, and Captain Louis La Grenade's regiment departed Gouyave and Revolution Hall Estate in hopes of crushing Fédon and his rebels in Belvedere. Arriving at Morne Felix Estate around one, Lindsay "thought it proper to rest the troops … to three o'clock P.M." Colonel Gordon Turnbull believed that Lindsay made a colossal mistake by allowing his troops to rest. "This delay of only two hours was probably fatal to the expedition." Precious time was lost, resulting in their arriving at Belvedere too late.[12]

⸻ ❧ ⸻

The troops reach Belvedere's northern border, Chadeau or Mount Saint John, around late afternoon to find an empty Lacroifade boucan and great house. They seize the buildings and quickly march to Belvedere House (Fédon's home), about a mile-and-a quarter away, to rescue the prisoners. To Lindsay's dismay, there are no prisoners and no rebels at Belvedere House. The prisoners, except for Rev. M'Mahon, were never even in Belvedere House. They were always in a boucan, hidden by coffee and cocoa trees, about a mile away.

Although Lindsay finds nobody in Belvedere House, he leaves Captain Louis La Grenade and his regiment of Loyal Black Rangers to protect the area. Lindsay realizes that the revolutionaries are in the Belvedere valley; he even sees some running into the woodlands around Belvedere House. So, he divides his troops into two columns to fight Fédon's forces and personally leads one of the columns.

Since midday, the prisoners have been hearing cannons echoing in the distance. They know that the British are approaching and will soon rescue them. Fédon orders the prisoners out of the boucan. Now, standing outside but in the vicinity of the boucan, the prisoners can see British troops descending from the hills of Chadeau and Belvedere House in order to attack Fédon. The British fighters get closer.

"We were marched along the pasture, and from thence could see … three men on horseback were reconnoitering … it did not appear to us that they observed a large detachment of the insurgents, drawn up along the skirts of a wood in their front," writes Dr. John Hay.[13]

Lindsay's troops, the revolutionaries, and the prisoners are now close to each other, but Lindsay's forces are not aware that the prisoners are among the revolutionaries. Also, the prisoners cannot run toward their rescuers. If they do, the guards will kill them.

Realizing his likely defeat, Fédon orders the prisoners to be shot, as he warned would happen since the start of the rebellion. Michel, a major in Fédon's army, ignores the order, telling the prisoners, "I take it upon myself to spare your lives."[14]

⎯⎯ ❧ ⎯⎯

THE BATTLE AT BELVEDERE PROGRESSED in Lindsay's favor, according to British reports. Prisoner Dr. John Hay, however, indicated that Fédon was winning. Revolutionaries began to scatter into the nearby hills and dark woods—taking with them, on the orders of Fédon, Governor Home and other prisoners.

Lindsay's men chased the revolutionaries into the mountains, and many from both sides were killed or wounded as darkness descended. At sundown, around 6 p.m., a confident and rather flamboyant Lindsay suspended the fight for the day.

Lindsay subsequently sent a letter to Mackenzie boasting that he and his men had captured the house and boucan of Mount Saint John, Belvedere House, and chased the revolutionaries into the mountains. The report, though, was unintentionally misleading. Lindsay addressed the letter from "Post at Fédon's House," leading Mackenzie to believe that the troops were actually occupying Belvedere House, Julien Fédon's home. Instead, Lindsay was in Jean Fédon's house, Lacroifade Estate, in upper Chadeau or Mount Saint John! It was the same house and boucan that Captain Gurdon saw occupied by revolutionaries on the previous Sunday. Lindsay corrected the address the next day, referring to "Post Before Belvidere House" in his next report to Mackenzie.[15]

Lindsay's decision to return to the outskirts of Belvedere and occupy the boucan and house at Lacroifade Estate, rather than occupying Belvedere House, is rather baffling. Belvedere House had been secured, since Lindsay had ordered Captain Louis La Grenade and his black militia to defend Belvedere House and its vicinity. Was Lindsay afraid that, by sleeping in Belvedere House, Julien Fédon would come back and attack? That question comes to mind, because Lindsay didn't sleep in the comfort of Lacroifade's great house; rather, he slept in a nearby hut.

⁓⦿⁓

Torrential rain poured over Belvedere and Mount Saint John for days, both day and night, triggering landslides, waterfalls, muddy ravines, and ferocious rivers—and making it impossible, from Lindsay's perspective, to wage war. The weather also affected Lindsay's spirit.

Writing to Mackenzie on March 21st, Lindsay noted, "Sir, upwards of one-half of the militia having left me, contrary to the most positive orders … I thought it advisable to give the part of the militia that remained behind, and who bore cheerfully much hardship from the badness of the weather, to return to St. George's to refresh themselves." And he added, "I must request a supply of blankets and shirts for my troops, as, when they laid down their haversacks to engage the enemy, the negroes stole them." The letter reflects a disillusioned Brigadier General Colin Lindsay. After his death, however, his officers denied that the soldiers deserted in droves.[16]

Colonel Gordon Turnbull, one of the last persons to converse with Lindsay, painted a different picture. "He came out of the miserable hut he had chosen for his quarters … with great composure and complacence. He seemed then to be perfectly collected."[17]

Hours later, Brigadier General Colin Lindsay was dead. His troops were stunned, and chaos erupted. The troops quickly retreated, as revolutionaries and former enslaved people hastened to Chadeau—on Fédon's orders—to plunder whatever the British had left behind.

The second attempt to crush Fédon in Belvedere ended in embarrassment for the British. Once again, Julien Fédon had been victorious—but wise enough to not rest on his laurels.

NINETEEN

No Time for Celebrating

Based on the unexpected death of General Colin Lindsay and the hasty retreat of British forces from Mount Saint John and Belvedere, one might assume that Fédon and his revolutionaries would bask in glory—but quite the opposite.

Between the evening of March 17 and March 22, the prisoners were held on a steep mountain peak near Fédon's military headquarters, which overlooked Belvedere's flatlands and cultivated fields. Rev. M'Mahon's and Dr. Hay's narratives about those frustrating days, although not intending to praise Fédon, describe an adroit, visionary, and intelligent Julien Fédon exhibiting both administrative and military prowess.

British records and anti-Fédonists unceasingly blame the weather for derailing Lindsay, as if Fédon were immune to the elements. The unusual monsoon-like rain in the middle of the colony's dry season prevented direct combat between both armies. In spite the weather, Lindsay sent daily messengers to Acting Governor Mackenzie in St. George's, and Fédon found ways to send aides to La Baye and to wage sporadic guerilla attacks on Lindsay's forces in Chadeau.

The topography was disadvantageous for Fédon and his forces, as well as for their prisoners. Though he chose rugged mountain peaks in a virtual jungle for his military headquarters, the deteriorating weather from the night of March 17th placed him in a more precarious spot than it did Lindsay, who occupied the rolling, cultivated hills of Chadeau and the northern area of Belvedere including Belvedere House. Yet, Lindsay made no attempt to attack Fédon, and that allowed time for Fédon to coordinate his strategies.

Climbing the mountains from the flatlands of Belvedere—which Hay described as a "pasture," Rev. M'Mahon described as a "savannah," and 20th-century Belvedere laborers called "Pasteur Field"—one quickly encounters treacherous ridges and precipices. Grenada's second-highest mountain peak, now known as Fédon's Camp, is part of this mountain range. Fédon's military headquarters, which consisted of huts hidden in the jungle and protected by two cannons, was on one of the hazardous ridges overlooking the pasture (Pasture Field), the "slave houses," and the two-story boucan where Governor Home and other prisoners were first kept.

Fédon wisely ordered the prisoners brought to his headquarters as dusk descended on March 17th. "We were then marched up a steep hill, which we could only ascend by the assistance of roots and branches of trees and, with infinite labour and difficulty, at last reached the General's camp," according to Dr. Hay.[1]

Upon seeing the 47 prisoners, Fédon realizes that there is no space in the huts for the prisoners to sleep. He halfheartedly suggests sending them back to the boucan, but darkness and the hazardous terrain makes that impossible. Moreover, he knows that's an irrational idea, since the British could rescue them. A few prisoners find room in a hut used to store ammunition. Most of them, however, endure the "excessively cold and rainy" night in the open air, as torrential rain, lightning, and thunder engulf the entire area—including Lindsay's location.[2]

The next few days and nights are similar: raindrops by the bucket. The prisoners are hungry and cold, but so are the revolutionaries. There are not enough huts for everyone. The prisoners are exposed to the elements, except for a few—including Hay and M'Mahon—who are allowed to shelter in the huts.

Thinking Lindsay may resume the battle and rescue the prisoners, Fédon sends them to a peak above his headquarters at sunrise on March 18th, where they are exposed to the weather—sun, rain, and wind. The prisoners continually beg for a place to shelter, but Fédon again explains, it is "Fortune de la guerre" (Fortune of war) and he has "no other lodging to spare." The weather deteriorates throughout the night.[3]

Dr. Hay takes refuge under a tree, where a sergeant escorts him (on Fédon's orders) to headquarters to spend the stormy night. Dr. Hay is graciously welcomed by Fédon and given "two or three glasses of Madeira." Hay persuades Fédon to send rum to the prisoners and to allow revolutionaries with space in their huts to accommodate prisoners. A few fortunate ones, such as Governor Home, are allowed into the huts of "coloured people"—but there's not even space to lie down.[4]

In Fédon's makeshift headquarters, mulatto leaders and influential white Frenchmen—such as Father Pascal Mardel, the Roman Catholic priest from Gouyave, and French planters Clozier d'Arceuil and Pierre Labat—are conducting business, notwithstanding the dismal weather. They are counting money and preparing financial documents to send to Spanish Trinidad for purchasing weapons. Father Mardel contributes 40 Joes. A letter is drafted to send to Victor Hugues in Guadeloupe, recommending promotions for some men, including Africans, who are providing excellent services for the revolution and for the French Republic.

DR. HAY'S FIRST-HAND DESCRIPTION OF those horrific days and nights, as well as observations by Rev. M'Mahon, reveal a realistic and diligent Fédon. The revolutionaries were not solely depending on financing from Victor Hugues and the French revolutionaries. In fact, Fédon may have lost confidence in Hugues. Two weeks after the start of the rebellion, Hugues had still not sent a sizeable battalion. Fédon was unaware, however, that British ships were cruising around the island, thus preventing French ships from entering Grenada's numerous bays to deliver arms.

THE REVOLUTIONARIES RAISED THEIR OWN money and used their own connections to purchase arms in Trinidad, even though Trinidad's Governor Don Jose Maria Chacón was assisting efforts to crush the rebellion in

Grenada. Why was Spanish and Roman Catholic Trinidad—where most resident French planters and their offspring immigrated from Grenada, Saint Vincent, and other French-speaking islands after refusing to become Protestants in what had become British colonies—against Fédon's rebellion in Grenada?

Governor Chacón had no choice. France and Spain were at war, and Spain was an ally of England; therefore, Chacon had to support the English over the French in Grenada. Mackenzie, in his appeal to Chacón for assistance, clearly stated that the French were responsible for the rebellion and that French-speaking people were leading it.

Don Jose Maria Chacón dispatched "two armed Spanish Brigs and a Schooner ... with forty soldiers" to Grenada. The soldiers protected St. George's, and the brigs cruised around the island to prevent Julien Fédon from getting external help. Two enemies—the English and the Spanish—now confronted Fédon's men. The presence of both British and Spanish soldiers in St. George's may have been a reason why Fédon didn't even attempt to capture the capital, although no archival evidence validates that assertion.[5]

Chacón's participation in Grenada was brief but effective; he inflicted irreversible damage on Fédon and his men. Fortunately for Fédon, however, Chacón was concerned that uprisings in Grenada, Saint Vincent, and other islands would encourage French people in Trinidad to do likewise. As rumors of an impending rebellion at home reached Chacón's ear, he withdrew his soldiers and warships from Grenada. They were needed at home to protect Trinidad.

———

BEFORE THE REBELLION, AS MENTIONED earlier, Fédon chose a boucan in the cultivated coffee and cocoa flatlands of Belvedere to imprison his captives and the almost inaccessible mountains overlooking Belvedere for his military headquarters. Taking prisoners to higher and more unreachable areas in the mountains of Morne Vauclain, though, became a necessity after the March 17th assault.

On March 18 or 19, Fédon ordered a prison built near a mountain peak that was much higher in the mountains and much farther from his headquarters. Approximately 150 Africans completed it on Saturday, March 21, and prisoners arrived the following day. According to Dr. Hay, "We began our march through defiles of standing wood up a precipice ... We were obliged to rest every ten to fifteen minutes." The prison, made from tree trunks, branches, and leaves, barely held 28 of the 47 prisoners. The others either "stand or sleep on the wet ground."[6]

Dr. Hay's vivid description of the climb from the vicinity of Fédon's military headquarters (which Belvedere's 20th century laborers called "First Camp") to the prisoners' final stop (called "Second Camp" or "Morne Qua Qua") is quite accurate. Between the military headquarters and the prisoners' final destination were several more mountain peaks and valleys covered in mud, stagnant water, and thick vegetation. The cold winds constantly howled. In November 2017, I hiked with two family members from First Camp to Fédon's Camp in the midst of torrential rains, high winds, and thick mist. It took us about two hours to ascend and longer to descend. One can only imagine how dangerous those mountains were in the 18th century.

⸙

Fédon may be faulted for placing too much trust in Julien Lussan, a French merchant living in Gouyave. Fédon made a grave mistake sending Lussan to Trinidad to procure arms and ammunition—a mistake that changed the course of the revolution.

At midnight on March 2nd, when the revolution began, Lussan was detained and brought to Belvedere. He was one of the few French persons arrested by the revolutionaries in Gouyave but released the next day to manage food supplies and ensure that everyone was fed. Was he a decoy aimed at getting information from Fédon's British captives? Did the revolutionaries have hesitations about Lussan's loyalty to the French cause? Did Lussan trick the revolutionaries by allowing them to release him from custody by seeming to join their cause?

Two weeks into the revolution, on March 18, Fédon selected Lussan and Pierre Alexandre (who was born in Toulouse, France) to go to Trinidad to purchase arms and solicit additional help. To send Lussan and Alexandre to Trinidad signified Fédon's faith in Lussan, who had become part of Fédon's inner circle.

In spite the continuous rainstorm on March 19th, Alexandre and Lussan ride on horseback to La Baye, where they take a fishing boat with six others to Trinidad. They arrive at the Carenage, the Spanish colony's main port, on the evening of March 20th. Leaving Lussan aboard, Alexandre disembarks to take money to Michel Beleran, Fédon's brother-in-law, to purchase munitions. At daybreak, Lussan plans to take letters of credit to his business contacts in order to purchase additional arms.

Instead, during the night, Lussan takes a rowboat and heads to Governor Chacón's home in Port D'Espagne (Port of Spain) to betray Fédon and the revolutionaries and, eventually, cause the execution of Alexandre. Lussan advises Governor Chacón that Alexandre would be going directly from Trinidad to Guadeloupe, carrying Fédon's letter to Hugues asking for weapons. Lussan reveals Fédon's contacts in Trinidad and hands over the letters of credit that the revolutionaries gave him to present to businesspeople in Trinidad. Lussan then requests a vessel to transport him, as soon as possible, to St. George's, Grenada, to apprise Acting Governor Mackenzie. Lussan even identifies white Frenchmen who are supporting Fédon such as Clozier D'Arceuil, Clozier Saint Marie and "their Commissary of war, a son of Chevalier De Suze.[7]

LUSSAN TOLD GOVERNOR CHACÓN THAT Fédon had a force of 610 men, divided into seven companies and "on the 18th of March, when he left them, their numbers had increased in men, women and children to about 7,000 souls." Based on that briefing, Alexandre's movements in Trinidad were closely monitored. [8]

Lussan arrived in St. George's on March 23rd. Alexandre was captured on March 26th aboard the Spanish schooner *Félicité*, bound for Guadeloupe. Using Lussan's testimony, on March 31, "Alexandre was tried by a Court Martial and found guilty of taking up arms … to subvert His Majesty's Government in this island." He was hanged on April 2nd "about noon in the Market-Place" (St. George's). [9]

In his letter requesting that a Roman Catholic priest administer last rites, Alexandre insinuated that Lussan betrayed him to save himself. The British badly wanted the head of Pierre Alexandre, as he and another white Frenchman, Cadet de Suze, had brought the second Flag of Truce to Acting Governor Mackenzie on March 6th, demanding surrender of the island to the rebels.

Learning from Lussan about the connection between Hugues and Fédon, the British captured a French vessel off Grenada and retrieved a letter from Hugues to Fédon. As a result, Fédon never received the letter. Neither did Hugues ever receive Fédon's letter, which had been carried by the captured Alexandre. Trusting Lussan—who had, in better times, participated in a land transaction with Fédon—had dire consequences.

Various sources over the centuries mention that Lussan told the British that approximately 7,200 persons assembled in Belvedere and that they consumed eight to 10 cattle a day, but those statistics have never been fully corroborated. Lussan spent the first 17 days of the revolution in Belvedere, so that is the period he described. Even in the 21st century, Belvedere remains thickly wooded, large trees, thick vegetation, numerous rivers, ravines and streams flowing from steep hills and deep valleys. Therefore, one can only imagine what Belvedere was like in 1795. Lussan's estimate of the amount of people flocking to Belvedere and cattle consumed although accepted carte blanche by scholars is highly questionable by this writer.

By the end of March 1795, most of the cultivated land and dwelling areas of Belvedere (Camp Liberty) were abandoned. The revolutionaries and former slaves were either staying in the mountains of Belvedere, including at Fédon's military headquarters, or had left the area to fight the British in other parts of Grenada.

Fédon became aware of the capture and hanging of Pierre Alexandre and must have been pleased that his prisoners were in Belvedere mountains and beyond the reach of the British. He knew, though, that the British would attack again in Belvedere. He also had to defend other revolutionary bases and strongholds such as Telescope Point, La Baye, Battle Hill and elsewhere. And he had to prepare his own attacks on the British in various other towns and ports.

TWENTY

British Blunders – Fédon's Ingenuity

Another battle to dislodge Fédon from his military headquarters came sooner than expected. Council President Mackenzie—resuming his roles as the leader of government, as well as acting governor and commander-in-chief—grasped what he imagined to be a golden opportunity to annihilate the revolutionaries.

Mackenzie was convinced that the majority of Fédon's forces were building and defending bases at Pilot Hill, Telescope Point, Madame Ache's, and other locations, therefore, Fédon's army in the mountains of Belvedere was stretched thin. Mackenzie quickly attacked Fédon's military headquarters (First Camp,) on April 8th against the advice of Lieutenant Colonel Augustus Campbell, who was dispatched to Grenada to assist Mackenzie. The April 8th battle stretching from Mount Saint John and Belvedere to Fédon's military headquarters was the climax of several battles the week before. And it was the defining moment of Fédon's Revolution.

***

After Lindsay's daring but failed attack on March 17th, Fédon realized that he urgently needs ammunition for upcoming battles and makes a crucial mistake by sending Lussan, a turncoat, to Trinidad to procure them—a slip-up with ramifications that may prevent Fédon's rebels from occupying the colony's principal town, St. George's.

***

LUSSAN HAD EMPHASIZED TO THE British that Granville Bay (Grenville) and nearby areas were strategically important to Fédon. Vessels transporting arms and reinforcements from Guadeloupe were sailing into bays protected by Fédon's forces, which were stationed on the hills overlooking the bays. Whoever controlled the hills controlled the bays, so Mackenzie decided to fight Fédon's forces in those areas in order to regain control of Grenville Bay and Pilot Hill.

One of Mackenzie's mistakes was trusting Lindsay's optimistic and misleading report that only darkness prevented him from defeating Fédon on March 17th, allowing Mackenzie to mistakenly believe that he could otherwise defeat Fédon in the mountains of Belvedere.

Mackenzie also made a slew of other errors between the third week of March and early April. The outcome of the skirmishes prior to April 8th favored Fédon but also served as a forewarning to Mackenzie—who nevertheless remained resolute. Unwilling to admit that the rebellion by mulattos, with the support of most slaves and French people, was both strong and united, Mackenzie underestimated their strength and made numerous blunders when battling Fédon.

⁂

OVER THE CENTURIES, BOTH EUROPEAN and colonial writers have neglected to list military blunders by the British, including those revealed by Colonel Augustus Campbell and Colonel Gordon Turnbull, two senior British officers who participated in several battles in the rebellious colony. As professional soldiers, Campbell and Turnbull abided by Acting Governor Mackenzie's decree—even though they disagreed with his strategies. Mackenzie was determined to fight Fédon in areas that Fédon's forces occupied, such as Paradise, Grand Bras, Pilot Hill, Telescope, Simon (Seamoon), and Morne Horne. Militias from Saint Patrick and Saint Andrew gathered in La Baye to try to quell the rebellion and then were dispatched to Belvedere via Gouyave and Mount Saint John, leaving La Baye and nearby estates unprotected.

On March 18th, while Lindsay was resting his troops in Mount Saint John and blaming bad weather for what became an unwise decision, Fédon was burning down what was left of La Baye after the initial fighting on March 2-3. Fédon's forces also burned to ashes Pilot Hill House, which overlooked Grenville Bay.

The revolutionaries may have regretted burning Pilot Hill House once they realized the strategic importance of its location, as they immediately established a base there. With the help of former slaves, the revolutionaries dragged a number of cannons up Pilot Hill—one nine-pounder, two six-pounders, and a four-pounder—that were capable of destroying vessels entering Grenville Bay. In the many battles for control of Pilot Hill that took place throughout the 16-month Fédon's Revolution, hundreds of revolutionaries and British forces would die.

On March 24, the gravity of the situation at Grenville Bay and Pilot Hill suddenly dawns on Mackenzie and his Council of War, so they declare that "a post is immediately to be formed at Grenville Bay for the protection of that quarter." A permanent base at Grenville Bay will help the British protect neighboring estates—where sugarcane fields, great houses, and boucans were burned nightly— and also prevent Fédon from receiving weapons via Grenville Bay.[1]

MISGUIDED BY LUSSAN'S REVELATIONS, MACKENZIE believed that Fédon dispatched his troops from hideouts in the mountains of Belvedere to defend his strongholds around La Baye, procure arms arriving from Guadeloupe, and attack British fortifications. Lussan also reported that "about 6,000 Negroes, but few of whom had any arms at all … those few having cutlasses, and most only pikes" had joined Fédon. Mackenzie felt positive; therefore, he could defeat a weakened Fédon in Belvedere.[2]

Mackenzie's officers, however, didn't always execute his commands. On March 6th, for example, Mackenzie admonished Colonel Isaac

Horsford, an old and highly respected planter and leader of the Saint Andrew Regiment, and Major Commander John Stewart, leader of the Saint Patrick Regiment:

> "The critical situation of the island required your instant obedience to my orders and not your debates on the eligibility of them."[3]

Also, on March 8th, Captain Philip Gurdon declined to attack Fédon's men occupying the Lacroifade boucan in Mount Saint John.

Regardless of the all-too-frequent insubordination of his officers, Mackenzie conceived several battles in his attempt to defeat Fédon: one in the Grenville Bay-Pilot Hill area, another at bases at Michel and Madame Ache's estates, and another in the mountains of Belvedere.

To reinforce Pilot Hill and establish the base at Grenville Bay, Mackenzie created a combined army—50 members each from the Saint Andrew and Saint David regiments and from newly arrived British troops stationed in Gouyave—that, "under the command of Captain Philip B. Gurdon, embarked in the *Flying Fish* and *Pegasus* armed vessels" for Grenville Bay. What Mackenzie didn't know was that Julien Fédon already occupied Grenville Bay and had demolished Pilot Hill.[4]

Simultaneously, Mackenzie dispatched 50 men from Saint Patrick Regiment, also stationed in Gouyave, "along with a detachment of the light cavalry" to march to Observatory Estate in Saint Patrick, about six miles from Grenville Bay. They arrived at Observatory almost two days before the two battleships that were transporting Captain Gurdon and his troops. Sailing through high winds and rough seas, the two ships had drifted to Isle De Ronde, a small island located between the islands of Grenada and Carriacou.[5]

When the two ships eventually arrived at Grenville Bay, a partially sunken British cargo ship, The Roman Emperor, blocked the harbor. The British claimed that the ship became stranded on the rocks when leaving the harbor laden with sugar and rum. Others said that the revolutionaries deliberately brought the captured ship to the mouth of the harbor and partially sank it.

Captain Gurdon realized that the sunken ship made it too dangerous to land at Grenville Bay. Moreover, Fédon had fortified Pilot Hill with a "nine-pounder." The ships then sailed to Levera Bay, a few miles north, where the soldiers disembarked and marched from Levera Bay to Observatory Estate to join the regiment from Saint Patrick.[6]

Beginning on April 2nd and led by Captain Gurdon, the attack on Pilot Hill was a fierce battle; lives were lost on both sides. Fédon was in the vicinity, commanding his forces, but misled the British by ordering his forces to disperse.

Believing that they had routed Fédon from Pilot Hill, the British marched toward Grenville Bay. To their astonishment, "about one hundred men at Paradise negro-houses" attacked them on Paradise Estate. Captain Gurdon made a written report to Mackenzie, explaining that Fédon's forces fired a "nine-pounder" twice, forcing his own troops to take refuge "under the cover of a hill."[7]

Gurdon further informed Mackenzie that he and Major Stewart both climbed the "hill called Telescope House when, to their great surprise," they observed that Fédon "had two pieces of cannon and two hundred men, and all the adjoining heights were covered with men principally armed with muskets."[8]

Convinced that he did not have enough men to defeat Fédon, Gurdon abandoned his march to Pilot Hill and Grenville Bay and ordered his troops to return to Observatory Hill. Later, apologizing to Mackenzie, Gurdon emphasized how the insurgents "appeared so strong and so well prepared for them." He also claimed that the wife of a rebel had given him inside information, telling him that Fédon sent two regiments from Belvedere to La Baye. In conclusion, Gurdon wrote, "They [the insurgents] evidently have had information of the intended attack."[9]

Meanwhile, Mackenzie still remained confident that he could "save the colony" by destroying the rebellion. He believed that even though Fédon's forces occupied La Baye, professional soldiers expected to arrive from abroad would ultimately defeat Fédon in Belvedere.

Appropriating professional soldiers and sailors was not a problem for Mackenzie. Thousands of troops were assigned to the powerful British fleet that protected the British West Indies, and more were stationed on the various British colonies. The fleet was not concerned about France, their arch enemy in the region, because France was occupied with the revolution at home. The British navy could sail freely around the Caribbean and were able to send their ships and sailors to Grenada. Miscommunication, disobedience, and disorganization, however, continued to plague Mackenzie—to the advantage of Julien Fédon.

The 25th and 29th British army regiments, led by Lieutenant Colonel Augustus Campbell, were dispatched to Grenada via Barbados. Campbell was expected to act as Mackenzie's principal military advisor. Rather than awaiting Campbell's arrival in Grenada, Mackenzie dispatched a brig to meet Campbell on the high seas and deliver a message. Mackenzie recommended that Campbell have the 25th and 29th regiments disembark in three different locations upon arrival off Grenada: 250 soldiers at Gouyave, 250 at Grenville Bay, and 300 at St. George's.

From Mackenzie's perspective, it would be fruitful to have the soldiers land simultaneously in three different locations and then, following three different routes, all march to Belvedere to attack Fédon at the same time. In addition, soldiers landing at Grenville Bay would eliminate Fédon's strength in La Baye and his control of Pilot Hill. Perhaps Mackenzie was unaware that Campbell's troops had just arrived in Barbados from England, had no idea of tropical conditions, and were not acclimatized. The march across Grenada would certainly be difficult for them.

Moreover, Mackenzie had no military experience; he was not a planter, manager and owner of estates. Unlike, Governor Ninian Home, Alexander Campbell, James Campbell, Dr. John Hay and others who dwelled in the colony for decades, Mackenzie arrived in Grenada late and remained in St. George's earning a living as a lawyer, bureaucrat and politician. Evidently, he did not understand the ruggedness of Grenada's interior, therefore, his orders were frequently ignored because they were impractical.

Colonel Campbell received Mackenzie's message but, instead, "took the fleet to Charlotte Town, where the two regiments" went ashore at 5 a.m. on

April 1st. Had Campbell followed Mackenzie's directive and landed 250 soldiers at Grenville Bay, the British may have won the battle on April 2nd. On the other hand, Julien Fédon and his two astute commanders in Saint Andrew, Charles Nogues and Stanislas Besson, may have succeeded anyway.[10]

On April 1st, Mackenzie welcomed Colonel Campbell's arrival in Gouyave, briefed him, and outlined strategies for defeating Julien Fédon once and for all. They ordered 300 men from the 29th Regiment to re-embark and sail to St. George's, where the men would rest for a day or two before strengthening a base at Michel Estate — "about two miles beyond the grand étang, or great lake, on the Saint Andrew's side ... to cut off the communication between Grenville Bay and the camp of the insurgents."[11]

The next day, April 2nd, 250 soldiers and sailors led by Major H. A. Wright of the 25th Regiment, "with proper guides," marched "through the woods" to support the militia at Observatory, Saint Patrick.[12]

After his meeting with Mackenzie on April 1st, Colonel Campbell "with eight hundred men immediately" went to Mount Saint John— or "the camp before Belvedere." Many of those 800 soldiers belonged to Campbell's 29th Regiment, so he remained with them in Mount Saint John.[13]

Fédon's network of spies kept him apprised of the British military buildup, but he wanted the British to bring the war to him. Fédon told his illustrious prisoner, Governor Ninian Home, that he knew "the mode of making war in the woods."[14]

⸎

On April 4th, the 300 soldiers from the 29th Regiment originally sent to St. George's left for Michel Estate. The base at Michel's was located east of Grand Étang Lake closer to Mount Sinai. Led by Major Mallory, the primary duty of the soldiers was to prevent supplies from getting to Fédon's headquarters in Belvedere and to his military headquarters in the mountains. But Mackenzie made a huge blunder. As one British planter observed in his report to London, "Michel's does not lie upon any road between Grenville and Belvidere." Mackenzie was not a longtime resident of Grenada; he was a planter in Demerara (Guyana) and not a planter Grenada.[15]

While Mallory's troops were still in Saint George parish, they received an unpleasant welcome by Fédon's snipers at Madame Ache's, a strategically located base. "They were attacked by a party of insurgents, who killed a sergeant and wounded an officer and four privateers." The troops quickly seized the base when Fédon's forces ran away, and Major Mallory and his men spent the night there.[16]

The next morning, while reconnoitering at Madame Ache's and unaware that Fédon's forces were still around, Major Mallory was "attacked by a negro and a mulatto man" and he died from his wound weeks later in St. George's. Blindsided, Britishers explained that Mallory "fell victim to the contagious fever," meaning dengue. Today, a plaque in Mallory's memory is installed in St. George's Anglican Church.[17]

On April 6th, Mackenzie replaced Major Mallory with Lieutenant Colonel William Este, who had recently arrived in war-torn Grenada and was stationed in Gouyave. Accompanying Colonel Este were other officers, 50 marines from the battleship *Resource*, a detachment from the Grenada militia, and two cannons. That night, they arrived at Madame Ache's, where Mallory's battalion was awaiting them. The combined military expected to march to Michel the following morning to capture Fédon's base. In a letter to Mackenzie, Colonel Este explained what happened:

> The night proving rainy, with heavy showers in the morning, I was informed there would be no possibility of moving before the roads got somewhat dry. I therefore proposed to march about ten.[18]

As they were leaving Madame Ache's for Michel, Fédon's forces attacked and blocked the road. Several Britishers were killed and many more wounded. Este was still surrounded by Fédon's forces at Madame Ache's the next day and night, April 8th. Este could hear the sounds of cannons echoing far away and had no idea that the invasion of Belvedere and Fédon's military headquarters were underway and that Governor Home was being slaughtered.

Based on Fédon's strength and strategic locations, Colonel Este refrained from going on the offensive. He was afraid of the Fédon contingents were awaiting his troops along the route and one "about two hundred yards from

Grand Étang house." On April 9th, Este advised Mackenzie to abandon the quest for Michel. "Upon the whole, the expedition against Michel's proved unsuccessful," explained Colonel Este, who was "not thinking it safe and advisable to proceed."[19]

In addition to repulsing the British, Fédon had also outwitted them. The revolutionaries "had no fewer than four roads, or ways of communication, from Grenville to their camp at Belvidere." They used routes through "Grand Bras River below Renaud's and through the lands of La Force to Peschier's Estate" (modern-day Grand Bras, La Force, Windsor, Fraze, and Ferme Peschier.)[20]

Meanwhile, Major Wright and his soldiers from the 25th Regiment were not faring any better. On their way to Observatory, Saint Patrick, the battalion encountered "great hardships, losing twelve men … fallen into the hands of the barbarous enemy." Fédon's forces attacked them at Mirabeau, Grand Bras, Morne Horne, and other estates on the route to Observatory. At Morne Horne, Major Wright and Captain Gurdon's battalions merged. The combined professional battalion, 400 strong, failed to stop Fédon's ragtag forces. On April 7th, Fédon was still in control of Grenville Bay, Pilot Hill, and virtually the entire Saint Andrew parish.[21]

Since his arrival in Grenada, Colonel Campbell had been reinforcing the base at Mount Saint John on Belvedere's northern border, where sections of the 25th and 29th regiments were stationed. By April 7th, hundreds of men were positioned between Lacroifade (upper Chadeau) and Madame Chadeau (lower Chadeau) estates. Although Campbell's new base at Madame Chadeau provided a better view of Fédon's military headquarters and was closer to Belvedere House than Lacroifade, Fedon's forces had already burnt down Madame Chadeau's great house.

As a youngster in the 1950s, I always looked forward to visiting my godmother, Nenen Dee Campbell, living in the Chadeau great house, and enjoying the view of the magnificent evergreen mountain peaks of Fédon's Camp (Morne Qua Qua) even when they were draped in mist.

⸎

Mackenzie remained optimistic. He stubbornly believed that he could use the bases in Mount Saint John to defeat Fédon, forgetting that two attempts from Lacroifade had already failed: Captain Gurdon's attempt on March 8th and Brigadier General Colin Lindsay's attempt on March 17th.

Mackenzie apparently overlooked the battle at Madame Chadeau at midnight on April 3rd, when Fédon's forces stealthily attacked the British and mortally wounded Captain Ewan, commander of the base. A sergeant and one private were also killed, and nine others were wounded.

⸎

It is the first week of April, and Fédon has triumphed in every skirmish. The British blame the heavy rain in Grand Étang and Mount Saint John for their defeats. Colonel Campbell, commander of all British forces on the rebellious island, is not pleased. Mackenzie, however, is making all the decisions in his capacity as commander-in-chief.

Encamped at Mount Saint John, a worried Colonel Campbell requests that Mackenzie visits him at Mount Saint John to discuss "future operations." Mackenzie arrives on Tuesday, April 7th, to issue an order rather than evaluate the situation with the colonel. He advises Campbell to launch "an immediate attack upon the enemy's post at Morne Quaqua on the heights of Belvidere." The attack is planned for the next morning, less than 12 hours after Mackenzie's arrival.[22]

Based on Fédon's advantageous location in the mountains, especially at his military headquarters (First Camp) and on Morne Vauclain or Morne Qua Qua (Second Camp), Campbell believes it is impossible to win a battle against Fédon's forces without thorough planning. He informs Mackenzie that "the attack proposed might be attended with very serious consequences."[23]

Mackenzie, however, rejected Campbell's notion. Mackenzie believed that the dwindling numbers and weakness of Fédon's forces were more significant than their location. "From the best authority possible," Mackenzie claimed, he was informed that Fédon dispatched his forces from the mountains of Belvedere to defend their posts at La Baye and Madame Ache's and that "very few fireworks were left at Morne Qua Qua and hardly any ammunition."[24]

There is no archival evidence identifying who briefed Mackenzie nor did he divulge to Campbell who was "the best authority possible." Perhaps it was the highly respected mulatto, Louis La Grenade, who was posted at Mount Saint John with his militia of Loyal Black Rangers.[25]

Truly believing that Fédon no longer had a large force at his military headquarters, Mackenzie perceived the moment as "the most favorable opportunity" to end the rebellion by controlling the mountains of Belvedere. "Success seems now to be reduced to an absolute certainty," he stressed to Colonel Campbell.[26]

After convincing the reluctant Colonel Campbell to attack Fédon the next morning and before leaving Mount Saint John, Mackenzie tried to lighten Campbell's pessimism. He promised Campbell that about 200 sailors from *HMS Resource* and from commercial ships anchored off Gouyave would be immediately sent to help him.

Unlike the late General Colin Lindsay, who assumed the dual roles of head of government and commander-in-chief, Campbell had not taken those titles. Although he was a professional soldier and a senior military leader dispatched to Grenada, he considered himself the top military advisor to Mackenzie. He refrained from eclipsing Mackenzie and, instead, reluctantly followed his orders—as council president and acting governor—to attack Fédon on Wednesday, April 8th—despite expecting a military defeat.

Why was Mackenzie so adamant? Why the haste to annihilate Fédon and his forces on April 8th, 1795? Over the centuries, scholars have speculated about Mackenzie's reasons.

And where was Julien Fédon? Based on letters from his two principal commanders, Charles Nogues and Stanislas Besson, that were addressed to General Fédon and captured on bases and from messengers, it appears that Fédon was conducting the war from his military headquarters at Belvedere.

The British, however, were mocking Fédon. They considered his title of "General" to be laughable; but Fédon had, in fact, outmaneuvered them. Mostly on the defensive in Belvedere, he was definitely on the offensive in Saint Andrew during the first days of April.

TWENTY-ONE

Night of April 7, 1795

Rev. Francis M'Mahon describes the dreadful scene on Tuesday, April 7, 1795 at Morne Qua Qua.

> From the strict guard kept before the door, as also from the women coming from the lower post with their children and passing the house, which we could see through the crevices, and from the continued influx of the rebels, we could well conceive our troops were approaching.[1]

MORNE VAUCLAIN, ALSO KNOWN AS Morne Qua Qua, was then believed to be the highest mountain peak in the colony. Today, that peak is called "Fédon's Camp" or Morne Fédon.

On the night of April 7th, Julien Fédon did not reveal his state of mind or his strategies for defeating the British the following day. Whatever was revealed came from eyewitness accounts by two of his prisoners, Dr. John Hay and Rev. Francis M'Mahon, and from reports dispatched to England, Scotland, and the United States by civilians, government officials, and military personnel.

Mackenzie's determination to attack Fédon once again in the mountains of Belvedere did not surprise Fédon. Enticing the British to bring the battle to him in the Belvedere highlands was his plan, because he and his insurrectionists knew about "making war in the woods, and that any European force brought against them would fail of success." Fédon may have been mentally prepared but was not expecting another attack that soon, April 8th, after Lindsay's debacle of March 17th and Captain Philip B. Gurdon's failure to recapture Pilot Hill on April 2nd.[2]

During the week prior to April 8th, British troops battled Fédon on Pilot Hill-Grenville Bay, Observatory, and Madame Ache's areas; but to decapitate the "head of the serpent," Mackenzie felt that he had to defeat Fédon at his military headquarters. Although Fédon had repulsed the earlier British attack in Belvedere, he expected future attacks to be more aggressive.

Rev. Francis M'Mahon and Dr. John Hay unintentionally provided a glimpse of Fédon's activities and mindset in the mountains during the first week of April and, in particular, the night of April 7th. The two men were not glorifying Fédon's actions, but their writings do reveal a certain admiration.

Hay and M'Mahon were privileged prisoners, because they were acquaintances of Fédon. As residents of Grand Pauvre and Gouyave, they all did favors for each other. Some historians allege that Dr. Hay once saved Fédon when he had an acute fever, although archival evidence of that remains undiscovered. Fédon held no grudges against Hay and M'Mahon; rather, he respected them. But they were loyal Britishers, after all; so, they were treated as prisoners for both security and military reasons. Still, except on days of tension or battle when Hay and M'Mahon were housed with the other 49 prisoners, the two men socialized with the revolutionaries. Sometimes they slept in the revolutionaries' huts, as long as there was room.

Hay saw Fédon often; and when Fédon was not at his military headquarters, Hay left written messages with Fédon's secretary. Fédon may have been in the Pilot Hill-Grenville Bay locale on April 2nd, when Hay gave Fédon's secretary a note asking "General Fédon" to satisfy seven requests from the prisoners, including:

> 1st That the prison may be enlarged and new-thatched …
> 6th That they have liberty to go out, under a guard
> (which has been frequently denied them), by night or by
> day, as often as the calls of nature may require.
> 7th That a person may be appointed to bring water,
> as the guards consider it as no part of their duty.[3]

In his vivid description of the night of Saturday, April 4th, Dr. Hay revealed General Fédon's disposition and his whereabouts during that challenging week: "The General, his Secretary, Le Riche, Deputy Rapier, and myself sat down to supper."[4]

Hay also indicated that two revolutionaries, Ollivier and Marucheau, who arrived from Grand Roi, joined them. "Ollivier brought some canes and a bottle of liqueur, a present from his wife to the General." The dinner participants chatted about family life, and Olliver boasted about his nine-month-old son.[5]

Le Riche, meanwhile, proclaimed that liberty could not be confined only to France and its dominions "but must gradually extend to every corner of the globe." He also stressed how "the tyrannical government of Home" denied liberty to French-Grenadians. That statement attributed to Le Riche indicates that the revolutionaries were fighting for the rights of disenfranchised people and that Governor Home denied their liberty.[6]

Fédon inquired about Dr. Magnival, a white French revolutionary, and about "the health of all the ladies at Good Chance," an estate located below Fédon's military headquarters on the Saint Andrew side, where the wives, their children, and other women camped and prepared meals for all—including the prisoners. Food and water were brought to the camp daily, because there were no streams or waterholes on Morne Qua Qua. After the revolution ended in 1796, the British hanged Dr. Magnival.[7]

Writing that Fédon and his aides appeared relaxed at supper, Hay gave no hint that the British soldiers and Fédon's forces had waged battle just days before at Pilot Hill, Grenville Bay, Telescope Estate, and Madame Ache's Estate. He was not aware. Perhaps Fédon's high spirits at the dinner party were the result of his victories in all those battles.

After supper, Hay wrote, "a mattress was allotted for three of us: Mr. Ollivier, a mulatto, and myself." Fédon's secretary and Deputy Rapier were given a second mattress alongside them.[8]

"Fédon was first in bed, or rather a hammock, which he always made use of," observed Dr. Hay. It was not surprising that "Fédon was first in bed." He was likely exhausted for multiple reasons, including the almost nightly climb by foot to his military headquarters. Horses could not negotiate the steep, slippery, and thickly wooded mountains. Fédon had to dismount or mount his horse in the flatlands of Belvedere or Madame (Ferme) Peschier's when he traveled to or from his military headquarters.[9]

Hay reported that "Fédon slept in his clothes, with his pistols and musket alongside of him, attended by two of his own negroes armed." His "negroes" followed Fédon wherever he went. Two other men—Louis St. Hilaire, a mulatto from Gouyave, and André, a former slave—helped Fédon with his personal needs. A security detail protected him.[10]

"A guard was provided very early next morning (before I had an opportunity of conversing with Fédon) to conduct me back to prison," Hay continued. By then, Fédon had already vanished. He couldn't remain in one area too long and also had to visit bases as far as Saint Patrick. Based on Hay's observations, Julien Fédon was brave, busy, and cunning.[11]

Fédon's military headquarters (First Camp) and Morne Qua Qua (Second Camp) were areas with rugged peaks and deep valleys. At First Camp, Fédon built huts on the ridges overlooking Belvedere, where they slept during the struggle; they knew that Fédon's home, Belvedere House, would be an easy target for the British and it was.

⸺⚬⚬⚬⺆⸺

REV. M'MAHON AND DR. HAY rarely saw each other due to the large size of the area, yet their accounts are similar. But on April 7th they were placed in the prison hut that housed the governor and other Britishers.

Rev. M'Mahon: "I could well perceive that another attack was expected, from the unusual alacrity of the rebels and from the preparations that were made. … Fédon and the other mulattos boasted they could defeat the English, trusting to the difficulty of the ground they had fortified." On April 6, M'Mahon was prohibited from sleeping in the huts of revolutionaries and roaming around. "I was ordered from my hut to the prison to join Governor Ninian Home, Alexander Campbell, and others in their misery."[12]

Dr. Hay: "On the afternoon of the 7thof April, a cannonading was heard which lasted near an hour." Already in the makeshift prison, Hay felt that the cannonading confirmed "the truth of the report" of an impending attack.[13]

Rev. M'Mahon: "Neither was the door of our prison once opened after twelve o'clock, when the small quantity of provisions was thrown in." The provisions would be the last meal for 48 of the 51 prisoners.[14]

Mothers brought their children to Morne Qua Qua for safety. They knew British forces camped in Mount Saint John would be passing through the Belvedere valley to attack Fédon and would shoot anyone in sight, including children.

AT MORNE QUA QUA AND Fédon's military headquarters, the night was tense for both the prisoners and the revolutionaries. "The prisoners passed a horrible and dreadful night, for there was a strange confusion around the house, much talking, and the steps of numbers continually passing," Rev. M'Mahon explained.[15]

Julien Fédon spent the night at his military compound or First Camp, preparing for the attack expected by sunrise. He may have seen bonfires used by the British soldiers to warm themselves and dry their clothes at Mount Saint John's two bases, Lacroifade and Madame Chadeau. He may have heard the echoes of cannons, as British troops made their way to Chadeau from ships anchored off Gouyave. Fédon's network of spies, mulattos, Africans, and white Frenchmen, which stretched from Gouyave to Belvedere, may have constantly updated him.

Acting Governor Mackenzie was correct when he claimed that Fédon did not have massive forces and weapons in the cold, damp mountains. Mackenzie did not realize, though, that the revolutionaries in Saint Andrew would use other routes to carry ammunition and reinforce Fédon's rebels. Further, Fédon intuitively knew of alternatives to his lack of weapons and troops. He had learned and implemented strategies from maroons and slaves who had been through similar battles.

Rev. M'Mahon observed:

> They had cut down the face of the Hill at the post, and the palmetto and other trees nearly in two, and bent them in such a manner that a child, at liberty to do so, could hardly creep

through, much less a soldier with his arms and ammunition, and at the same time exposed to all the fire they could bring on them at particular points.[16]

During the day and night of April 7th, Fédon ensured that his most destructive weapons, three cannons (a nine-, a six-, and a four-pounder) were placed in otherwise inaccessible positions on the cliffs near his military headquarters overlooking Belvedere's flatlands. The positioning of the weapons would enable the revolutionaries to target British troops on their way to Fédon's base from Mount Saint John.

Nevertheless, Fédon was likely nervous, cautious, tired, and sleepless as he awaited the attack by newly arrived soldiers, marines, and sailors, along with local regiments—including a black militia led by his nemesis, Captain Louis La Grenade.

But Julien Fédon was ready.

TWENTY–TWO

Massacre

"Captain Joseph, the General orders you to 'kill all the prisoners!'—Let the reader judge of our horror and consternation at this command." —Rev. Francis M'Mahon.[1]

Britain's loss of its 13 North American colonies in 1776 and its forced recognition of the United States of America—on September 3, 1783, by the Treaty of Paris—was embarrassing. A mere 12 years later, on the morning of April 8, 1795, the massacre of Governor Ninian Home and 47 other Britishers in the mountains of Belvedere had to be equally disconcerting for the mighty British Empire. Worse still, Home's execution was ordered by a person of color and carried out by other mulattos and Africans.

Although gruesome by today's standards, the atrocities at Morne Qua Qua—variably known as Morne Vauclain, Camp of Death, Morne Fédon, Fédon's Camp and Second Camp—were the norm in 18th-century West Indian slave colonies. Barbarism was extreme, especially in the French colony of Saint Domingue and even in France, where King Louis XVI and Queen Marie Antoinette were guillotined. Yet, 18th-century British reports portray Julien Fédon as the "Monster of Monsters."[2]

In his narrative of the rebellion, published on May 1, 1795, Thomas Turner Wise shared his opinion:

> Julien Fédon and his nefarious band of Ruffians, a scene which for its diabolical Atrocity, its barbarous, savage Cruelty, equals, if not exceeds, Any Thing, as I believe I have already said, that has not yet been exhibited on the Stage of the World.[3]

Colonel Gordon Turnbull, who fought in the battle, added:

> The mind is struck with horror and recoil at the collection of an event, which, for its atrocious barbarity, has not, perhaps, been paralleled in the history of the most savage nations.[4]

For more than two centuries, most European and Caribbean historians accepted such descriptions of Julien Fédon's behavior. What history has preserved about one of the most humiliating days for the powerful British Empire, though, was written by Britishers and British sympathizers. Their accounts of April 8, 1795, were focused on the coldblooded murder of Governor Ninian Home and other Britishers.

Even today, Julien Fédon's prowess as a military commander has been ignored. Fédon's victory on that Wednesday morning, April 8, 1795, prolonged the rebellion for another 14 months—making it the longest and most destructive upheaval in a British slave colony in the 18th century.

Throughout the past 227 years, writers have focused principally on the causes and consequences of the revolution while ignoring the battles won by the rebels and the personality of Julien Fédon. He has not been credited for successfully defending against mighty British armies during the early months of the rebellion, as well as on that infamous Wednesday, April 8, 1795.

———

ACTING GOVERNOR MACKENZIE WAS FIRMLY convinced that it was time to "sever the head of the serpent," the rebel leader, Julien Fédon. On the afternoon of April 7, 1795, Mackenzie hurried to Mount Saint John to order Colonel Augustus Campbell to attack Fédon, but Mackenzie did not remain at Mount Saint John to witness "the severing" or to provide moral support to the troops. Instead, he spent the night in Gouyave and, about 10 p.m., dispatched newly arrived sailors to Mount Saint John. Mackenzie assigned their responsibilities rather than allowing Campbell to do it, resulting in the troops disregarding Campbell's command.

On the following day, April 8th, despite feeling certain of victory, Mackenzie did not return to Mount Saint John to witness the action in

Belvedere and the surrounding mountains. He remained in Gouyave and was informed of the devastating defeat before returning to St. George's later that evening.

To PREPARE FOR THE ATTACK, Lieutenant Colonel Augustus Campbell, commander of all military forces in Grenada despite having arrived in the island only five days before, created three columns consisting of hundreds of troops. Within each column were regiments rushed to Grenada from fleets protecting the British West Indies, along with local militias.

The right column, led by Lieutenant Colonel Hope, was comprised mainly of soldiers from the 25th, 9th, and 68th regiments and the St. George's militia.

Lieutenant Colonel Dickson led the left column, "composed of the corps of seamen, the light company of the 29th Regiment," and other battalions.[5] The center column, led by Campbell himself, consisted of "two Grenadier Companies of the 25th and 29th Regiments."[6]

The center column or reserve remained in the flatlands of Belvedere, below the towering mountains, to protect the right and left columns in case the troops had to retreat in haste and knowing he was not confident about securing victory. That decision turned out to be a blessing.

Going south from Mount Saint John (Chadeau) to Belvedere, the columns used separate routes. The left and right columns planned to converge at Fédon's military headquarters (1st Camp or 1st Post), where they would seize his cannons and turn them around in order to fire on rebel forces on the higher peaks.

With Belvedere and Mount Saint John sharing a common boundary, the battle began as soon as the troops entered Belvedere (Camp Liberty). The British effortlessly recaptured an abandoned Belvedere House, Fédon's home. The mulatto Captain Louis La Grenade, who fell from his startled horse during the early stages of the battle, was left with his colored regiment to protect Belvedere House—located about a half-mile from Chadeau.

Knowing that the British had to pass through Belvedere in order to attack Fédon's military headquarters, about two miles away in the second-highest mountain range in Grenada, the revolutionaries nervously waited for the battle to begin. Revolutionary and British forces clashed around slave huts and in the cultivated fields in Belvedere's flatlands, including the area where the prisoners were originally held. Some revolutionary troops hid in the thick vegetation and woodlands to wage sniper attacks on the British troops before deliberately running away. The revolutionaries knew that, by encouraging the British troops to pursue them to the foot of the mountains, they could wage a better fight. The rebels also expected the British troops to encounter difficulties climbing the steep, wet hills.

The battle intensified as the British troops got closer to the foot of the mountains. From the cliffs at Fédon's military headquarters (1st Camp), the rebels used cannons to fire on the approaching enemy down below. Some rather daredevil soldiers from the two British columns converged on the cliffs near the revolutionary's military headquarters but were unable to seize the cannons. Captain Stopford, who had earlier killed Jean-Pierre, Fédon's brother, "got within 20 yards of the gun, when he fell" either in crossfire by his troops or Fédon's troops. Another commissioned British officer, Enfign Baillie, from the famed 29th Regiment, was also killed at lower Morne Qua Qua or 1st Camp. Some troops got above Fédon's headquarters and closer to the highest peak of Morne Qua Qua mountain range, known today as 2nd Camp, where the prisoners had been moved.[7]

The majority of British troops did not ascend the hills leading to Fédon's military headquarters. The rebels "rolled large stones upon our men," Campbell reported to Sir John Vaughan. "The troops now being exposed to a heavy and galling fire from the enemy, and finding it impossible to make their way through the fallen trees, were forced to retreat."[8]

A company of revolutionaries, observing the British retreating, shouted words of triumph. A British regiment that was stealthily approaching thought that the jubilant shouting meant that the British were defeating the rebels and returned shouts of joy themselves, thereby revealing their location. Many in that regiment were instantly killed.

The fatalities on the British side were enormous. Several officers were killed. When the three prisoners that Fédon spared—Dr. Hay, Rev. M'Mahon, and William Kerr—descended from Morne Qua Qua ("Camp of Death"), they saw many bodies scattered at Fédon's Military Headquarters ("Camp Equality") and in the Belvedere flatlands ("Camp Liberty").[9]

"I counted ten men killed, most of them stripped and hacked with cutlasses," Dr. Hay wrote. While there is no certain evidence of the total number that died that day, an estimated 200 persons were killed on the British side, including the 48 prisoners, and far fewer on the revolutionary side. Today, one can see plaques in St. George's Anglican Church that were mounted there in 1799 in memory of the British officers and rank-and-file soldiers who died in action on April 8, 1795.[10]

The British presented lofty excuses for their embarrassing defeat but never acknowledged Fédon for outfoxing their military commanders—and Acting Governor Kenneth Francis Mackenzie.

As an officer in St. George's militia, Colonel Gordon Turnbull eagerly made himself available to quell the rebel revolt as early as March 3, 1795. Returning to Scotland shortly after the April 8 battle, Turnbull listed reasons for the crushing defeat in his book published in Edinburgh on November 9, 1795:

> The failure of the enterprise may be attributed to several causes. The heavy rains which had fallen, the inaccessibility of the ground, and the trees, which had been cut down, rendered it almost impossible for the men to march or to use their arms. The seamen and troops employed to bring forward a six-pounder had no share in the action; and this gun, owing to its great distance from the ridge, was of no service whatever.[11]

Turnbull revealed that the troops that had arrived in Grenada "were raw and undisciplined young men." As a result, the British troops left Mount Saint John late, at sunrise, rather than earlier in the morning in order to attack the revolutionaries while they were asleep. So, the element of surprise never occurred. At sunrise, the revolutionaries at the ridges above Fédon's military headquarters and in the Belvedere flatlands clearly saw the British troops departing Mount Saint John—and were ready for them.[12]

The battle lasted three to four hours. By midmorning, hundreds of British soldiers and sailors were fleeing Morne Qua Qua Mountain range, Belvedere, and Mount Saint John. "Soldiers … threw down their arms and ran away, which were immediately seized by the negroes," Hay emphasized.[13]

Fédon and Hay—still standing near the highest peak of Morne Qua Qua, close to the bodies of approximately 67 persons who were shot and hacked to death—would speak to each other for the last time. Hay wrote:

> He [Fédon] observed to me that the English troops employed against them were raw, undisciplined country people, who had never seen service or perhaps fired a musket before."[14]

The written accounts of the two eyewitnesses, Dr. Hay and Rev. M'Mahon, and two British writers living in Grenada—Henry Thornhill and Thomas Turner Wise—underlined a central reason for the humiliating British defeat. They each wrote that the British troops could not climb the mountain cliffs, because Fédon's men had uprooted trees, shrubs, and boulders. And that turned out to be a brilliant strategy. Fédon knew how to make "war in the woods." Those loose boulders and partially uprooted trees prevented the British troops from reaching their target; most lost their balance and fell down the slippery hills and precipices.[15]

⁂

EVEN IN 2017, PROBABLY DURING this writer's final hike to Fédon's Camp, I slipped and fell down numerous times when ascending and descending the hills in the rain. The branches, shrubs, and boulders that I grabbed onto were of minimal help. One can imagine how bad it must have been in 1795 with all of those removed.

⁂

Thomas Turner Wise and others who informally spoke to Colonel Campbell claimed that Campbell laid the blame on Mackenzie for the failure and that Campbell felt misled by an "impatient" Mackenzie. Henry Thornhill penned:

> General Campbell says, that he was induced to hope for success, particularly when he considered the weakness of the opposing Force, as the President had been so strongly assured of; he was, however, too well convinced by fatal experience that the President had been grossly misinformed, and the assurances given to him, totally erroneous.[16]

In his official account to Sir Vaughan of the defeat, Campbell faulted Mackenzie, "The President, having come on the 7th to the post at LaCrusade, (Lacroifade) represented, rather in strong terms, the necessity of attacking the enemy Camp without delay."[17]

GOVERNOR NINIAN HOME AND OTHER prisoners may have been saved had Mackenzie allowed Campbell to use his military expertise and delay the attack for at least a day. Instead, the decision to seize Fédon's weapons, especially the powerful 9-pounder, and use them against his forces is an example of how much the British underestimated Fédon's ability and the fortitude of his troops.

On the evening of April 8th, a few hours after the massacre, a mulatto named La Grange arrived from Guadeloupe with an order to relieve Fédon of his command and to send Governor Home and other prisoners to Guadeloupe. Governor Home was already dead, but Hay, M'Mahon, and Kerr were on a vessel bound for Guadeloupe, as prisoners of war, the following morning.

Where was General Julien Fédon during the April 8 battle? Evidently, he spent the afternoon and night of April 7 and the early part of Wednesday morning, April 8, at his military headquarters (1st Camp, lower Morne Qua Qua.) He may have strategized that his first line of defense was preventing the British from capturing his headquarters and cannons and, therefore, remained there to ensure that everything was thoroughly secured and defended. He must have left his headquarters for Morne Qua Qua (2nd Camp, upper Morne Qua Qua) when the British troops were getting closer, though, to protect his wife and daughters and, if necessary, to order the execution of Governor Home and the other prisoners.

Meanwhile, at Morne Qua Qua, Rev. M'Mahon, Dr. Hay, and the other prisoners could hear the musket fire and echo of cannons. "At one time, the firing appeared nearer to us," Rev. M'Mahon wrote. He then heard the dreadful instruction, shouted in French: "Captain Joseph, the General orders you to kill all the prisoners!"[18]

No document has been found to validate why Fédon ordered the killing of the prisoners. Did he believe that the British were getting too close, that they would defeat him and rescue the prisoners? That's possible. Since March 3rd, when Governor Home was captured, Fédon repeatedly warned that he would kill the prisoners if his camp were attacked. Now, as Rev. M'Mahon wrote, "the firing appeared nearer to us." Everyone was nervous at Morne Qua Qua—prisoners, revolutionaries, women, and children.[19]

The few British soldiers and sailors who almost seized Fédon's cannons climbed behind his headquarters but couldn't find a trail leading to the exact location of Fédon or the prisoners. They fired into the hills of Morne Qua Qua, but the musket fire fell short of the target. When Fédon spared Dr. Hay, he told Hay that, if he were killed, it would be by his own people firing at them.

⸺◈⸺

It was in the valleys between Morne Qua Qua's highest peak or Fédon's Camp and Fédon's military headquarters that this writer, then a teenager, and many others frequently found musket balls and old guns decaying beneath the soil. An aging Father Raymund Devas stood in the deep valley below Fédon's Camp one day in the early 1960s and explained to us that we were standing in the area where most muskets fell on April 8, 1795, when the British and revolutionaries aimed at each other—the revolutionaries at upper Morne Qua Qua and, below, the British in the area of Fédon's military headquarters or lower Morne Qua Qua. They were shooting at each other but couldn't see one another.

—⁂—

WRITING ABOUT THE BATTLE ABOUT three weeks afterwards, Wise speculated on Fédon's decision to order the killing of the prisoners:

> The Fall of Fédon's brother, who Captain Stopford shot, I believe, was a Circumstance, too, that is stated not only to have affected the Monster, but to have caused some Consternation in many of his fellow traitors.[20]

That speculation—also made by others, such as Henry Thornhill and Samuel Cary, Jr. writing to his parents in Massachusetts—has led historians to accept the notion that the rebels murdered the prisoners to avenge the death of Fédon's brother Jean-Pierre. In his vivid description of Julien Fédon's mindset at Morne Qua Qua that awful morning, however, Rev. M'Mahon never implied that Fédon had the prisoners killed in order to avenge the death of his brother. Neither did Dr. Hay, who described the temperament of Julien Fédon and the scene at Morne Qua Qua. Those two men both survived Fédon's wrath, lived and died in Grenada many years later but never wrote that Fédon ordered the prisoners killed to retaliate for the killing of his brother.

When Dr. Hay pleaded with Fédon "to have mercy on the innocent" by stopping the massacre of the other prisoners, Fédon replied, "They have none on our people below"—but did not mention his brother's name.[21]

Colonel Turnbull wrote:

> ... but his [Fédon's] principal motive for so horrible a deed was probably his fears that they would have been relieved by our troops or might have made their escape during the engagement.[22]

Dr. Hay further observed, "Fédon began the bloody massacre in presence of his wife and daughters, who remained there, unfeeling spectators of his horrid barbarity." Fédon has been disparaged over the centuries for allowing his family to witness the massacre, but he had no choice. Rev. M'Mahon stated that he saw women and children coming there during the night of April 7th in order to escape the wrath of the British, who were expected in Belvedere the following day.[23]

When Julien Fédon descended from Morne Qua Qua, he must have been exhausted. Evidently, he did not have the energy to descend to the Belvedere valley or to Camp Liberty, where the body of his slain brother remained. Instead, Fédon got as far as his military headquarters, Camp Equality, where he fell asleep.

THE BRITISH LOST THE BATTLE on April 8, despite some soldiers scaling lower Morne Qua Qua and coming closer to Fédon and the prisoners at Morne Vauclain or upper Morne Qua Qua. In fact, only a few hazardous hills and deep valleys separated the two opposing forces. By midmorning, the British were running back to Gouyave after Fédon ordered them chased from Morne Qua Qua, Belvedere, and Mount Saint John. The nearly naked revolutionaries, many of whom were Africans emancipated by Fédon, combed the battlefield for anything valuable. They grabbed boots that were stuck in the mud and stripped clothes from the dead, immediately putting them on. Weapons and bullets left by the British troops were the most valuable items. British soldiers lost in the woods and severely wounded remained there to depart this life.

The cannons had been silenced. The cries of agony had ceased. The mountain peaks remained evergreen. The rhythmic sounds of Belvedere's rivers and ravines continued as if nothing had happened—except for Wilson Ravine, whose waters ran red with the blood of the dead for days.[24]

Julien Fédon would control most of Grenada for the next 14 months.

TWENTY—THREE

Pilot Hill

A disconsolate Acting Governor Kenneth Francis Mackenzie departed Gouyave and arrived in St. George's during the night of April 8th only to receive more depressing news. His commanders in the Madame Ache's and La Baye areas still had not created a base at Michel, which Mackenzie had ordered in order to cut off the rebel supplies from La Baye. When communicating with his commanders on April 9, Mackenzie did not mention his humiliating defeat and the murder of Governor Home and other Britishers.

In any event Mackenzie did not comprehend the importance of alerting his commanders "where the others were" and their mission. For example, on April 8, Col. Este still trapped between Madame Ache's in Saint George and Grand Etang on his way to Michel heard the sound of cannons but he did not realize that a fierce battle was happening in the mountains of Belvedere.[1]

Mackenzie was determined, more than ever, to drive the revolutionaries from Pilot Hill and secure Grenville Bay. He was convinced that if Fédon were prevented from getting arms through Grenville Bay, the rebel forces would be weakened. In Mackenzie's mind, the free flow of weapons to Fédon through La Baye prevented the British from winning the April 8th battle.

Colonel Gordon Turnbull wrote:

> In every instance, the best plans which his Honour the President could devise for the reduction of the insurgents have been defeated. Unfortunate and unforeseen accidents … and a want of strict discipline and obedience prevented those plans from being carried into execution with that vigour and alacrity which he wished.[2]

An unhappy, unsuccessful, inexperienced, and exhausted Mackenzie then requested from General Sir John Vaughan, commander-in-chief of British forces in the West Indies, "a general officer, vested with the full command, in whom the military establishment, the militia, as well as regular troops, might have full confidence."[3]

British-Grenadians greeted Brigadier General Oliver Nicolls on April 13, similar to the welcome they gave General Colin Lindsay a month before. "None could be more pleased on this occasion than the President," Turnbull explained. "He was, by the arrival of General Nicolls, relieved from a load, under the pressure of which he was ready to sink." Everyone was confident that General Nicolls would crush the rebellion due to his experience in Grenada when he commanded the 45th Regiment earlier in his military career.[4]

After visiting the base at Madame Ache's, a mulatto-owned coffee estate in Saint George, General Nicolls went to Mount Saint John for a close view of Belvedere and Fédon's military headquarters. Nicolls withdrew troops from Madame Ache's and Mount Saint John and dispatched them to Observatory Estate in Saint Patrick in preparation for driving "the enemy from Pilot Hill, where they were now in considerable force."[5]

The base at Observatory Estate, Saint Patrick, under the command of Major Henry Addison Wright, was now the epicenter of activities. More troops had gathered there, but Fédon's forces soon gave General Nicolls a rude awakening. On the morning of April 22nd, a group of cavalry soldiers went to nearby Tivoli but were ambushed by Fédon's forces on their return to Observatory Estate. Robert Turnbull and a Mr. Langan from the local regiment were both killed. Major Wright immediately "ordered a detachment of the regular troops under Captain Gurdon, and the militia under Captain M'Caskill, to march against the enemy."[6]

The British did not have to march far. Fédon's forces were on a nearby hill, armed with a six-pounder that they were able to fire before running from the approaching British troops with Captain Philip Gurdon in the lead. Captain Gurdon was instantly killed by the six-pounder.

Captain Gurdon's death was a shock to everyone, including those who had belittled him for permitting his soldiers to get drunk and behave in a disorderly manner in Gouyave and then go to sleep there instead of proceeding to Belvedere; for allowing his regiment to sleep at Revolution Hall Estate the following night; for not going to Mount Saint John on the day that President Mackenzie had ordered; for not attacking Fédon's forces in Belvedere when he arrived at Mount Saint John; and for not landing his troops at Grenville Bay, as commanded. Nevertheless, a plaque in Gurdon's memory, placed at the Anglican Church in St. George's in 1799, is still mounted there today.

Before he fell ill with dengue fever and subsequently recovered, General Nicolls established a regiment of "three hundred faithful and trusty Slaves … equally divided into five companies …. being accustomed to labour, fatigue, and travelling in the woods" to help attack Julien Fédon's forces at Pilot Hill and elsewhere.[7]

Mackenzie and other leaders certainly must have briefed Nicolls on their own failed attempts at stopping the revolutionaries, beginning on March 24 and ending in a fierce battle during the first week of April. Therefore, Nicolls must have understood the strength of Fédon's forces at Pilot Hill and how difficult it would be to win a battle there.

The retaking of Pilot Hill began on April 26th, when the remaining British troops at Mount Saint John were dispatched to nearby Grand Bras Estate. Soldiers from the large base at Observatory Estate also moved to that location.

An amphibious assault was in the making, as well. "Two gun-boats, each carrying an eighteen-pounder [and] twenty small vessels, escorted by the *Resource* frigate, assembled at Gouyave." On April 27, the fleet left Gouyave for Grenville Bay "with about nine hundred troops."[8]

From St. George's, a troop of light cavalry and a black volunteer corps traveled to Marquis via Saint David, Crochu, and Grand Bacolet. Most likely, the black volunteer soldiers marched and the British rode horses. Meanwhile, the naval fleet from Gouyave landed its 900 troops at Marquis Bay, about two miles from Grenville Bay.

General Nicolls and his commanders meticulously planned the attack. Pilot Hill was surrounded. Hundreds of soldiers from Observatory and the 900 who came ashore at Marquis Bay were camped at Grand Bras and other nearby estates to cut off the retreat of any of Fedon's troops escaping north, south, or west. East of Pilot Hill, the armed fleet from Gouyave, sailing off Grenville Bay, completed the circle. The armada off Grenville Bay and Marquis Bay would capture any revolutionaries trying to escape by sea. General Nicolls not only looked to retake Pilot Hill and control Grenville Bay, he also aimed to demolish Fédon's powerful force by leaving no avenue of escape.

As a precaution, General Nicolls routed Fédon's forces at neighboring Battle Hill, located less than three miles from Pilot Hill. That mission was fairly easy, since Battle Hill was neither heavily fortified nor manned. Later, Battle Hill would become more strategic.

Excitement built as anxious British troops awaited the command to rout the revolutionaries. Fédon's troops were now completely surrounded and couldn't escape. They expected to catch Julien Fédon in the net. No escape for him. Optimism filled the air—in contrast to the mood a month earlier at Belvedere and Morne Qua Qua.

On the morning of May 4th, British troops were stunned when they discovered that the revolutionaries had vanished into thin air. Young, anxious British soldiers and sailors looking for "action" were disappointed, as were an embarrassed General Nicolls and his commanders. Fédon's troops had not been annihilated. Not a single shot was fired.

One more time, Julien Fédon and his brother-in-law, Charles Nogues, had outmaneuvered a high-ranking British military officer. The night before the "battle," while British forces were fast asleep, the revolutionaries silently spiked the cannons, making them unusable, and then—just as stealthily— returned to Belvedere and Morne Qua Qua.

Nonetheless, Pilot Hill and Grenville Bay were once again controlled by the British—but Julien Fédon and his revolutionaries had escaped to fight another day.

TWENTY–FOUR

Fédon Takes Back Gouyave

By mid-May 1795, Julian Fédon and his revolutionaries controlled all of Grenada's parishes in the island's interior. General Nicolls, meanwhile, expanded surveillance around the colony's coastline in order to intercept ships delivering supplies and soldiers from Guadeloupe. For General Nicolls, occupying Pilot Hill and Grenville Bay had been essential—but he needed additional bases in coastal areas to provide island-wide security. So, he created new bases in Saint Patrick and Saint David and strengthened those around the vital port of Charlotte Town as the British insisted on calling Gouyave.

British bases in other parishes were left depleted and weak due to the fact that General Nicolls had sent most of his troops and ammunition to the garrison at St. George's to discourage Fédon from invading the capital. That strategy enabled Julien Fédon and his revolutionaries to roam the interior of the island with minimal fear. Sometimes, the rebels went close to Nicoll's bases—daring the British to attack them.

During the remaining months of 1795, British-Grenadians became increasingly frustrated with General Nicolls. They felt that he was not being aggressive. By now, British-Grenadians expected Nicolls to have crushed the revolutionaries. They did not realize he was a man of vision or understand why he created approximately eight regiments with more than 500 loyal black soldiers, most of whom were slaves.

While General Nicolls had revamped the militias, he remained on the defensive. Clearly, he respected Fédon's ingenuity and did not want Fédon to outfox him again. The general preferred to wait for additional weapons and soldiers expected from England before making another attempt.

Thursday, October 15, 1795, was a rainy, windy night evidently a late summer storm. The British had occupied Gouyave for months. During that day in October, an African man deserted Fédon's forces at Morne Felix, a mulatto owned estate halfway between Belvedere and Gouyave, to inform the British of a pending attack. (During the 1950s, when children walked from Belvedere and Clozier to attend school in Gouyave and when coming back, we often quenched our thirst with the crystal-clear water from a waterhole off the Morne Felix Main Road.)

The African man explained that Fédon's troops consisted of seven companies, with each company having 60 to 80 men, plus soldiers from Guadeloupe. The troops assembled at Morne Felix to attack Gouyave the night before, but torrential rains prevented them from carrying out the plan. They were determined to attack that night—October 15—regardless of weather conditions.

The deserter also reported that a company of Fédon's soldiers planned to occupy the northern part of De l'Ance in order to trap the British in Gouyave and prevent them from escaping to Saint Mark. Another regiment would go to the mouth of Gouyave's southern river (near today's cemetery and Cuthbert Peter's Park) to thwart anyone looking to escape toward St. George's. He even revealed the exact time and place of the attack— "at the first cock-crow"—and that Fedon's troops would invade the British principal base on the hills of Gouyave Estate (today, the site of St. Rose Secondary School.)[1]

To authenticate the African's information, Lt. Col. B. Schaw, commander of British forces in Gouyave, dispatched a reconnaissance team to the outskirts of Morne Felix—where they did, indeed, observe Fédon's troops. Rather than thanking the African, the British imprisoned him; they couldn't understand why this slave from Barbados, freed by Fédon, would betray him. They thought he was a spy sent by Fédon to mislead them.

As a precaution, Colonel Schaw placed all troops on alert and sent an urgent message to Brigadier General Nicolls about the stunning new development. Colonel Schaw was also quite concerned, because his force in Gouyave was weak.

Grenada's 68th Regiment, comprised of 100 men, occupied the base located on the highest peak of Gouyave Estate, overlooking the town and the sea. The base had massive cannons faced toward the sea for firing at enemy ships; therefore, it was ideal for Fédon's forces to attack from the rear. The Loyal Black Rangers, totaling 55 Africans, and the St. John's militia, consisting of 83 men, were positioned in three places: De L'ance in the north, the marketplace in the middle, and near the river at the southern end of town. The British troops were not positioned there to defend Gouyave but, rather, to escape if Fédon invaded.

⸎

Dr. John Hay, who amazingly returned to Grenada from Guadeloupe in a prisoner exchange that July, had reorganized the Saint John militia by October. Just as how Julien Fédon loved Grenada, Hay also loved Grenada—particularly Charlotte Town, as he called Gouyave. When Fédon spared his life on April 8th, Hay was sent to Guadeloupe as a prisoner-of-war. Given his splendid relations with the French and with people of color in Grenada, Victor Hugues and others in Guadeloupe afforded him respect and special privileges. Hugues promised him his release as soon as an opportunity arose. So, in July, Hay—along with several other men, women, and children—were all sent to British Martinique, aboard two ships, as part of a prisoner exchange.

Based on Dr. Hay's ordeals in Grenada between March 2nd and April 8th, along with his imprisonment in Guadeloupe and current state of health, Hugues must have expected that Dr. Hay would sail on the first ship headed for England, his homeland. Instead, Hay boarded the next vessel out of Martinique bound for Saint Vincent and Grenada. About his return, he wrote:

> My return astonished many, but more particularly the negroes … A negro of my own, at first seeing me, laid hold of my hand with both his, and after looking in my face, burst in a flood of tears … nothing could be more expressive of his feelings, or more sensibly affect mine.[2]

Hay, a man of courage, had arrived in St. George's but was anxious to return to his adopted hometown, Gouyave. He continued:

> I proceeded to Gouyave by water, where I had spent the greatest part of my life happily amongst my friends … the scene … instantly struck me with a deep melancholy, and required my utmost exertions and fortitude to conceal it from the numerous bands of negroes, ready to receive me on landing … I remained for a considerable time in the midst of the crowd, before I could open my mouth to return thanks for their affectionate welcome.[3]

Julien Fédon and his revolutionaries couldn't believe that Hay was back in Gouyave and were infuriated to learn that Hay was raising a company of blacks to defeat them. How could he? A fuming Fédon now sought Dr. Hay—even if he were hiding in a "rat-hole." According to Hay:

> Whereas, from the lenity shown me in sparing my life on the 8th of April, they never expected I would take up arms against them. They offered a considerable reward for any person who would deliver me up, or discover where I could be found.[4]

Would Fédon capture Hay on October 15? Awful weather dominated the night of Thursday, October 15; moreover, it was pitch dark, not a star to be seen. In spite the howling winds and high sound of waves and gushing water, "the cry of *Vive la République*" was "distinctly heard." The British in Gouyave never thought that Fédon would attack in the middle of a fierce storm. Instead of invading "at the first cock-crow," as the African had warned the British, Fédon astonished everyone by attacking at midnight. His army, which had marched from Belvedere via Morne Felix, captured the British base on the hills of Gouyave Estate. Fédon knew all of the trails leading to the base, because months earlier they had created the base themselves but had quickly abandoned it in March, when the British invaded Gouyave by both land and sea.[5]

The weather was so dismal during that night that, upon capturing the base in the hills overlooking Gouyave, Fédon's forces did not even bother to enter the town—opting to do so the following morning. For Schaw, everything happened very quickly. There was no time to offer even token resistance. Upon realizing that Fédon had captured the fort in spite of the weather, Schaw ordered the weak British forces to evacuate Gouyave.

Dr. Hay, who was camped near the base at the foot of Gouyave Estate, narrowly escaped. He, along with several British and French women and soldiers, hastened to St. George's by foot, through the storm, arriving there around 8 a.m. Several persons, including Richard Muir, the town doctor, drowned in the angry sea when the group attempted to board canoes and head toward the capital.

Left in Gouyave to fend for themselves were several women and children and wounded British soldiers who had been brought to a hospital in Gouyave from other parishes. Dr. John Hay and other Britishers wrote that, the following day, French soldiers from Guadeloupe, who had joined Fédon in conquering Gouyave, prevented the revolutionaries "and negroes…. savage to a degree" from butchering those who had not escaped.[6]

General Julien Fédon, with the help of those French soldiers, had scored a significant victory. And while the British were eager to disparage him as the "Monster of all Monsters," they praised "the men from Guadaloupe" for obeying the rules of war. Regardless of how much he was maligned by the British, Julien Fédon had now outmaneuvered another high-ranking British officer—this time, General Nicolls—in the battles at both Pilot Hill and Gouyave.[7]

Fédon stunned Nicolls by easily capturing Gouyave, brashly renamed it Port Libre, and established the town as the capital of Grenada. But instead of recognizing Fédon's success in reoccupying Gouyave, historians focus on Schaw's loss of Gouyave. In a surviving letter to Samuel Cary in Chelsea, Massachusetts, penned on November 18, 1795, by Samuel Cary, Jr.—his son, a member of the St. George's militia, and manager of Mount Pleasant Estate—describes the fall of Gouyave and his frustration with Schaw, although he did not mention Schaw by name:

> …although the hill above Gouyane House was fortified, and that above 200 effective men were stationed on and about it, it was taken in the night without a dozen shot being fired … The Officer commanding at that post had warning the day before

> of the preparations making by the enemy, yet he placed only 36
> men on the hill, the rest slept below at the Gouyane House and
> in the town … So shamefully precipitate was the retreat, that
> 100 sick men were left in the hospital; and even after they left
> Gouyane so fast did 200 men armed and accoutered hurry to
> town that several women and others who attempted to follow
> them were left by the way, and some were killed by the negroes,
> and some taken up along shore by Cruisers.[8]

British Grenadians and General Nicolls were embarrassed for "the loss of the important Post of Gouyave … It furnished the enemy with a Seaport," and an attempt to court martial Schaw for dereliction of duty was unsuccessful. Nicolls' strategy of a naval blockade around the island continued, but Fédon's control of Gouyave, made it easy for French ships to enter and depart "Port Libre." French naval ships from Guadeloupe and armed canoes from Gouyave routinely captured British commercial ships and escorted them to Port Libre.[9]

While the French never invaded Grenada, as Julien Fédon had promised in the early days of the rebellion, the French did assist him throughout 1795. With the capture of Gouyave, French soldiers from Guadeloupe occupied nearby estates near Port Libre, such as Morne Nesbit, Morne Granby, and Dougaldston. The French never attacked St. George's but frequently waged sniper attacks on ships in St. George's Harbour. Why Fédon's rebels and the French soldiers did not invade St. George's remains a topic of speculation. Because he was policing the entire Eastern Caribbean out of Guadeloupe, perhaps Victor Hugues did not have a force that was capable of seizing St. George's.

The French presence in Grenada did allow their commanders to ask the British in St. George's for prisoner-of-war exchanges. The British responded to the French requests but not to Fédon. The British accepted the French as a legitimate foreign enemy and practiced the protocols of war but did not feel the same about mixed-race General Julien Fédon. To the British, he was a British subject who revolted against his king.

DURING THE LAST TWO MONTHS of 1795, sporadic battles between the British and the revolutionaries occurred around the island, especially in Saint Andrew and Saint David. To compensate for his loss of Pilot Hill and Grenville Bay, Fédon established a new base three miles away at Post Royal, overlooking Marquis Bay, which allowed him to get supplies from Guadeloupe and Spanish Trinidad. In December, however, Fédon failed to recapture Pilot Hill during a fierce 12-day battle; hundreds on both sides were killed.

Two weeks before the year ended, Fédon's forces now occupied most of the colony. A dispirited Council President Kenneth Francis Mackenzie—having failed to stop the rebels—resigned and departed Grenada.

When 1795 began, people in the United States and Europe had never heard of Julien Fédon. By the end of the year, Fédon was mentioned in publications across France, Britain, and the United States. At first, the articles focused on how Fédon led a slave revolt, which was not uncommon in West Indian slave colonies—but readers were puzzled to learn that Fédon, who murdered the island's governor, was mixed-race and the owner of a large coffee plantation. Why would a rich plantation owner, who owned more than 100 slaves, free all slaves in the colony and lead an insurrection? People were baffled.

Julien Fédon was a very curious character.

Relationships
Influences
Inspirations

TWENTY-FIVE

The Enigmatic Julien Fédon

Little did people know in the 18th century that Julien Fédon would remain an enigma more than two centuries later—partly the result of fiction writers. Like their earlier counterparts, 21st-century novelists have contributed to Fédon's mystique and his somewhat surreal life.[1]

Scholars in almost every continent, from Europe to Australia, have cited Fédon's Revolution as a topic of their academic papers. Most of those scholars focus on the cause and consequences of Fédon's Revolution, while others compare it to other 18th century rebellions in the Caribbean—but seldom do they focus on the man himself, Julien Fédon. It's not surprising that biographies of Toussaint Louverture—leader of the Haitian Revolution— are still being written, as he was one of the greatest leaders in history. It is folly to place Fédon in the same league with Louverture, yet Julien Fédon certainly deserves more than an essay or a chapter in a book.[2]

While historians have not completely ignored Julien Fédon, information about him is scarce. There is little known about his daily activities during the 16-month revolutionary period or his whereabouts afterwards, except what a few Britishers documented. We know about the battles but not about the man. Most of what has been written or said about Julien Fédon is speculation shamelessly disguised as fact, such as claiming that he was born in Grenada. There is no archival proof of where he was born; Martinique remains a possibility.

Little is known about "General Julien Fédon," and less has been documented. That said, understanding the relations between him and his contemporaries (such as Ninian Home, Victor Hugues, Louis de La Grenade, and self-emancipated slaves or maroons), along with the impact of contemporaneous events (such as the American, French, and Haitian revolutions), can contribute to an insightful biographical sketch of the enigmatic Julien Fédon.

TWENTY–SIX

Governor Ninian Home

On March 3, 1795, during the first 12 hours of Fédon's Revolution, Governor Ninian Home was captured. Julien Fédon visited Home in the rebels' makeshift prison, a two-floor boucan hidden in the flatlands of Belvedere Estate and not too far from the Belvedere Main Road. Fédon rebuked his prisoner: "Here you, Home, Tyrant of the French, my prisoner. You must make them deliver up the forts."[1]

Fédon ordered guards to place irons around the legs of his two prized prisoners, Governor Home and Alexander Campbell, as they were too important to have even the slightest chance of escaping or being rescued. Fédon ordered the guards to kill them if an escape or rescue attempt was made.

The next day, March 4th, Fédon asked Home to send a message to the British authorities in St. George's, ordering them "to surrender, and to offer honourable terms" to him and also to inform the authorities that the prisoners, including the governor, would be killed if the British did not surrender the island. An adamant Ninian Home refused, telling Fédon that "being their prisoner deprived him of all power and authority." Home either did not understand the gravity of the situation or simply continued his customary disrespect toward French Grenadians and mulattos of French ancestry.[2]

Fédon visited Home during the afternoon of March 5th and asked him again to request the surrender of the island. Home refused once more but did agree to write to the caretakers in St. George's, informing them of Fédon's request. Before leaving the prisoners, Fédon reminded the guards "to put all the prisoners to death," except for Dr. John Hay, if the need arose. At that time, Rev. M'Mahon was still a "guest prisoner" in Fédon's home.[3]

About 9 p.m. on Saturday, March 7th, Fédon sent for prisoners Home, Farquhar and Campbell. They walked through the flatlands of coffee, cocoa, and plantain fields, crossed swamps and ravines and then scaled the perilous mountains, finally arriving at Fédon's military headquarters only to be told by Fédon that he was surprised to see them "at so late an hour." Home and Campbell stood all night in the cold and pouring rain. Was that a message to the arrogant governor of what would happen if Grenada was not surrendered?[4]

Fédon reiterated his demand for the British to surrender the colony to the French Republic. Addressing the governor and Mr. Campbell, Fédon said, "The island was theirs by right, and you are only intruders; you came from England, that is your country, where you ought to have remained."[5]

That bold statement implied that Fédon considered himself Grenadian, whether he was born in Grenada or elsewhere. The French developed Grenada; therefore, Grenada belongs to people of French ancestry. Fédon resented the British "occupation."

On the first Sunday of the revolution, March 8th, hundreds of French inhabitants, mulattos, maroons, and newly emancipated Africans all marched around the prison celebrating the events of the last few days. That display of joyfulness and solidarity, however, did not change the resolve of Governor Ninian Home and Alexander Campbell.

During another visit to the prison, Fédon took valuables from the prisoners to use toward purchasing arms in Spanish Trinidad. In an act of benevolence, Fédon returned Governor Home and Campbell their "Joes" (coins). Realizing that Fédon urgently needed money, Dr. Hay and some other prisoners concocted a plan to pay a ransom for their release, but Alexander Campbell promptly rejected the idea.

The frequent contacts between Fédon and Home during the first week of the rebellion implied that Fédon understood Home's power. Fédon may have felt that the leadership in St. George's, with Council President Kenneth Francis Mackenzie now at the helm as acting governor, would honor a letter from Home urging surrender. Mackenzie disregarded the letters. Fédon's continuously insulted Home when he visited the prison. He detested Home and Campbell more than he hated other Britishers.

Ninian Home was governor for just two years and one month, so why did Fédon detest him? Why did Fédon refer to him as "Tyrant Home?" The answer is fairly simple. Like other French Grenadians, Fédon had endured Governor Home's tyrannical governance for decades.

NINIAN HOME LIVED IN GRENADA for 31 years, and that was the crux of the problem. Throughout his residency, Home never bonded with the French population. So, like other people of French ancestry, Fédon dealt with the consequences of Home's anti-French legislation.

NINIAN HOME WAS ABOUT 32 years old and a wealthy lawyer when he left Wedderburn Castle, Berwickshire, Scotland, for Britain's new colony of Grenada—a spoil of war. It is believed he lived for a short period in the British Colony of Virginia. Like so many affluent European adventurers at the time, Home was looking to create wealth for himself in the West Indies. In October 1766, Home was "one of the thirteen Scots elected to the new assembly" and became British Grenada's first Speaker of the Assembly. As such, he became an architect of Grenada's government and its laws.[6]

Home was appointed a judge of the Court of Common Pleas in 1771, the same Court that ratified property transactions—and he was a frequent purchaser. Home became Assistant Judge in 1784 and Colonel Commander of the Troops of Horse Militia in 1785.

A staunch Protestant, Home steadfastly opposed Roman Catholicism. He also made it known that he did not favor any French people remaining in the British colony—although many were Grenada-born and/or descendants of 17th-century French settlers.

A mere eight months before Julien Fédon decided he had enough of Ninian Home's rule, Home dispatched a letter, dated June 17, 1794, to his friend George Logan in Scotland. "White people are much wanted in this island," Home said, insinuating that British Protestants should emigrate to Grenada. "For many of the French … are gone and many more must go soon, and it would be happy for the Island if we were rid of them all." Governor Home's abhorrence of the French was creating increasing tension between the British and the French citizenry.[7]

Home slightly turned the other cheek during the French Revolution. He reluctantly invited French Royalists living on colonies governed by French revolutionaries to settle in Grenada—on one condition: They were not allowed to bring their slaves, who most likely also spoke French.[8]

Throughout his three decades in Grenada, Ninian Home was a prominent planter and politician. One of the most conservative members of the Assembly, he enacted legislation over the decades that denied the French their political, civil, and religious liberties. For example, Julien and Marie Rose Fédon and other Roman Catholics were forced to marry in an Anglican Church due to the laws spearheaded by Home and other Scots.

Home also may have used his expertise as a lawyer and his hatred of the French to rob French landowners of their properties. When reviewed, Home's real estate transactions—such as indentures, mortgages, and lease and release deals—lead one to believe that Home exploited French landowners and concocted schemes to take their property. Small French planters had no way to complain, because the British were in control of everything.

***

ISLE DE LA GRENADE WAS easily captured by England in February 1762. By the time the colony officially became British by the Treaty of Paris in 1763, British investors, especially the Scots, were already in Grenada purchasing estates from the French or making deals in London and Scotland to acquire them. Two of the first group of Scots to arrive were Alexander Campbell and his friend Ninian Home in 1763.

The government in England declared all lands in Grenada to be crown property, meaning that all lands now belonged to the King of England.

The French, resident in Grenada for more than 100 years, had a choice of leasing back their property from the British for 40 years or selling their property and emigrating. They were given 18 months to decide. The Scots, in particular, acquired property quickly. Prime estates were gobbled up by Britishers, including Ninian Home.

From his home in picturesque Paraclete, Home continued to purchase land in Grenada's other parishes and in nearby Carriacou. With European investors speculating in sugar as the next lucrative commodity, Home dreamed of getting a lion's share of the profit. Amassing a fortune was, of course, why he went to the West Indies in the first place.

GRAND PAUVRE, AS ITS NAME implies, was the poorest and smallest parish in Grenada. Many underprivileged French people settled there upon arriving in Grenada. They had little or no wealth and no connection to the French monarchy or aristocrats, which was needed to purchase large pieces of property to develop into estates. The people in Grand Pauvre parish were perfect targets for the Scots to exploit.

A 1764 deed is the first evidence of Ninian Home and his wife, Penelope, owning lands in Grand Pauvre. On June 4, 1763, through a letter of understanding with Home's agent, the owners of an estate—two French couples, Anthony Bonis and his wife Jane Ferary and John and Catherine Elizabeth Reubin—agreed to sell their property to Ninian Home. Conceivably, the couples preferred to sell and leave Grenada rather than stay as "adopted" subjects and lease the property that they had cultivated for years.[9]

On September 10, 1764, Home purchased that property as two separate estates, a coffee and cocoa estate and a sugar estate, although the two purchases were deeded as one transaction. The indenture, submitted to the Grenada Registrar's Office on November 13, 1764, was an "indenture of three parts between John Reubin …. and Catherine Elizabeth his wife of the first part, Anthony Bonis and Jane Ferary his wife of the second part, and Ninian Home of the said island, Esquire of the third part."[10]

The sugar estate (128 quarreys, or 410 acres), together with the coffee-cocoa estate (36 quarreys, or 115 acres), gave Home 168 quarries, or 525 acres of cultivated land in Grand Pauvre.

The British government forbade anyone from purchasing estates larger than 500 acres, but Scottish and English planters found a way to circumvent the law. That may have been the reason why Home bought the property as two separate lots. Each lot was less than the maximum 500 acres but, when combined, totaled more than 500 acres.

Home paid £21,764.14s for the properties. Included in the price were the buildings, equipment, 151 enslaved, 21 mules, 12 cattle, and two horses. The indenture's "schedule" (attachments) listed the names of slaves and, as recent as January 2021, the writing was still legible.

The sugar estate had 111 enslaved; the schedule did not indicate how many were male, female, or children. The second schedule contained "the Names of the Negroes on the Coffee and Cocoa Plantation" and included 14 males, nine females, and 11 children for a total of 34—plus an additional six slaves.[11]

The sugar estate, previously called Bonis, and the coffee-cocoa estate together became known as Bonair Estate. The land began "from the sands of the sea" at the mouth of the River Grand Pauvre and then spiraled east and then north. The property also included a second river, Ecrivise.[12]

In the 21st century, Victoria River (River Grand Pauvre) and its bridge, the playing field, the primary school, the river near the primary school (Ecrivise), and Jouvay chocolate factory (Diamond Estate) are all located on land once owned by Ninian and Penelope Home.

⁕

As a member of the Assembly, Home consistently voted for laws denying the French their civil liberties while, at the same time, acquiring their properties. No property was too small for Home, and he got lands by any means necessary. Sometimes he bought, rented, leased, or exchanged lands in complex transactions that the French owners could not understand, since many did not speak English and/or were illiterate.

October 5, 1764, deed: An attachment to the deed listing the 34 slaves included in the sale of estate sold to Ninian Home by French owners, Jean Reubin and Catherine Elizabeth wife and Antoine Bonis and wife. The area is today's Bonaire in Victoria. (*Courtesy Supreme Court Registry archives, Grenada.*)

At an auction on December 10, 1767, for example, Ninian Home bought "11 quarries of land … formerly belong to Monsieur Gibon late of the said island of Grenada and was sold at publick outcry by the Deputy Provost Marshall for the satisfaction of the debts of the same Monsieur Gibon when the same was bought by the said Ninian Home." The Gibon property was not in boundary with Home's other properties, but Marie Catherine Deslanades Gilles, a French widow, had "10 quarries, 32 acres … in boundary in the east and north with lands of the said Ninian Home." He exchanged his newly purchased 11 quarries, the Gibon property, with widow Gilles for her 10 quarries, which were adjacent to his own. The indenture, written in English, was filed in the Registry.[13]

Marie Catherine Deslanades Gilles's entire estate was larger than the 10 quarreys, and Home gradually leased and rented her remaining land, along with her slaves, animals, buildings, and equipment, with the intent to buy. By 1769, he owned the vast estate that is today the Village of Diamond in Saint Mark (Grand Pauvre.)

Most properties in those days were bought with a down payment, and the buyer promised to pay the seller in annual increments. Many sellers did not receive the annual payments, however, and their cases dragged on in the British and French courts. After Home's execution, his brother George and other shareholders in Britain discovered questionable aspects in Ninian Home's and Alexander Campbell's transactions, but no evidence has ever appeared indicating that Home did not pay the sellers.

Home and other Scots had no major problems raising money. Abundant evidence of how Home financed his affairs shows, for example, that on June 9, 1767, he obtained financing through his connections in Britain to convert the coffee and cocoa estate that he purchased in 1764 into a sugarcane estate. The agreement was "between the Honorable Ninian Home of the said island of Grenada, Esq. and Penelope his wife of one part, Henry Douglas of the City of London, Esq. and Sir James Cockburn of the said City of London Baronet of the other part." Douglas and Cockburn invested £3,000 sterling into that venture. After Home's murder in 1795, his brother, George, became liable to Cockburn for £5,000.[14]

While Home was visiting Scotland and England in 1768-69 with the express purpose of raising capital, his agents in Grenada were busy purchasing lands from the French.

⚬⚬⚬

THE FRENCH AND HAITIAN REVOLUTIONS triggered Governor Home to pass more stringent laws against the French and mixed-race people. One can only imagine Home's contempt for French-speaking mulattos, many of whom were faithful Roman Catholics.

⚬⚬⚬

HOME'S ORDEAL AS FÉDON'S PRISONER and his eventual execution still evoke sympathy two centuries later. One wonders if Home received similar sympathy from the caretaker government in St. George's or whether the Council President Kenneth Francis Mackenzie truly cared about rescuing him. Historical records show Mackenzie often speaking of "rescuing the colony," "saving the colony," and "crushing the insurgents"—but very few instances where he talked about rescuing Home. On March 6, 1795, a mere three days after the capture of the governor, Mackenzie informed the leaders of the Saint Andrew militia that "the island is to be saved" by their "united exertions."[15]

In his letter to Mackenzie that same day, Home emphasized Fédon's frequent threats to kill him, together with all prisoners, "the instant an attack is made … We therefore hope you will take this, our representation, into your most serious consideration and not suffer, if possible, the lives of so many innocent persons." Mackenzie disregarded Home's pleas. Instead of negotiating, Mackenzie went forward with his attempts to crush the insurgents.[16]

The Saint Patrick and Saint Andrew regiments voluntarily assembled at La Baye when they heard about an invasion and, later, a rebellion. Mackenzie, who had no military experience, soon lost the officers and soldiers moral support by upbraiding them. From "St. George's, 6th March 1795," only three days after the insurrection commenced, he dispatched a letter to Colonel Isaac Horsford, Colonel John Stewart, and Lieutenant Gordon Turnbull who had assembled at La Baye with their militias:

> The island is to be saved by your united exertions against the enemy, and not by hiding your regiments on board ships at La Baye.[17]

With England and France at war, Mackenzie had the option of surrendering Grenada to save Home's life, thus allowing the British and French governments to negotiate a peace treaty. Instead, Mackenzie became solely focused on defeating the revolutionaries and saving the colony. That was his principal objective in the battle with Fédon on April 8th; it was not on rescuing Ninian Home.

You see, not everyone in Grenada's ruling class was pleased about Home's appointment by British Foreign Secretary Henry Dundas. Some aspired for the governorship themselves. "I have the mortification to see a man put above my head who for 18 years has been under my command.…and in the very place, which 14 years ago was promised to me by His Majesty," wrote a disappointed Acting Governor Samuel Williams, on two occasions, to a friend in London. It is not surprising, then, that nobody in the Council pressured Mackenzie to rescue the governor first and defeat the rebels afterwards. Moreover, the aristocratic lifestyle of Ninian Home—and Alexander Campbell, as well—offended other Britishers, especially the English.[18]

A letter from Ninian Home while on vacation in Scotland, rebuking the manager of his Paraclete Estate for the ill treatment of slaves, continues to be used as an example of Home's benevolence. It's just as likely that Home simply understood that a healthy slave provided more labor and increased production.

Slaves on other estates were not taken in by Home's so-called benevolence; they were interested only in freedom. It was Oronoko, a house slave in the great house of "Lafortune Estate," who precipitated Home's easy capture. Oronoko ran from Lafortune Estate in Saint Patrick to inform revolutionaries in Gouyave that Home would be sailing to St. George's. Oronoko was one of the executioners of prisoners on April 8th.[19]

—∞—

DID HOME OPPOSE JULIEN FÉDON purchasing property in Saint Mark and other parishes? Did Home force the French and French-speaking mulattos in Saint Mark, including Pierre Fédon, to sell certain properties to him or to exchange theirs with his? What is most interesting is that Julien Fédon purchased Belvedere in 1791, when Home was in Britain for an extended period (1788-1793). Would Home have blocked the sale of Belvedere to Fédon if Home had been in Grenada? We'll never know the answers to these questions, but they're interesting to consider.

When Belvedere laborers of the 1950s chatted about Julien Fédon during "rum talk" or socializing, my Papa, Frederick Adams, always repeated, "De people in Town [St. George's] did not like the governor, so dey did not save him."[20]

—⁂—

REASONS FOR THE ENMITY BETWEEN Home and Fédon will remain a topic of speculation. Nevertheless, the two men did share one thing in common: a love of plantains, the principal staple in colonial Grenada. During his first week of imprisonment, Home asked to have his plantains roasted. Plantains were his last meal, too.

Victor Hugues, the French Commissioner in Guadeloupe, had weapons sent to Fédon but no food. Plantains sustained the revolution.

TWENTY–SEVEN

Victor Hugues

If Jean-Baptiste Victor Hugues (1762-1826) were alive today, he might say, "They are giving me more praise than I deserve for the rebellion in Grenada."

On May 21, 1794, when Hugues sailed into the Eastern Caribbean to recapture and assume the governorship of the French colony of Guadeloupe and to conquer nearby British colonies, especially those previously owned by France, Julien Fédon and other free, mixed-race, French-speaking people were already planning their rebellion.

In neighboring Saint Vincent, Saint Lucia, Dominica, and other British colonies, discontent had come to a boiling point among people of French ancestry, who were dissatisfied with British governance. In Grenada, in particular, free French people of color, with the discreet support of French whites, were seeking their civil rights.

Internal problems were the driving force behind a possible rebellion. Like the mulattos of Haiti, landowning free coloreds in Grenada expected to participate in politics and to exercise their rights. Only when those expectations were repeatedly ignored by Governor Ninian Home and other Grenadian politicians, Julien Fédon and most mixed-race landowners escalated their approach from exerting peaceful pressure to advocating violence.

External factors played a role, too. Both the French Revolution and the abolition of slavery in Saint Domingue (Haiti) encouraged French-speaking people to rise up against the British colonists. Memories of the success of the American Revolution, which occurred about 20 years prior, may have been a consideration, as well. Chances are, French mulattos with Julien Fédon's stature evaluated all of those developments, took note, and may have thought, "Why can't we seek our liberty, too?"

In 1793, more than a year before Victor Hugues was appointed by the French Republic to be a commissioner in the Eastern Caribbean, fields of plantain and other crops were planted on Fédon's Belvedere Estate and other neighboring, mulatto-owned estates for harvesting during the upcoming rebellion.

One day in March 1795, as the rebellion was underway, Julian Fédon assigned Dr. Magnival, a confidant and a Frenchman, to assist Dr. Hay in taking care of the wounded. Dr. Hay, who had a knack of getting information without asking direct questions, offhandedly commented to Dr. Magnival that the revolutionaries soon would not have enough food to feed everyone. Dr. Magnival casually explained to Dr. Hay that, while planning the rebellion, the revolutionaries took many factors into consideration. As the two doctors were riding through a large plantain field on their way to visit the wounded, Dr. Magnival pointed out to Dr. Hay that the field, about 11 quarreys (more than 20 acres), was cultivated about 18 months before "from which it is evident that the present measures have not been entered into, without first being maturely considered, and their plans deeply laid."[1]

It was a wise decision by Fédon, Dr. Magnival, and other plotters to plant crops in advance even on estates such as Madame Peschier owned by mixed-race planters. Realizing how essential food was to the revolutionaries, however, Council President Mackenzie, on April 12, 1795, ordered Colonel C. W. Este to dispatch "50 Negroes with cutlasses," protected by a cavalry and 100 soldiers, into the interior to destroy the plantain fields.[2]

THROUGH THE CENTURIES, THE WIDELY accepted narrative has been that Victor Hugues was the principal architect of Fédon's Revolution. Alas, he was not. Hugues added fuel, but the branches, sticks, and dried leaves required to make a fire had already been gathered and laid by Fédon and other disgruntled French Grenadians—including white French planters such as Clozier Darceuil and a handful of Britishers. It was French-Grenadians who conceived the rebellion, the uprising, the revolt, or—as the British preferred to call it—the insurgency.

Calling Victor Hugues the instigator of the rebellion in Grenada, an idea underscored by generations of historians, was simply recycled British propaganda. Yet, it wasn't only historians who blamed Hugues. Fédon's revolutionaries themselves promoted Hugues as a prime mover. As soon as the fighting began in Gouyave and La Baye, for instance, Fédon and his plotters pompously displayed French support. They wore colorful French national cockades, epaulets, and uniforms. They displayed "swords and pistols," shouted the slogans of the French Revolution, and sang the French national anthem—all inspirational gimmicks to get people to support the revolt.[3]

HISTORIANS AND OTHERS, THOUGH, REFERENCED documents as the main evidence that Hugues initiated the revolution. Fédon's first direct communication with the government in St. George's, for example, was the message that he sent to Council President Kenneth Francis Mackenzie demanding the surrender of Grenada in the name of the French Republic. That convinced everyone that Fédon had the support of France:

> We summon you, and all the Inhabitants of this Colony
> of every denomination to submit yourselves ... to the
> forces of the Republic under our command ... We will
> warrant you the safety of your lives and properties.[4]

A second document—"Declaration of the Commissioners delegated by the National Convention of France" issued by Victor Hugues, Gaspar Goyrand, and Alexandre Lebas in the Eastern Caribbean and addressed to the commanders of British forces in the region, Vaughan, Caldwell, Thompson, Stewart, and Lindsay—was delivered along with Julien Fédon's letter to Council President Mackenzie. The Declaration, created on February 21, 1795, did not even mention Grenada; rather, it cited Saint

Lucia. Hugues warned the British command, based in Martinique, of grave consequences if French nationals in Saint Lucia were attacked. Yet, Fédon apparently included that Declaration in order to impress Mackenzie and other Grenadian politicians.[5]

The two documents presented to the government in St. George's on March 5th by Fédon's emissaries, Joachim Philip and Charles Nogues, appear to be the basis for the public and various governments back in 1795-96, as well as historians and Caribbean writers through the centuries, to credit Hugues for the rebellion in Grenada that became known as Fédon's Revolution.

Thomas Turner Wise, a British lawyer living in Grenada, published a book on May 18, 1795, a mere 10 weeks after the revolution began, in which he focused on "la Déclaration ci-jointe" from the French Commissioners. That reference led many to believe that Victor Hugues did ignite the rebellion.[6]

Lieutenant Colonel Gordon Turnbull of the St. George's militia, who fought Fédon during the first two months of the war and returned to Scotland soon after, published his account on November 9, 1795—only nine months into the revolution.

> It was probably owing to the success of the Republican arms in Guadaloupe [Guadeloupe] that the free coloured people and other malcontents in Grenada conceived the design of subverting the government and murdering all the British inhabitants.[7]

Turnbull was not completely sure, as he said "probably." In any event, his conclusion was inaccurate. Fédon was planning to overthrow the Grenadian government long before Victor Hugues and other French Republicans in Guadeloupe ever entered the scene.[8]

In an article in *The London Gazette* on June 23-27, 1795, General John Vaughn, commander of all British forces in the West Indies, wrote that "many acts of barbarity" in Grenada were orchestrated by Victor Hugues. So that served to validate the allegation against Hugues, as well. (Let's not forget that there was no love lost between the British and the French!)

No documents show that Britishers ever acknowledged the ingenuity of Julien Fédon and his revolutionaries or that Britain's overall mishandling of Grenada—denying civil and political liberties to free mixed-race people— was the incentive for the rebellion. After all, would the British ever admit that a mixed-race planter, a subject of their king, had destroyed their prosperous sugar colony? Likely not. It would be easier and more politically "acceptable" to assign the blame to the Frenchman, Victor Hugues.

In early 1794, the National Convention, a parliament of revolutionary France, abolished slavery in all French colonies. The decree stated: "All men living in the colonies, without distinction of color, are French citizens and enjoy all the rights guaranteed by the constitution." Upon his arrival in Guadeloupe in May of that same year, Victor Hugues promptly abolished slavery there. His other priority was to encourage people of French ancestry on British colonies to take up arms against the British. He found Grenada, Saint Lucia and Saint Vincent perfect candidates for that campaign.[9]

—⟨⟩—

As they secretly met in remote Belvedere to formulate ways to seek their rights and possibly take up arms against the British colonists in Grenada, Julien Fédon and his cohorts were depending on French-speaking Grenadians residing in Spanish Trinidad for weapons. Marie Beleran, one of Fédon's sisters, and her husband Michel lived there. News of Victor Hugues activities in Guadeloupe, however, may have changed Fédon's mind from a possible armed insurrection to a definite one. He no longer had to depend solely on families and friends in Trinidad for assistance. He was now optimistic of getting support from Victor Hugues in Guadeloupe, who appeared anxious to help without even being asked.

In February 1795, Julien Fédon sent Charles Nogues, his brother-in-law, and Jean Pierre Lavallee to Guadeloupe to win support from the French Commissioners. Some pundits feel Fédon made a monumental mistake by not going to Guadeloupe himself, since Hugues would have more clearly understood their common objective. But Fédon had confidence in his associates and delegated the responsibility to them. There is no other clear reason why Fédon decided not to go, unless he wanted to avoid suspicion. Grenada's Governor Ninian Home was already wary of the activities of French-speaking people in the colony. If the owner of one of the largest French mulatto-owned estates secretly went to Guadeloupe, that would arouse Home's suspicion—something that Fédon couldn't afford. Or, Fédon may have stayed in Belvedere in order to supervise plans for establishing his military headquarters.

Charles Nogues and Jean Pierre Lavallee's mission to Guadeloupe was fruitful. The two men returned to Grenada, with the "Declaration" from the French Commissioners, along with sundry items that may have been more valuable than weapons: cockades, epaulets, uniforms, and even the colors of the French Republic, which impressed almost everyone.

During the first weeks of the revolution, correspondence between Victor Hugues and Julien Fédon was captured by the British. Fédon's first letter to Hugues after the revolution commenced, carried by Pierre Alexandre, was seized following Alexandre's capture. A letter from Hugues to Fédon was seized around the same time. That event may have been a turning point in the relationship.

It won't be surprising if archival evidence is eventually found that proves Hugues was committed to invading Grenada once the rebellion had begun. Fédon's inner circle continually boasted of an imminent French invasion. And when that didn't happen, Jean Pierre Lavallee, then Fédon's second in command, lost his life by a disappointed rebel named St. Bernard, who felt misled.

Between 1794 and 1796, however, Victor Hugues was extremely busy. Grenada was just one of several priorities on his list. He had to administer Guadeloupe, attack the British in the Eastern Caribbean, and encourage the rebellion of the maroons in Jamaica. He had taken on so much responsibility that his attack on Barbados was canceled. Moreover, he did not have much weaponry. Those weapons that he did amass were the booty of privateers who captured American and British ships.

Rev. M'Mahon and Dr. Hay, when sent to Guadeloupe as prisoners of war, met Victor Hugues on occasions and were aware of Hugues's hectic schedule. Based on their observations, Grenada was not his number one priority. Hugues delegated Grenada's affairs to co-commissioner Gaspard Goyrand who monitored and aided the revolutionaries from French Saint Lucia. Further, Hugues biographers have not found any convincing documentation to substantiate his focusing on developments in Grenada.

⸙

BY THE MIDPOINT OF THE revolution, relations between Fédon and Hugues had worsened. French forces in Grenada controlled Gouyave and what today are the villages of Morne Granby and Morne Nesbit, but they never attacked St. George's. Speculation is that, by October 1795, the deteriorated relationship of Hugues and Fédon made it impossible to successfully attack St. George's. In a letter to Fédon, Hugues wrote, "We are pained to see how divided you are; the enemy will hear of it, and will take advantage of it to fall upon you and defeat you. Let ambition give way to love of the Republic."[10]

Another letter from Hugues said, "We reiterate that as long as your motivation remains an ambition to wear epaulettes, and as long as your passions take precedence over your devotion to the Republic, you will suffer defeat." It is unknown whether Fédon ever received either of the letters or replied.[11]

Based on Hugues letters, Hugues was bent on upholding the honor of the French Republic. He may have believed that Julien Fédon's aimed to make Grenada a French colony once again, although there is no evidence to indicate that Fédon planned to do such a thing. Except for restoring the rights of French-Grenadians, Fédon never fully divulged his plans. He wanted to overthrow the British government and replace it with a government associated with France but did not reveal if he planned to declare the colony an independent nation similar to the relatively new United States of America.

⸙

FÉDON'S LACK OF KNOWLEDGE OF military protocols was apparent. He did not understand, for example, how Governor Home and other British elites, who were his prisoners, could put France in a better negotiating position in a prisoner-of-war exchange than Fédon could himself. Fédon wanted weapons and other support from Hugues but did not want to take orders from him. For Victor Hugues to have informed the leaders of the French Republic that he had custody of the governor of Grenada as a prisoner-of-war would have been a feather in his cap and, mostly likely, cause for promotion. That may have been another reason for Hugues becoming less interested in working with Julien Fédon.

Before 1795 ended, three separate forces were influencing Grenada: French and Fédon's forces, which operated independently, and British forces that quietly expanded as they watched the revolution self-destruct.

But the Fédon-Hugues relationship couldn't be as bad as one is led to believe. When the British gained the upper hand in Grenada, Fédon requested a safe passage to Guadeloupe, not to Spanish Trinidad where his sister resided. Were Fédon's wife and daughters in Guadeloupe? That's yet to be discovered. Dr. Hay and Rev. M'Mahon did not see them because they certainly would have included the news in their memoirs. They may have arrived after the two British prisoners left Guadeloupe. To this day, 2022, nobody knows what happened to Marie Rose Cavelan Fédon and her daughters.

TWENTY–EIGHT

Philippe-Rose Roume

Julien Fédon and Philippe-Rose Roume de Saint Laurent grew up in neighboring parishes: Fédon in Paroisse Du Grand Pauvre; Roume on his parents' Belvidere Estate in the Paroisse Des Sauteurs (Saint Patrick). Roume may have also visited his parents' other estates, along with Waltham Estate in the Paroisse Du Grand Pauvre, which was owned by his grandfather, Simon de Gannes.

As children, Fédon and Roume probably didn't cross paths. Philippe-Rose, about ten years older than Julien, was rich and white; Julien was mixed-race and poor.

Fédon remained in Grenada, where he carved his name in Grenadian and Caribbean history. Roume left Grenada, and his name became enshrined in one of the most notable revolutions of all time, the Haitian Revolution.

Philippe-Rose Roume may be regarded as the first Caribbean who understood the geopolitical and socioeconomic structure of the islands, from Spanish Trinidad in the south to Cuba in the north. Roume's name is prominent in the history of Tobago (then French), Trinidad (then Spanish), the French Revolution, the Spanish Court, Spanish San Domingo and the Haitian Revolution.

Roume was instrumental in opening Spanish Trinidad to Grenadians and people from other former French colonies, such as Saint Vincent. White French families escaped to Trinidad with their slaves. The consequences of Roume's vision would impact the economy, politics, and culture of Trinidad for centuries. Members of the dominant French Creole society of the 20th century nation of Trinidad & Tobago were descendants of French Creole planters who settled in Trinidad as a result of Roume's initiative.

Toussaint Louverture, Roume's friend and foe, his subordinate and then his superior, was a witness at Roume's divorce hearing in 1799 and a guest at his wedding to Marie-Anne Elisabeth Rochard that same year. Louverture was also the godfather of their daughter. By then, of course, Fédon's Rebellion had ended.[1]

Contemporary Grenadians have heard very little of Philippe-Rose Roume de Saint Laurent. Along with Julien Fédon, Roume was one of the first Grenadians to leave their footprints in the post Columbian island's history—yet, Roume is barely mentioned.

As of this writing, documents authenticating the Roume family's presence in Grenada remain, although decaying, in the Grenada Registrar's Office. One of those documents is a real estate deed:

> This Indenture made the Sixteenth Day of February in the year of Our Lord One Thousand Seven Hundred and Sixty Seven.... Between Dame Rose de Gannes de Saint Laurent of the Parish of Saint Patrick in the island of Grenada, widow of the late Laurent Phillipe Roume De St. Laurent of the parish and island spouse and esquire deceased, and Phillipe Roume De St. Laurent of the same Parish and island esquire of the one part and Antonine Andres and Jean Louis Andres of the City of London merchants of the other part.[2]

The property, along with slaves, animals, and buildings, was mortgaged on May 18, 1767, to Antonine and Jean Louis Andres and accepted in the Court of Common Plea on June 19, 1767. A British agent obtained the property for Antonine and Jean Louis Andres, who were not in Grenada. [Throughout the deed, Roume's first name is spelled "Phillipe" and Roume is sometimes spelled "Roumet."]

Apart from clearly showing that Rose (Rosa) and her son had mortgaged one of their estates to British investors, the indenture provides some background on the French family. Like other French property owners, the Roume family may have been coerced by the British to sell or mortgage their properties to Britishers, a practice that sparked tensions and, in part, led to Fédon's Rebellion 32 years later.

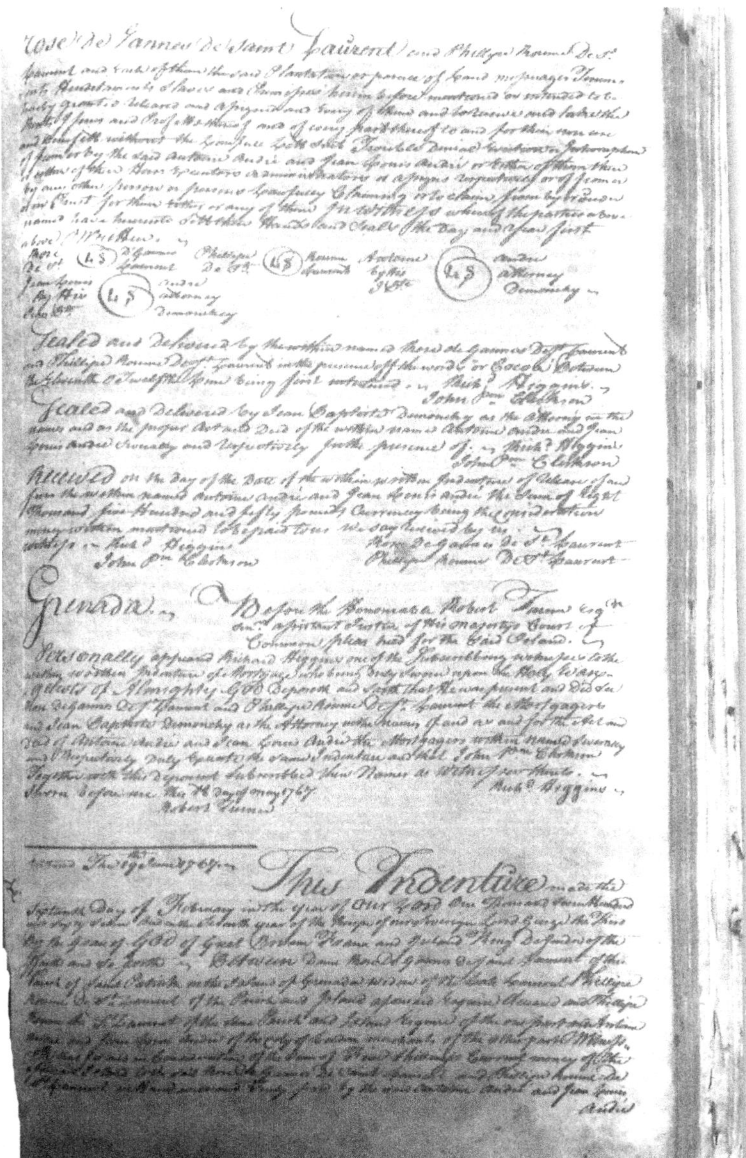

May 18, 1767, deed: Widow, Rosa de Gannes De Saint De Laurent, and her 22-year-old son, Phillipe Rosemet De St. Laurent, owners of Waltham Estate in Saint Mark, mortgaged one of their plantations in Saint Patrick to Antonine Andres and Jean Louis Andres residing in the City of London. By 1767 the seeds of the Fédon's Revolution were planted. Phillipe (Philippe) Roume is forever associated with Tobago (then French) and the Haitian Revolution. *(Courtesy Supreme Court Registry archives, Grenada.)*

For Rosa and her son, both born in Grenada, Grenada was home. For arriving Britishers such as Ninian Home and Alexander Campbell, both born in Scotland, all people of French ancestry born in Grenada, whether white or of mixed race, were considered "adopted" subjects—including the De Gannes, Roume, and Fédon families.

Historians such as Dr. Eric Williams, who led Trinidad & Tobago to independence in 1962, and others writing about the Haitian Revolution mentioned the involvement of Philippe Roume. Since Roume was once a French Commissioner of Tobago, 20th century writer C. L. R. James erroneously wrote, "Roume was not even a Frenchman, but a creole from Tobago." James should have said, "a creole from Grenada."[3]

Today, Roume is a mere footnote in Grenada's history. Some estates that the family once owned are now villages, such as Lataste in Saint Patrick and Waltham in Saint Mark. The St. Mark's Secondary School is on the site of the Waltham Estate great house, where Roume's mother, Rosa de Gannes, was born. Philippe may have been born there or his mother's home, Belvidere Estate, in Saint Patrick.

⸻⸰⸻

THE DE GANNES AND ROUME de Saint Laurent families settled in Isle de la Grenade during the 1720s or before. As French aristocrats, they had enough wealth to purchase or create large estates. Approximately three decades later, Pierre Fédon and his mulatto wife arrived in Grenada as ordinary people who could only afford to purchase eight and a half acres of land.

If Ninian Home did not know the adolescent Philippe-Rose Roume de Saint Laurent, he certainly knew his prominent parents and his grandparents from Saint Patrick and Saint Mark. Home was active in both parishes, purchasing property from French Grenadians for himself and for investors in Britain. As an adult, Philippe-Rose was well-known by Home and other affluent British planters and politicians, because he had become a thorn in their backside! They were relieved when he went into self-exile in neighboring Spanish Trinidad.

⸻⸰⸻

Roume and two other commissioners were sent by France to take over strife-torn Saint Domingue (Haiti) in November 1791; the rebellion in British Grenada was not yet conceived. Roume's first tour of duty in Saint Domingue was brief. A proponent of French values, Roume lived in France. He sailed to and from Saint Domingue on behalf of French revolutionary governments to help administer what was then the richest slave colony in the world. Did he keep abreast of happenings in his native Grenada, where his mixed-race sweetheart, Marie-Anne Rochard, was born in 1761.

In June 1792, Roume abruptly left Saint Domingue and sailed back to France to save his life. The other two commissioners had already fled. All three had encroached upon Saint Domingue's white powerful estate owners:

> Proclamation au nom de la République, de la loi et du Roi," by Philbert-François Rouxelde Blanchelande and Philippe-Rose Roume.[4]

The "Proclamation in the name of the Republic, the law, and the King," by Philbert-François Rouxel de Blanchelande and Philippe-Rose Roume, dated February 11, 1791, granted freedom to the mulattos—much to the chagrin of white planters, who dominated the local Assembly. Roume and his two colleagues arrived in Saint Domingue in the midst of the Boukman Rebellion, named for an early leader of the Haitian Revolution and leader of the maroons, Dutty Boukman. The compromise that they offered through the proclamation did not free the slaves; it only freed the landowning mixed-race people. Yet, the three white Frenchmen fled to prevent themselves from becoming dead men. A Dutty Boukman coordinator, Toussaint from Bréda, was observing Roume's actions and his sympathy toward slaves and people of color.

By 1796, slavery had been abolished in Saint Domingue. Toussaint from Bréda—later called Toussaint Louverture—fought those who dared to restore slavery. He fought the enemies of France, commanded armies, and controlled regions in Saint Domingue. By demonstrating his loyalty to France, some historians describe Louverture as "a black man with a white heart." He was influential enough to have the French government dispatch Roume back to Saint Domingue.

By May 11, 1796, when Roume arrived in the port of Le Cap to take control of Spanish San Domingo, once again under French rule, Fédon's Rebellion had almost ended. It would be Roume's second and final assignment on the island of Hispaniola.

Roume had been living in France when the rebellion in Grenada began, and the French government did not directly encourage Fédon's revolutionaries other than through the involvement of Victor Hugues in Guadeloupe. No records indicate that Roume and Victor Hugues ever communicated or that Roume participated in Fédon's Revolution. As a Grenadian, a white French Grenadian, one can only think he must have been interested, fascinated, even excited by it.

TWENTY–NINE

Toussaint Louverture

When Julien and Marie Rose Cavelan Fédon purchased Belvedere Estate in May 1791 and, a month later, moved there with their two girls, the slave rebellion that broke out in northern Saint Domingue (Haiti), considered the beginning of the Haitian Revolution, was three months away. Toussaint Bréda, who later changed his enslave last name to Louverture, was a mere participant at the August 14, 1791, clandestine meeting where slave leaders organized the rebellion. It is doubtful that he went to the mountain of Morne Rouge for the second meeting, August 21-22, since a voodoo ceremony was part of the assembly. Louverture disavowed voodoo. As a slave child, he was drawn into the Roman Catholic Church and remained a staunch follower of the faith until, deprived of food and water, he died in prison in the French Alps in 1803.

It is unlikely that Toussaint heard of Julien Fédon in 1791, but Toussaint may have heard about Grenada-born Philippe-Rose Roume de Saint Laurent who arrived in Saint Domingue from France on November 29, 1791, to restore law and order. The chaos of the French Revolution, which began in 1789, had washed ashore in Saint Domingue. On the largest and most profitable slave and sugar colony in the world, it was royalist vs. non-royalist, "big whites" feuding with "small whites," white planters fighting free mulattos planters, and politicians disavowing laws enacted in the French National Assembly. The slave rebellion commenced while Roume and two other French Commissioners were on the high seas, heading for Saint Domingue. Eventually disembarking at Cap-Francias, in the province of Haut-du-Cap, the three commissioners faced a new and unexpected problem: a slave revolt.

Meanwhile, in Grenada, 800 mile south, Julien Fédon and his family were settling down in Belvedere. Fédon's Rebellion, a similar uprising, was not yet conceived. It would not begin for another three and a half years and would not be led by slaves.

While there is no evidence that Julien Fédon and Toussaint Louverture ever even communicated, Louverture may have heard of Fédon through Philippe-Rose Roume or by Louverture's protégé, Henri Christophe, who left Grenada as a youth. On the other hand, Fédon—like most others in Grenada—had to be very much aware of the slave rebellion in Saint Domingue in 1791, other upheavals between 1791-1795, and Toussaint Louverture in general.

Fédon's Revolution started at the midpoint of the Haitian Revolution. Unlike Commissioner Victor Hugues in Guadeloupe, who was directly involved in Fédon's Rebellion, Louverture was preoccupied with his own responsibilities. Most likely, he was not even aware of the revolt in Grenada because, by then, Henri Christophe was busy fighting or may have lost ties with his homeland. We just don't know.

Some 20th century scholars have surmised that Julien Fédon and his revolutionaries had connections with Louverture and his fighters, who then inspired Julien Fédon to insurrection. That is mere speculation, as there is no archival evidence for any such connection. The famed C. L. R. James, in *The Black Jacobins*, and Philippe Girard, in his more recent *Toussaint Louverture: A Revolutionary Life*, did not mention Julien Fédon or Grenada. Neither have other historians of the Haitian Revolution. Nevertheless, a brief comparison of Julien Fédon and Louverture is relevant.

"Louverture alone left behind thousands of letters, reports, and other documents. Many of his fellow revolutionaries did the same." For Fédon and his ringleaders, it was the opposite. They left virtually nothing, as the revolt was crushed within 16 months and Fédon never administered Grenada.[1]

⸺◦⦵◦⸺

FÉDON WAS BORN A FREE mulatto around 1752-53. (His birthplace or exact birth date remains a mystery.) He married once, had two daughters, and may have had a son outside his marriage. Like Louverture, Fédon was a devoted Roman Catholic and close to his family. Fédon embraced French values, but we do not know if he considered himself a French subject. Evidently, he had no problem living in British Grenada, as long as the colony granted equal rights to French-speaking people and gave them the same privileges extended to Britishers. Fédon was a slave owner until the morning of March 3, 1795, the day the rebellion began.

Toussaint Louverture, born a slave on Bréda plantation in northern Saint Domingue, perhaps in 1743, was 100 percent African. Originally called Toussaint Bréda, he later owned slaves— mostly family members whom he bought chiefly to free them. Later in life, when he governed the entire colony and had to administer and sustain the economy, Toussaint forced former slaves to return to their plantations, including his own plantations, for a pittance. As Toussaint Bréda, he married a woman named Cécile, a union that produced three children. He had three more children with his second wife, Suzanne Simon-Baptiste. In all, Toussaint was blessed with 16 children, some by other women and others that he adopted.[2]

The origins of the Haitian Revolution and Fédon's Revolution were quite different; so were the strategies of Fédon and Louverture. Fédon created a revolution, whereas Louverture inherited a slave revolution led by Dutty Boukman.[3]

The Haitian Revolution began around 1789-90, when powerful whites attempted to seek autonomy from France, and then evolved. It ended when the slaves rebelled, won their freedom, and led Saint Domingue to independence. The new nation renamed itself "Haiti" and became the first black republic in the Americas. Although Louverture had been kidnapped before the revolution was over and died in France, a prisoner of Napoleon Bonaparte, Louverture has gone down in history as the liberator of the slaves and the architect of independence in Haiti.[4]

Fédon's Revolution, on the other hand, was too short-lived to evolve and Grenada too small to sustain a revolution similar to the one in Saint Domingue. Haiti covers 27,750 square kilometers, while Grenada covers only 310 square kilometers.

In 1789-90, when the white population of Saint Domingue failed in their violent bid to wrest control of the colony from France, they realized the importance of having the support of the powerful mulatto planter class in order to succeed. The two groups united and were victorious, but the whites reneged on their promise to give political rights to the free mulattos. It was then that the free mulattos allied with the slaves to fight the white plantocracy and politicians. The alliance was successful; but when victory was attained, the mulattos "chose some of the bravest slaves and offered them freedom if they would lead the rest back into slavery."[5]

Tired of being pawns—and realizing that they were not part of the liberty sought by whites and free people of color, the slaves took up arms in their own quest for freedom. They claimed they were fighting for the French King, who had granted them their freedom. The massive slave uprising of August 1791 is considered the formal beginning of the Haitian Revolution—an opportune time, since France itself was in turmoil.

When Dutty Boukman—a maroon from Jamaica, a high priest, and the principal leader of the revolution—was killed in action on November 7, 1791, the time was right for moderate Toussaint Louverture to lead, after months of observing and strategizing behind the scene. Louverture had been a free man since the 1770s.

In Grenada, there was no major insurrection by slaves but the island was tense especially in the early 1790s when Home became governor. The British-run government purposefully did not extend civil rights to its white French population and to free people of color. On the morning of March 3, 1795, a French-speaking mulatto named Julien Fédon became the leader of a rebellion against the island's British government. Fédon and his rebel army invited other mulattos, slaves, white French planters and sympathetic British planters to join them. A few British planters did.

Given the large size of Saint Domingue, the slave rebellion of 1791 did not occur across the colony all at once. While it began in Louverture's home province, Haut-Du-Cap, it was fairly easy for the former slave to encourage slaves in the other two provinces to revolt. When he was a slave, Louverture was a muleteer and was responsible for the well-being of live-stock on Bréda Plantation in Haut-Du-Cap. In that position, he developed managing skills and the art of delegating—and earned respect. "Toussaint from Bréda," his enslaved name, was an excellent rider and trainer of both mules and horses. As a coachman and slave driver, he knew the provinces, their towns, and estates.

When Louverture became a leader of the rebels on Saint Domingue, he would "fly" on his horse across the provinces to stir up slave uprisings, coordinate with other leaders, and forge alliances with adversaries. His friends and enemies were astounded by how fast Louverture could ride from region to region. His horsemanship, along with his familiarity with the three provinces, enabled him to encourage slaves in northern, western, and southern parts of the colony to agree to revolt, coordinate, and ultimately achieve freedom.

Grenadian folklore recounts Fédon riding a white horse. Eyewitnesses such as Rev. M'Mahon and Dr. Hay wrote of Fédon mounted on his horse (but did not specify the horse's color). Grenada is too mountainous and small, especially in Belvedere, for Fédon to have galloped at breakneck speed from parish to parish, as Louverture had done in Saint Domingue. Besides, there was no need. Mulatto planters in all of the parishes and on the nearby islands of Carriacou and Petite Martinique were involved in his planning. For example, Joachim Philip, whose family owned almost every acre on Petite Martinique, was the high-ranking rebel who brought Fédon's demand for capitulation to the Grenadian government.

Through alliances, diplomacy, military prowess, and conquest over a period of years—Louverture won control of the entire colony. He became the head of government and the military leader of each province, one by one, in order to mold the colony into one independent nation. At one time, he occupied Spanish San Domingo (Dominican Republic); he formed alliances with France, Britain, Spain, and the United States; and he switched sides when it was advantageous.

Once Fédon's Revolution failed, a few revolutionaries escaped to Haiti, according to Joachim Philip, who was captured in 1803 on Petite Martinique. Some scholars claim that Fédon also went to Haiti, although there is no archival verification that he did.

Julien Fédon detested the British-run Grenadian government, despite having pledged his loyalty to the British King, because the British in Grenada did not recognize the rights of anyone but themselves. When Fédon and other free people of color revolted in order to secure their civil and political rights, he told slaves that they were as free as he was in order to gain their support. But he never created a document that proclaimed their emancipation. Some scholars claim Fédon planned to restore slavery. They have no evidence. If they study Fédon's daily activities, they will realize most slaves supported the rebellion and the pressure of frequent battles prevented him from administering. But he couldn't administer because he never captured the seat of government.

Saint Domingue was a French colony when Louverture joined Dutty Boukman and others to lead the historic slave revolt. Louverture always considered himself a French patriot. He never fought against France but did concoct schemes to appease various French governments—a strategy that enabled him to succeed...until Napoleon Bonaparte became Emperor of France.

No archival findings confirm a linkage between Julien Fédon and Toussaint Louverture or between Fédon's Revolution and the Haitian Revolution. In the end, the two men and the two "revolutions" were quite different—but had a similar purpose.

THIRTY

Louis La Grenade

It is midmorning on Wednesday, April 8, 1795, the battle stretching from Belvedere to Morne Qua Qua is underway. Julien Fédon is standing near the plateau on Morne Qua Qua's highest peak managing the execution of Governor Ninian Home, Alexander Campbell and other prisoners. He spares Rev. Francis M'Mahon, shakes his hand, and says to him, "I am glad you are safe; if you are killed now, it will be by your own countrymen" and directs him "to remain with Dr. Hay." A special messenger ("an express") breathlessly and incorrectly informs Fédon that Louis La Grenade has been killed in the fierce battle waging in the Belvedere flatlands. Fédon explains that he is glad La Grenade is dead but he does "not blame La Grenade for being grateful to the English" since "they had always treated him well."[1]

Based on Fédon's acknowledgement of La Grenade's pro-British stance, would Fédon have taken up arms against the British had they also treated him well? The truth is the British (Fédon called them "English") *did* treat Fédon well. Whether or not he was duped into buying Belvedere, he did own one of the largest coffee estates in the colony—a remarkable achievement for a person of color. Chances are, though, that Fédon may still have revolted as long as civil and political rights were denied to free mixed-race and other French-speaking people. Between 1763-1795, except 1779-1783 when Grenada was French again, the land-owning mulattos and white French planters lobbied unsuccessfully for the reassertion of rights they enjoyed during French rule.

La Grenade and Fédon were radically different personalities. La Grenade did what was in the interest of La Grenade, as long as he gained status and made money. Fédon was wealthy, too, but was willing to lose his estate, family, and life to do what was in the interest of people of French ancestry—to assert their rights.

The possibility of Fédon pandering to the British for favors was remote. In 1790, to please the local government, he took an oath of allegiance to the King of England—but that was as far as he went. Of course, La Grenade and other mulattos also took that oath.

La Grenade and Fédon were opposites in many ways. La Grenade felt compelled to curry favor with the British in order to gain their largesse. He embraced the British values, etiquette, and lifestyle. As a mixed-race person of French ancestry, La Grenade grew up speaking French but spoke mainly in English to please the British. He rejected his Roman Catholic faith for Anglicanism. He sent his son, Louis La Grenade Jr., to England to be educated and to develop a British lifestyle.

La Grenade lobbied to become captain of a regiment composed of slaves and mulattos, a position reserved for British whites. A letter from a military observer evidently petitioning for La Grenade, dated 1790 and stored in a Colonial Office archive in England, summarizes La Grenade's interest in winning acceptance by the British. The letter said:

> I have had some conversation with Louis La Grenade, a Mulatto of this Colony, of considerable property, well-known for many years, and upon many occasions, for his active services against the Runaway Negroes. He is now employed in suggesting this idea to his Friends, over whom he has great influence, from his character, property, and situation as Captain of a coloured Company, attached to the St. George's Regiment.[3]

La Grenade subsequently became the only black person to lead a militia, which was comprised of mulattos, free Africans, and slaves.

Contrary to the belief of some historians, Louis La Grenade did not betray Julien Fédon and the revolutionaries. "He never conspired with Fédon to overthrow the English" and was never a member of the rebel force. Owing to his devotion to the British, it was unlikely that the plotters would invite La Grenade to join their cause.[4]

JULIAN FÉDON OWNED PROPERTY IN two parishes, Saint Mark and Saint John, whereas La Grenade invested in several parishes and owned a commercial vessel. One of his estates, Morne Jaloux, was in Mount Saint John and may have been in boundary with Belvedere Estate. Leaving Paradise Junction in Clozier and going east toward Chadeau and Saint Andrew, the flatlands on the right (with houses there today) is still called Morne Jaloux. La Grenade was buried on his other Morne Jaloux Estate in Saint George now called the Village of Morne Jaloux.

Morne Jaloux in Mount Saint John was not La Grenade's home. As the most successful hunter of maroons or runaway slaves in the history of Grenada, he sometimes slept there when hunting maroons, since they lived nearby in mainly inaccessible mountains. La Grenade made a fortune capturing maroons, dead or alive.

It is probably unfair to disparage La Grenade for his bounty hunting, as it was a big business. He once invoiced the government for £935 5s. Fédon's half-brother, Machaud, was also a bounty hunter; and some slaves trapped maroons in order to exchange them for the slaves' own freedom.[5]

When Council President Mackenzie urged Colonel A. Campbell to attack Fédon's forces in the mountains of Belvedere, based on information that Mackenzie had "from the best authority possible," that source was very likely Louis La Grenade. From the beginning of the rebellion, La Grenade volunteered his expertise to the British. His regiment was part of Captain Philip Gurdon's expedition to Belvedere on March 8, 1795, and General Colin Lindsay's attack on March 17, 1795, when La Grenade was left to protect the area surrounding Belvedere House. La Grenade fought with the British until Fédon was defeated. His regiment was part of the land and sea invasion of Post Royal on March 25, 1796, and he joined Graf Von Heillimer and his Löwenstein Jägers (German and Dutch mercenaries) in dispersing the revolutionaries on June 19, 1796, at Morne Qua Qua.[6]

The enterprising Louis La Grenade was the only prominent mixed-race person to cooperate with the British, and he was trusted by them. On the morning of the rebellion, as Governor Ninian Home remained briefly at Lafortune Estate, Saint Patrick, attempting to get a schooner to take him to St. George's, he hastily wrote instructions to his secretary, Mather Byles, in St. George's, to be delivered by foot: "I think the Colored People ought not to have their arms, or at least none except Captain La Grenade's Company."[7]

After the war, Captain La Grenade rose to fame and fortune for his dedication and patriotism. Before 1795, of course, the British accepted La Grenade as trustworthy and satisfied his request by making him a Naturalized British New Subject or "Honorary British Citizen," It was "honorary," because La Grenade did not have 100 percent white blood. For the British, despite La Grenade's status, patriotism, reputation, and achievements, he was still a person of color, tainted by African blood. He gave his all for the British but did not get the respect from them that he deserved.

While Louis La Grenade died a very contented man in 1808, he was less satisfied before the rebellion. In 1776, for example, 43-year-old Louis La Grenade petitioned the Grenada Assembly seeking "Provision for myself and family and some small Pension to my wife" if killed while performing perilous services to the colony as a hunter of runaway slaves. La Grenade also requested that he and his male heirs "enjoy every Privilege as a free white person." Instead, the Assembly gave him a "pair of pistols valued at fifty guineas and a sword."[8]

Since 1763, except for the period 1779-1783, the British considered La Grenade and other mulattos as adopted subjects with limited rights. Although the British did make La Grenade an "Honorary British Citizen," he was still not accorded the same privileges as "natural born" subjects. Perhaps that's why he never sought a seat in the Assembly, as the legislature was only for Britishers and no more than two French whites.

La Grenade soon became dissatisfied and wished to leave Grenada. On January 24, 1791, he and three other French speaking planters—Jean Pierre

Saulger, Joseph Green, and Francois Julien—dispatched a letter to U. S. President George Washington seeking asylum for themselves and 60,000 additional "free Coloured Individuals." The letter, "From Louis Lagrenade et al" is preserved in the National Archives in Washington, D.C.[9]

In part, La Grenade's lengthy letter states:

> We The free coloured people of the Island of Grenada, having taken into consideration a writing, the purport of which (they are informed) is your Excellency's generous disposition of giving that unfortunate Class of people, an Asylum in the southern parts of the States … Such an Act of your Excellency's Generosity, will excite their deepest gratitude and they will deem themselves peculiarly blest, if their unhappy Situation in these Islands can have touched your Breast so as to move your Benevolence to furnish them with the means of coming out of their Captivity, and to introduce them into a new Canaan, where they will enjoy all the Happiness of that precious Liberty … Your Excellency's Rendering this Certainty, will determine Sixty thousand free Coloured Individuals to Settle in Your Country for the Honor and prosperity of their Family's, and there to enjoy a tolerable existence; them & their Slaves will be fully sufficient to form their Establishments.[10]

La Grenade wasn't referencing just the mulattos in Grenada as the "unfortunate Class of people" in "Captivity" seeking "a new Canaan," as the letter specifically asked George Washington for asylum for "Sixty thousand free Coloured Individuals to Settle" in the southern United States with "their slaves." The entire population of Grenada was less than 60,000 people. The letter also mentioned mulattos "in these islands," so "The Committee" (La Grenade, along with Saulger, Julien, and Green) was obviously seeking asylum for "free Coloured Individuals" in other British West Indian islands, as well.

Surprisingly, La Grenade's letter was written in French, even though he had denounced the French language in order to curry favor with the British. He spoke and wrote only in English. Did he deliberately write Washington in French in order to gain sympathy?

President Washington received La Grenade's letter on June 12, 1791, and promptly referred "the very unexpected address" to Thomas Jefferson, Secretary of State, for an opinion. In his reply to Washington on June 20, 1791, Jefferson advised Washington to ignore the letter, because the authors "are parties in a domestic quarrel, which I think we should leave to be settled among themselves." George Washington did not reply.[11]

One wonders: Did Thomas Jefferson misjudge the deteriorating situation in Grenada, which would come to a climax four years later as Fédon's Rebellion and, as a result, financially affect Americans who owned estates in Grenada. The larger issue, of course, was freedom for people of color living on the British-controlled islands in the West Indies—although Washington and Jefferson, both being slave owners, may not have been moved by that argument.

Some revisionists of history believe that La Grenade did not draft or read the letter. Why would Louis La Grenade, who supported everything British including an allegiance to King George III, want to settle in a country that recently rejected the British monarchy and went to war in order to break its ties to England? In his letter to George Washington, La Grenade speaks of the "Happiness of that precious Liberty" enjoyed in the United States. He yearned for liberty.

Yet, the French Revolution—which commenced in 1789 and advocated liberty, equality, and fraternity—was in full stride in 1791. In the French colonies and among French-speaking people, including those in British Grenada, everyone was taking sides. If La Grenade truly favored liberty, he had an opportunity to identify with the French revolutionaries and the French-speaking community in Grenada; but he did not. He remained obdurately British while hoping to live in America. It's somewhat bewildering!

THE BRITISH GOVERNMENT BESTOWED A knighthood on white French citizen Francis Laurent but no similar honor for La Grenade. Born in France, Laurent was one of the richest planters in Grenada before the British captured Grenada. While many French planters left Grenada rather than live under British rule, Laurent remained. Like La Grenade, Sir Francis Laurent was pro-British; he adopted Anglicanism and accepted English as his native language. Sir Laurent did not risk his life to capture self-emancipated slaves; rather, he sat in the Assembly and was revered by Scots. Did that make La Grenade envious or disheartened? Perhaps he forgot he was mixed-race.

⸎

IN JANUARY 1792, WHEN HE realized President George Washington had snubbed his proposal and Grenada would be his home forever, La Grenade led a delegation of five other mulatto entrepreneurs to address Governor Edward Matthew on behalf of Grenada's free French-speaking mulattos. Unlike Fédon, La Grenade was a pragmatist. He reaffirmed his loyalty to Britain and informed Governor Matthew that the government was treating free mulattos too harshly and that Britishers must, instead, place trust in them. La Grenade knew how to walk a tightrope and survive politically.

The French and Haitian revolutions continued, and La Grenade was well aware of them. Perhaps that's why he decided it would be in his long-term interest to remain loyal to the British. In fact, that gamble paid off handsomely. La Grenade made more money and gained more respect and recognition after the Fédon's Revolution.

By late 1793, Fédon and his colleagues began planning their uprising against British hegemony but felt it unwise to bring Louis La Grenade to the table. Even if La Grenade had wanted to support his fellow mulattos, he was neither trusted nor welcomed.

Alas, it was inevitable! The two powerful mulatto planters were destined to fight each other in the 1795-1796 revolution. And both became popular characters for fiction writers well into the 21st century.

In the 20th century, one of Louis La Grenade's descendants, Maurice Bishop, became prime minister and Cécile Ellen Fleurette La Grenade was appointed governor general in the 21st century. As for the Fédon family, there are no known surviving members.

THIRTY-ONE

Self-Emancipated Africans

During the first week of the rebellion, a triumphant Julien Fédon must have been overwhelmed by the outpouring of support from the African and mixed-race people who had climbed mountains and crossed rivers to get to Belvedere from all parts of the colony.

One group did not go voluntarily. Some house slaves such as cooks and cleaners remained loyal to their British masters including Governor Home house slaves. Some stayed in the prison-boucan but they later abandoned him. Field slaves who did not forsake their masters were forcibly taken to Belvedere as prisoners. Fédon gave the enslaved an option. They could either remain his prisoners and slaves of their imprisoned owners or join the noble cause and become "as free as he was." Many accepted their freedom over bondage.[1]

On the other hand, slaves on estates owned by French-speaking planters, along with their masters, clambered to Belvedere to assist Fédon's effort. It was then that those slaves learned they were free.

Another group of Africans excitingly rushed to Belvedere "armed with pikes, some mounted with iron, others of hard wood, burnt and pointed, about eight feet long" to assist Fédon's revolutionaries. They had emancipated themselves from slavery and lived clandestinely in the interior of the island. European colonizers referred to the self-emancipated Africans as runaway slaves, or "maroons." Without support from those self-emancipated Africans, Fédon's Rebellion may not have lasted for 16 months. Surviving documents written by Dr. Hay verify the assistance of the maroons:

> Upon my entering the gate, five runaways were pointed out to
> me, then surrendering themselves, three men and two women,
> making part of thirty who had already come in: The three
> men were armed with muskets in very good order, one of them
> their chief.[2]

When Britain conquered Isle de la Grenade in 1762, it inherited a problem. Runaway slaves (maroons) had been a local threat and had lived elusively in the mountains since early 17th century French rule. For more than 100 years, the French had tried to annihilate them but were unsuccessful. Now it became Britain's turn.

In addition to collecting taxes from the French being a priority, British Governor Robert Melvill aimed at crushing the self-emancipated. He made catching maroons a lucrative activity by offering incentives to anyone capturing them, dead or alive. The more the maroons were killed, however, the more the slaves joined maroon groups.

The maroons were recalcitrant. They rejected servitude in favor of freedom. And they did not fear Europeans. For maroons, all Europeans were the same: They sustained slavery. Planters, free people of color, and even slaves were afraid of runaways. Sometimes, in the still of the night, male maroons raided estates to steal female slaves.

By the 1790s, the maroon groups of Grenada had grown in both size and strength and had also ventured onto the high seas. They built canoes and stole other boats to travel to other islands. Maroons in the Caribbean also joined up with European pirates. (You'll notice that movies about pirates in the Caribbean authentically include black characters.)

Like their counterparts in Saint Domingue (Haiti), where that island's innumerable factions and rebellion leaders bribed maroons for support, it may have been an open question as to whether Grenada's maroons would be asked to support whichever group spearheaded a rebellion.

Julien Fédon should have been aware of the sheer courage of the maroons from stories told by fellow planters, slaves, maroons themselves, and Fédon's own half-brother Machud, who was a bounty hunter. Fédon would have known that Grenada's maroons did not have an island-wide leader; rather, most parishes had groups, and each group had its own leader. Fédon may have realized, though, that the maroons, being considerably astute and cagey, were aware of the divisiveness between the French and British.

⸎

As a youth, Julien Fédon may have heard of Lafortune, Samba, Jacob, and other famed maroons of the 1720s, who dwelled in the mountains and valleys of Paroisse Des Sauteurs and Paroisse Du Grand Marquis on Isle de la Grenade. Before emancipating himself, it's likely that the maroon called "Lafortune" had been a slave on the estate that is today the Village of La Fortune.

Perhaps Fédon's father, Pierre, had told him about the maroon Pompey's serendipitous murder in 1764 by "two slaves named L'autriment and Vincent," the result of one of Governor Melvill's incentives. They killed "Pompey, the chief of runaway Negroes," and the colony granted L'autriment and Vincent their manumission, as promised by Governor Melvill.[3]

If Pierre Fedon told his son the rest of the story about L'autriment and Vincent, that may have implanted in young Julien the seeds of distrust toward the British. The two slaves belonged to Mr. Eustache, a planter, but it was Assembly member Mr. Pigott, on behalf of Mr. Eustache, who alerted Governor Melvill and the Grenada Assembly of the success of L'autriment and Vincent.

Shockingly, the manumission of L'autriment and Vincent was rescinded for a relatively minor reason: Mr. Eustache was unable to prove that he owned them! So, the British must have been both jubilant about the death of the notorious maroon Pompey and pleased that two more slaves were prevented from becoming free Africans.

⸎

Fedon lived most of his life in "maroon territory." As owner of Lancer Estate, located in the interior of Saint Mark, Fédon most likely came across self-emancipated Africans who lived in the Mount Saint Catherine

Mountain range, which stretches from west to east across the parishes of Saint Mark, Saint John, and Saint Andrew. Its highest peak is in Saint Mark. The self-emancipated forged relations with people who owned estates below that long mountain subranges. They also knew which properties were owned by Britishers or owners who were biased toward the British. French- and mulatto-owned estates, such as Fédon's Lancer property, would have been safe havens for the self-emancipated when they descended from their remote hiding places to raid British plantations or venture to sea.

By the time Julien and Marie Rose purchased Belvedere Estate in 1791, runaways were a force to be reckoned with despite the British continuing to hunt and kill them. The mountains of Belvedere, Morne Vauclain, and those south and southeast—such as Mount Saint Margaret, Mount Lebanon, and Mount Sinai—were maroon hideouts. As the mixed-race owner of mountainous Belvedere and with more than 100 slaves on his coffee estate, Fédon couldn't afford to defy or trouble the maroon. Most likely, he became acquainted with the maroon chiefs in the area. Maroons may have shown Fédon trails through the treacherous hills and valleys and strategies for evading or attacking the British. And that may be why Fédon boasted to his prized prisoner, Governor Ninian Home, that he was "perfectly acquainted with the mode of making war in the woods."[4]

Prisoner John Hay observed that General Fédon was always protected by Negroes. It is unlikely that Fédon used former house and field slaves to safeguard him. It is more likely that he used the self-emancipated, maroons, who knew the landscape and were experienced warriors.

Julien Fédon may have heard about a reward, advertised in the *St. George's Chronicle* and *New Grenada Gazette* issues of 19 August 1790, for anyone who captured two slaves who escaped from Carriacou, an island 40 miles north of Grenada, in a canoe. Further, fellow planters may have explained to Fédon that the government was asking them to pay the cost of two armed vessels to patrol the island's coast in order to prevent slaves from escaping by sea.[5]

There is no archival evidence revealing if Fédon was asked in 1793 to contribute a few slaves for the creation of a large slave force, led by captains in the British militia, to fight maroons in Saint Andrew. If asked, Fédon would probably have found a good excuse to decline. By then, slaves, mulattos, and French planters were all quietly cooperating with the maroons, who were brashly raiding British plantations in broad daylight.

For example, the self-emancipated knew that Mount Pleasant Estate in Saint Mark was owned by an American family, the Carys of Chelsea, Massachusetts, and that Samuel Cary, Jr., who managed Mount Pleasant Estate, was a member of the militia—as was his father years before. Moreover, as soon as the rebellion commenced, Cary, Jr. took up arms against the revolutionaries. In response, the self-emancipated burnt Mount Pleasant to the ground: buildings, slave huts, and sugarcane fields. Slaves who remained loyal to the Carys were instantly killed; those who escaped hid in the woods until Cary, Jr. rescued them and brought them to St. George's.[6]

The perseverance, adroitness, and aggressiveness that self-emancipated maroons had exhibited in Grenada since the early 17th century were traits that Julien Fédon later adopted. Fédon understood maroon history and customs. He needed the maroons, and they needed him.

PART V

1796 & Beyond

THIRTY–TWO

1796 – A Turning Point

By the end of 1795, the British had not surrendered Grenada to Fédon and Victor Hugues had not sent enough French troops to formally invade the colony, as Fédon had anticipated. Nonetheless, Julien Fédon controlled most of Grenada, and Victor Hugues was still committed to the cause. Hugues continued to send weapons and soldiers, although it was difficult getting them through the British navy patrols in the seas around the island.

After losing control of Pilot Hill and Battle Hill at the end of April 1795 and failing to retake the two bases in the 12-day battle in late December 1795, a forward-thinking Julien Fédon created a base in the hills of Post Royal overlooking Marquis Bay.

Then, in February 1796, the situation began to turn in Fédon's favor. He recaptured Pilot Hill—and whoever controlled Pilot Hill also controlled Grenville Bay, allowing ships to freely enter and depart. With that success, Fédon maintained four powerful bases about three miles from each other on the eastern coast—Pilot Hill, Battle Hill, Telescope Point, and Post Royal—in addition to Port Libre in the west.

On the other side, February 1796 was a dismal month for the British. Fédon was embarrassing the mighty empire on both land and sea. British military and merchant ships were captured by Fédon's rebels and French forces. The mulatto general was no longer focused on "making war in the woods," because the British had abandoned the strategy of bringing the war to him. Fédon's attention was now drawn to the colony's hidden bays, where vessels from Guadeloupe and Spanish Trinidad could unload supplies.[1]

Grenada's maritime maroons may have recommended the bays and peninsulas in Megrin (Saint David), Saint Andrew, and Saint George that Fédon discreetly utilized. It is hard to believe that Fédon, who lived in the parishes of Saint Mark and Saint John as a youth and later as a planter, would have known the numerous intricate bays on the island's southeastern coast, such as La Sagesse, Spitze des Fort Jeudi, Petit Bacaye and Isles Caliveny. For more than a century, the maroons had hidden in those bays, islets and elsewhere, using them to smuggle supplies from other islands and to escape. It appears rather certain that those maritime maroons aided Fédon and his revolutionaries, although there is no documentation of that fact.[2]

Meanwhile, the British continued to execute revolutionaries and suspected revolutionaries—whether white, African, or mixed-race—further hardening Fédon's resolve. The marketplace, what is today the St. George's Market Square, became a British killing field.

Anyone reported to be, or even suspected of, aiding the revolutionaries was tried in a special court, Court of Oyer and Terminer, which consisted of a panel of judges and a chief judge. A trial would last only a few minutes. The accused would be found guilty and quickly, viciously, and publicly executed in the marketplace.

The British, who disdained Fédon for his cruelty, were no better than he along those lines. Depending on the person's level of involvement in aiding Fédon, the rebel's arms, waist, and knees would be broken and then the body dragged around St. George's. Sometimes the body was divided into four parts and left out in the open for animals to feast upon. Other times, the person was shot or hanged and the head severed and displayed.

Revolutionaries continued to be caught, quickly tried, and executed for decades after the rebellion ended in 1796. During their trials, the accused individuals were not given an opportunity to testify on their own behalf. No documents were created, either, which is yet another reason why the story of Fédon's Rebellion has been chronicled over the centuries from a British viewpoint. The local British rulers were not concerned about understanding the cause of the rebellion; rather, they focused on swiftly executing anyone who dared take up arms against the British monarchy as an example to other would-be insurrectionists.

In spite of their successes in early 1796, did Julien Fédon and his inner circle realize that dark, fast-moving clouds were headed toward Grenada? That a crisis was brewing that would abruptly squelch their goals?

The crisis looming on the horizon resulted from the lack of a cohesive relationship between Victor Hugues and Julien Fédon.

THIRTY—THREE

Divided Purposes

The uneasiness between the enigmatic Julien Fédon and the flamboyant Victor Hugues, which had been brewing since the beginning of the rebellion, rapidly deteriorated and, by early 1796, two factions existed—much to the delight of the British.

The capture of Gouyave on October 15-16, 1795, enabled the French to establish their military headquarters at Dougaldston Estate. Gouyave, renamed Port Libre as the capital of revolutionary Grenada, seemed to have a semblance of a government administered by a lawyer, CHS Sugue, appointed by "Citizen Goyrand one of the National Commissioners."[1]

From Port Libre, Sugue boldly sent two emissaries to St. George's with a letter to General Oliver Nicolls about Sugue's "concern that many black citizens, having been surprised at Grand Bacolet, have been conducted to and hanged at St. George's." The British were executing captured slaves and free blacks who fought against them, while extending prisoner-of-war status to captured French soldiers.[2]

One day Sugue's emissaries carried a letter from Julien Fédon and Sugue to Nicolls. In his reply, Nicolls ignored Fédon by addressing only Sugue. He referred to Gouyave as Charlotte Town—ignoring the rebel's new name, Port Libre. Nicolls responded that if any blacks "have been hanged, they were (done) so by civil law, which is in force, and acts independent of the military. I have no power over it, nor can I make myself responsible for what they do … It was with pleasure I hear from you."[3]

Nicolls was willing to dialogue with Sugue but British policy was not to acknowledge any status for Fédon and his local forces which was disturbing.

As a result, slaves, mulattos and Grenada's French whites who were allied with Fédon and captured, despite being subjects of the British monarchy, were immediately hanged.

❦

Good relations and frequent communications between Victor Hugues and Fédon were absolutely essential in order to drive the British out of Grenada. Hugues accused Fédon of ignoring his letters and pleaded with him for unity.

> *To Citizen FEYDON, provisional commander of the armed forces in Grenada (20 prairial III, 08 06 1795)*
>
> We have received no news from you; however, it would be very useful to the Republic if we knew what successes or failures you have had; let us help you to increase the former and to make up for the latter... Make haste to let us know your needs and your situation.[4]

The chilly rapport between Hugues and Fédon continued, although Hugues did send additional troops and weapons to Grenada. Apparently, Hugues was not truly boosting Fédon's status; instead, he was supporting a movement to restore Grenada to France. As a result, his troops answered to the French commander and not to Fédon. In reality, Hugues controlled Gouyave and nearby estates and not Fédon, who maintained his footing in the interior of the island and along the eastern and southeastern coasts of Saint Andrew, Saint David, and Saint George.

Without a force of French soldiers from Guadeloupe bolstering Fédon's revolutionaries, Fédon had no chance of capturing St. George's. In spite of the policy differences between Fédon and Hugues, however, Fédon's army and French soldiers from Guadeloupe did consolidate their efforts to battle the British in some places—such as at Post Royal, Saint Andrew. And, Fédon and CHS Sugue met regularly.

Some historians claim that Julien Fédon was stubborn and blame him for the difficult association with Victor Hugues. That depiction may have resulted from his refusal to give up leadership of the effort just one month into the revolution. On the evening of the April 8, 1795 massacre, a mulatto named Jean La Grange, who arrived from Guadeloupe that afternoon, informed Dr. Hay, Rev. M'Mahon and others, "I am come to take the chief command. Had I arrived sooner, what you have witnessed to-day should not have happened."[5]

Is it "hardheaded" to think that someone who sacrificed his family, his property, and his life by starting a rebellion would agree to that?

As it turned out, Jean La Grange did not succeed in removing Fédon from command, and Fédon's confidantes—except for his brother-in-law, Charles Nogues—remained in solidarity with him and with his purpose.

No evidence exists of the reason(s) for the fallout between Julien Fédon and Charles Nogues, although many have speculated:

1) Nogues may have become spellbound by the inspirational Victor Hugues, whom he met in February 1795 as Fédon's representative. Nogues may have frequently mentioned the charisma of Hugues, leading to Fédon becoming jealous.

2) Perhaps Hugues promised Nogues that his French troops would invade Grenada once French-speaking Grenadians launched an uprising. And when that didn't occur, Fédon may have blamed Nogues for misleading him.

3) Nogues may have placed his confidence in Hugues and no longer in Fédon, creating a rift between Fédon and his brother-in-law.

4) Nogues may have felt that he was simply a better commander than Fédon, since the successful revolutionary battles in La Baye and the capture of Pilot Hill in March/April 1795 were due to the leadership of Nogues and Besson.

In any event, in the middle of the rebellion, Charles Nogues left Grenada for Saint Lucia—once again a French colony after being recaptured from the British—to work for Hugues. Rumors flew that an angry Victor Hugues demanded the arrest of Fédon and that he be sent to Guadeloupe for trial.

Jean La Grange failed in an effort to relieve Fédon of his command over the revolutionaries, but Hugues, now dominating the French Commission in Guadeloupe, dispatched Commissioner Alexandre Lebas to Grenada to meet with Fédon. Lebas narrowly escaped the British naval blockade and was forced, without ever landing in Grenada, to return to Guadeloupe and face the wrath of Hugues. Lebas, a notable French politician who had voted two years earlier for the execution of Queen Marie Antoinette and King Louis XVI, became weary of being harangued by Hugues returned to France.

It is believed that Gaspar Goyraud, another French Commissioner and administrator of recently conquered Saint Lucia, also attempted a landing in Grenada to meet with Fédon but sailed back to Saint Lucia when a British battleship nearly captured his vessel.

In the meantime, French forces in Gouyave and its outskirts continued taking orders from French commanders. They also remained on the defensive. Occasionally, they would send a "flag of truce" or a delegation to St. George's, requesting prisoner exchanges. And sometimes they dispatched canoes in the still of the night, heading for St. George's Harbour to capture British vessels. On the whole, though, the Hugues forces in Gouyave continued a wait-and-see strategy.

—∿—

THE AREA OF MILITARY ACTIVITY shifted from the interior of the colony to hills near the coastlines, and Julien Fédon focused on the coastal areas in the parishes of Saint Andrew, Saint David, and Saint George. His forces sometimes captured British merchant ships laden with ammunition and food, bringing the booty to hidden inlets—such as La Sagesse Bay, Petit Bacolet Bay and Requin Bay—for unloading.

Once captured, Fédon's forces would rename the British vessels and either dispatch them to Spanish Trinidad to purchase supplies or use them to trade with privateers on the high seas. That was the case on February 18, 1796, when the revolutionaries captured the *Hostess Quickly*, a military schooner loaded with weapons and food, in Grenville Bay. The rebels quickly brought *Hostess Quickly* to Marquis Bay (Port Marquis), relieved her cargo, and dispatched her to the coast of Trinidad with a new crew to purchase supplies from privateers. Three weeks later, on March 12th, the British recaptured the vessel and escorted her back to St. George's.

Interestingly, it was the astute Victor Hugues who discreetly arranged for Spanish and American privateers to use the seas off Spanish Trinidad to sell food and ammunitions to the French, as well as to Fédon's rebels. And Fédon apparently made use of that opportunity.

During the first three months of 1796, the revolutionaries continued to chalk up victories. For example, they defended their base at Post Royal, regained control of Pilot Hill and Grenville Bay, and forced the British soldiers at Observatory in Saint Patrick to retreat to St. George's. Nearly all British forces in Grenada hastened to St. George's in 1796, making it almost impossible for Fédon's rebels and French forces—whether alone or combined—to attack the heavily defended capital. Inadequate communication between Julien Fédon and Victor Hugues whether deliberate or consequences of British vigilance also prevented them from mounting a united army that could conquer St. George's and recapture British Grenada for the French.

Julien Fédon was fighting for the rights of French Grenadians by implementing the principles of the French Revolution and liberty for all, including the enslaved. He may have hoped that Grenada would become an associate of France and not its colony, but Fédon and his confidantes left no written objectives to confirm that. Documents captured by the British, however, do indicate that he believed in the French revolutionary slogan of "Liberté, Egalité, Fraternité"—Liberty, Equality, Fraternity.

Victor Hugues endorsed Fédon's freeing of the slaves but had his own plans for Grenada and the rest of the British West Indies. He was bent on making France stronger than Britain. By the 1790s, France had lost both colonies and status to the British. England had reaped the wealth of the West Indian sugar, molasses, rum, and slave trades. By capturing British West Indian islands and expanding French sovereignty, Hugues hoped to make them colonies of France— including, for a third time, Grenada. So Fédon and Hugues shared some similar motivations and had other quite different purposes for Grenada. Poor communication added to the divide.

AFTER MONTHS OF RUMORS THAT thousands of troops were expected to arrive from England to crush hotspots in Grenada, Saint Vincent, Saint Lucia, and other colonies, a massive armada of 200 battle ships—transporting nearly 30,000 soldiers and led by General Sir Ralph Abercromby—was definitely on its way. In late 1795, due to severe winter storms in the seas off England's southern coast, however, many ships were damaged and approximately 2,000 soldiers perished in the English Channel. As a result, Abercromby's soldiers were delayed by nearly three weeks.

Also, among those jeopardized by the ferocious English winter seas of 1795-96 was Lieutenant Colonel William Dyott, whose 25th Regiment disembarked from Portsmouth, England, in November but returned to port when the fleet was almost destroyed by a killer storm. Dyott's second attempt, on December 9th, was successful; he landed at Barbados on February 11, 1796, weeks ahead of General Abercromby. Dyott wrote in his diary:

> As soon as it was light, we discovered the long-wished-for island of Barbadoes ... the morning was cloudy with heavy showers of rain ... The appearance of the island as you come from the sea is in general low land, but on getting nearer to the north side there are some hills ... The island is picturesque almost to a degree of enchantment, and really makes you fancy it a fairy land.[6]

Throughout Dyott's military career, he kept a detailed diary that is now among the most treasured documents of British military history. Dyott's first "wartime" action was in Grenada, and his meticulous diary is filled with information about participating in battles against Fédon's forces.

It is doubtful that Julien Fédon—or even Joseph Chatoyer, the Carib leader in Saint Vincent—knew that Britain had committed its mighty forces to restoring law and order on its rebellious West Indian colonies and to invade war torn French Saint Domingue. The mighty British army, with its disciplined soldiers and sailors assisted by trained European mercenaries, were on the way.[7]

So now, with General Abercromby's forces approaching the region, General Oliver Nicolls was excited to go on the offense in Grenada against what was now the divided enemy of Fédon and Hugues. General Nicolls anxiously awaited the thousands of professional British soldiers that had been promised to him.

THIRTY–FOUR

The Battle for Post Royal

Scrutinized by apprehensive British Grenadians, General Oliver Nicolls knows, upon General Sir Ralph Abercromby's arrival, that he will have to account for his failure to end the rebellion. On February 26, 1796, a desperate General Nicolls dispatches Brigadier General Augustus Campbell on a reconnaissance mission to the Post Royal and Grenville Bay areas occupied by Fédon's forces. Henry Thornhill describes Campbell's troops:

> *A strong Party of Regulars and Militia, the 17th light Dragons under the command of Captain Black, and the Saint George's light Cavalry under the command of Captain McBurnie, with two companies of black rangers, the one under the command of Captain Branden, the other under the command of Captain Davis, accompanied by some volunteers.[1]*

By early 1796 almost every mission planned by Nicolls and Campbell had companies of black rangers consisting of slaves conscripted into the military.

It is not plausible that such a large force marched from the garrison at Richmond Hill, St. George's, all the way to Grenville Bay and back merely to reconnoiter. But it was the same General Campbell who attacked Fédon a year before on April 8th, when the revolutionaries murdered Governor Home and chased Campbell and his forces from Belvedere and Mount Saint John. Upon seeing how Fédon had fortified Post Royal, Battle Hill and

Telescope Point, Campbell most likely decided not to attack. Or, to satisfy an increasingly frustrated public who wanted the revolution crushed, Nicolls and Campbell may have just pretended that their intention was to prepare for an assault on Fédon.

Yet, three days later, in the still of the night on February 29th, Nicolls' soldiers under the command of Major Wright abandoned their Pilot Hill base and escaped to St. George's via Observatory Estate in Saint Patrick. As a result, Julien Fédon controlled all coastal bases in Saint Andrew, from Telescope Point to Madame Hooks (today, part of Village of Mount Sealey).

In the beginning of March, one year after the rebellion began, Julien Fédon controlled most of the colony except for the town of St. George's. It is not clear whether General Nicolls was disappointed in Campbell for not attacking Fédon at Post Royal and other bases, but Nicolls then personally led an attack against Fédon's forces in Post Royal—the same area where General Campbell's forces had reconnoitered—knowing, of course, that the no-nonsense Sir Ralph Abercromby would soon arrive in the region.

Nicolls probably felt that he had enough manpower to make the attack. Approximately 500 soldiers, including Lieutenant Colonel William Dyott who landed in Barbados in February, were dispatched to Grenada and arrived in St. George's on March 4th. A week later, on March 12th, 700-800 soldiers and sailors that were part of Abercromby's fleet sailed into Barbados. They were immediately (and inconspicuously) dispatched to Isle de Ronde, a small island off the northern part of Grenada, to join in the invasion of Post Royal.

While General Nicolls was concentrating on Post Royal and other bases in Saint Andrew, a battalion of Fédon rebels swiftly occupied part of Richmond Hill, near Fort Matthew, overlooking the town of St. George's. Nicolls commanded William Dyott to dislodge the revolutionaries; Dyott chose "a captain, 50 British soldiers, and 100 men belonging to a black corps." The mission was not easy, as Dyott noted:

> The party marched at four o'clock, and had to scramble up a hill
> more than a mile high, and in many places so steep as to make
> it necessary to use the bushes and trees to climb the precipice …
> The enemy consist chiefly of rebel negroes of the island, aided by

a few French, and mulattos from Guadeloupe, and encouraged and assisted by a great number of mulattos of the island who are united with the negroes.[2]

Although the revolutionaries ran away when Dyott's troops approached, General Nicolls was nervous about a Fédon battalion boldly coming very close to the town of St. George's to attack Fort Matthew, the British military headquarters at Richmond Hill. Fortunately for Nicolls, additional Abercromby soldiers were about to rush into Grenada from England, via Barbados, providing relief for the troops and hope for defeating Fédon.

At 7 p.m. on March 22nd, a confident General Nicolls marched from the garrison at Richmond Hill to Saint Andrew with a force of approximately 1,500 men. Five hundred were slaves that he trained in 1795-96 as part of the Loyal Black Regiments. The other 1,000 soldiers, including William Dyott's regiment, were part of Abercromby's early arrivals from England. The 1,500-strong force marched to Marquis and Madame Hooks, near Post Royal Hill, to await the 700-800 troops from Isle de Ronde for a combined land-and-sea attack.

Nicolls characterized Julien Fédon as a traitor and a criminal for betraying Britain, but he obviously respected his military dexterity by planning an attack on Post Royal and Grenville Bay, on both land and sea, with a force of more than 2,000 men. The buildup of troops also may have been intended as a deterrent to Fédon, hoping he would surrender or abandon Post Royal.

Nicolls also clearly understood that slaves were essential for defeating Fédon. They knew the landscape and places where revolutionaries could hide—which is why he developed the Loyal Black Rangers to hold the fort for him during most of 1795, when few British soldiers were located in the colony—and those who were there were dying from dengue fever.

Dyott carefully detailed the invasion of Post Royal in his diary:

> We marched all night and till 4 o'clock next morning, when we halted for two hours at a sugar work called Madam Sagesses [La Sagesse], which had been burnt and totally destroyed by the brigands, about eight miles from St. George's.[3]

The march to Post Royal resumed at 6 a.m. Along the route, the British were attacked by revolutionaries; but those who died on both sides were Africans. In most battles, the British put the Loyal Black Rangers, slaves and newly emancipated Africans, on the front line in case of attack by Fedon's revolutionaries. Dyott added:

> A few shots fired by the black corps in front, at some wretched poor devils in the cane fields, killed two of them. We came in sight of a party of the enemy about 2 o'clock, and attacked their advanced post, which was carried with the loss of a few men. The black corps had the principal share of dislodging them.[4]

Of the multiple descriptions of battles waged by the British few reports would give Africans or slaves credit as Dyott did.

> I was ordered on to their support with the 9th and 25th regiments. After we had got possession of the post they at first occupied (called Madame Hooks) ... that gave us a full view of their grand post at Post Royal.[5]

Although, it took General Nicolls almost all night and all the following day to march to the Madame Hook's/Post Royal/Marquis vicinity, and his soldiers were exhausted and sleepless, "He was determined to move forward and attack Post Royal that night," Dyott explained.

> We had proceeded about half a mile, when Brigadier General Campbell, who was in front, finding the night coming on very fast, and knowing how much the troops had suffered from being underarms for twenty-four hours ... proposed to defer the attack on Post Royal till next morning.[6]

The battle for Post Royal began on March 23rd with the occupation of Madame Hook's Estate, a minor base near Post Royal, and would last for several days. "The next day, the 24th, threw up our guns and mortars to bear on Post Royal," Dyott noted in his diary. "During the night of the 24th and in the morning of the 25th, our battery opened fire on Post Royal." The battle continued all day.[7]

From the hills of his Post Royal base, Fédon could see British forces in the flatlands of Marquis and British naval ships from Isle de Ronde landing soldiers in the bays of Grenville, Soubise, Marquis, and Madame Hook's. But Fédon was courageous. He had forces stationed on the beaches in order to greet the Britishers with gunfire. Adding to the intensity of the battle, two ships sent from Guadeloupe by Victor Hugues arrived with ammunition and troops and attempted to sail into Madame Hook's Bay. The British attacked the French ships, and several lives were lost. One British ship was wrecked on the rocks of Soubise and Marquis and then destroyed.

March 25, 1796, was "intensely hot." The firing of mortars caused the sugar boucan and slave huts at Madame Hook's Estate, where Nicolls and his officers had made their headquarters, to go up in flames. According to Dyott:

> The flames from the huts and the heavy fire from the ships alarmed the General [Nicolls] much. He told me he really concluded the enemy had attacked us in force and had set fire.[8]

Nicolls even thought he had lost yet another battle to Julien Fédon. Dyott noted:

> The consequence was the light infantry of the 3rd regiment suffered most severely; all the officers were killed or wounded... and as the enemy determined to dispute every inch, it was sometimes dubious how the affair would end.[9]

In this rare moment, the British lauded the revolutionaries for their "valiant defence of Post Royal." They said that Fédon had "about eight hundred men composed of their best and choicest troops, the very flower of their army."[10]

The strength, size, and superior weaponry of the British, however, were simply too much for Fédon's forces to overcome. He lost approximately 300 men, including soldiers from Guadeloupe and was himself slightly wounded when a shell exploded nearby. Yet, he hurried to Pilot Hill, about three miles away, to order the immediate evacuation of his troops, knowing that Grenville Bay was about to be invaded and whoever occupied the bay would control Pilot Hill.

The British lost about 50 soldiers, including four officers, and many more were wounded. Most of the rank-and-file soldiers who died were Loyal Black Rangers who, led by white captains, led the direct assault on Post Royal.

> The following day, Dyott's regiment was given a special assignment: March 26th - Employed in burying the dead, and sending away the wounded by sea to St. George's. I never beheld such a sight such as Post Royal Hill, etc. The number of dead bodies and the smell was dreadful … The side of the hill on which the enemy endeavoured to make their retreat was extremely steep and thickly covered with wood, and the only method of discovering the dead was from the smell. It was near a fortnight after the action that many bodies were found.[11]

The theater of battle for Post Royal compounded the problem of finding the dead and wounded. The area extended many miles, from the coast into the interior of Madame Hook's, Post Royal, Marquis, Battle Hill, Soubise, Pilot Hill, Grenville Bay, and Telescope Point.

Dyott, who later fought in wars across the mighty British Empire and rose to the rank of general, was frustrated with how the British treated Fédon's African revolutionaries:

> The negroes and people of colour can certainly suffer and endure far greater torture than white people … One in particular at Hooks Bay. Two negroes were taken prisoners the day we got possession of that post, and in order to secure them they were forced into a sort of arched place something like what I have seen under steps made use of to tie up a dog. There was just room for the poor devils to creep in on their hands and knees to lie down… two soldiers of the 29th regiment…fired at them… I made a negro draw out of these miserable victims of enraged brutality…I was most completely ashamed of the whole proceeding.[12]

Fédon's defeat at the two crucial bases, Post Royal and Pilot Hill, left him weak and no longer in control of Grenville Bay, Battle Hill, and Telescope Point. He retreated to Belvedere, and French forces continued to control Port Libre and its nearby bases.

For the first time since the revolution started on March 2, 1795, the British had won a resounding battle. Brigadier General Campbell shared the accolades with General Oliver Nicolls, who felt both exonerated and relieved. Everything was beginning to look good for the British and bad for Fédon and the French soldiers from Guadeloupe.

On the administrative side, a new lieutenant governor, Alexander Houston, arrived on April 6, 1796, to rebuild Grenada. He replaced the tyrant and late Governor Ninian Home, the pompous and inept Kenneth Francis Mackenzie who departed in December, and Council President Samuel Mitchell who succeeded Mackenzie. Evidently, Houston did not fully understand that Grenada was a complete war zone—and he was both surprised and angered that the governor's residence was occupied by soldiers, who did not want to give up the comfort of that house and make room for him.

British Grenadians, however, were awestruck. They knew Alexander Houston very well. He had once lived in the colony, and they held no grudges against him as they had held against Ninian Home. Everyone was willing to help Houston return normalcy to the stricken colony. And they hoped Sir Ralph Abercromby would put an end to the revolt in Grenada as soon as he was able to restore tranquility in Saint Lucia and Saint Vincent.

With the pivotal British victory at Post Royal and on the other bases in Saint Andrew, though, the war moved once again to Gouyave.

THIRTY–FIVE

Gouyave Falls

Unlike Victor Hugues who, upon arriving in the region in 1794, attempted to intervene simultaneously in several British colonies, Sir Ralph Abercromby preferred to focus on one group of colonies at a time. Spanish Trinidad and the Dutch and French colonies in South America were on his list, but crushing insurrections in British colonies instigated by the French was foremost. His first target was retaking Saint Lucia, which Victor Hugues had conquered in April, 1795.

Having succeeded in recapturing Saint Lucia in May 1796, Abercromby now set his eyes on ending the Carib uprising in Saint Vincent and then dealing with Fédon's Rebellion. He dispatched Adjutant General John Hope from Saint Lucia to Grenada to assist General Nicolls. Abercromby then sailed to the Grenadines and used the island of Carriacou as a staging point for the assaults on Saint Vincent and Grenada.[1]

Arriving in Carriacou from Saint Lucia with "between three and four thousand men," Abercromby summoned Nicolls to meet him there. Nicolls immediately sailed from Post Royal to Carriacou, where Abercromby gave Nicolls "his orders and instructions for his military operations against the rebels in Grenada." Putting the Grenada operations fully in the hands of Nicolls, Abercromby sailed north to Saint Vincent.[2]

Abercromby provided Nicolls with thousands of troops and "the reinforcement that had arrived from St. Lucia, consisting of the 27th and 57th regiments, the corps étrangers, and the Löwenstein Jägers." The étrangers and Jägers were paid European mercenaries who had accompanied Abercromby to the West Indies.[3]

Nicolls had fallen into disfavor for not ending the rebellion, but his stature had been on the rise ever since he defeated Fédon at Post Royal. Nicolls now had a chance to redeem himself by using the thousands of soldiers that Abercromby apportioned to the Grenada operation when the two met in Carriacou.

Did Fédon realize that he was up against nearly the entire British fleet in the West Indies? Did he think that someone like the late Brigadier General Colin Lindsay or Colonel Augustus Campbell, with weak and disobedient forces, would venture into the Belvedere mountains and try to attack him? He may have remembered how he described those earlier efforts to Dr. Hay on April 8, 1795:

> That the English troops employed against them were raw, undisciplined country people, who had never seen service, or perhaps fired a musket before, and mostly pressed from their wives and families.[4]

If Fédon believed that was still the case, he was soon in for a rude awakening!

Victor Hugues knew that it was not business as usual and that his forces were no match for the mighty Abercromby fleet. Moreover, having been defeated in Saint Lucia, having abandoned his plan to conquer Barbados, and having his operation in Grenada and Saint Vincent thwarted, Hugues' ego was quite bruised. He probably anticipated that Abercromby would unleash his forces on Fédon's revolutionaries and the French forces in Grenada—especially those in the town of Gouyave (Port Libre), capital of revolutionary Grenada.

⸙

THERE WAS LITTLE SURPRISE ON June 9, 1796, when General Oliver Nicolls, "with his troops from Carriacou, arrived early in the morning off Gouyave." Nicolls did not approach the town silently; he demonstrated his power with blasts from the cannons on his battleships, which must have startled the civilians and soldiers on shore. The French military on bases around Port

Libre responded, but their cannons couldn't reach the ships.[5]

Nicolls did not land his troops in Gouyave but, instead, at nearby Champion's Bay (Palmiste Beach). The troops then marched to French bases at Morne Nesbit, Morne Granby, and Port Libre, capturing them with little resistance.

Dougaldston Estate, headquarters of the French military, did not fall without a fight. During the night, the British aimed their cannons at Dougaldston from Morne Nesbit. By midday the following day, Jossey de Tournecy, the French commander headquartered at Dougaldston, surrendered and turned over all French bases to the British. On June 9-10, 1795, after a 16-month war, Gouyave and its neighboring estates were once again—and finally—in the hands of the British.

The British reverted back to "Charlotte Town" as the official name of Port Libre, or Gouyave. Regardless of their hard-earned power, though, the British couldn't control the town's name. They were the only people who used the name "Charlotte Town"; others continued calling the town "Gouyave," "Gouave," Goyve, Gouyavene or "Goyave," which were alternate spellings of the name that early French settlers had given the area. Today, the name of the town is spelled "Gouyave" but its legal name in an independent Grenada remains Charlotte Town.[6]

The terms of surrender that Commander Jossey de Tournecy was forced to sign at Morne Nesbit granted prisoner-of-war status only to soldiers sent to Grenada from Guadeloupe and other French colonies. From the beginning of the rebellion, the British considered Fédon and his revolutionaries' British subjects who took up arms against the king; therefore, those who fought with Fédon, including slaves, were left to fend for themselves after Jossey de Tournecy surrendered.

The locations for French soldiers to surrender and deposit their weapons were Dougaldston and Gouyave. Many revolutionaries gathered there in an unsuccessful attempt to be considered as soldiers from Guadeloupe thereby saving their lives in a prisoner-of-war exchange. Others knew that was a weak scheme and instead escaped into the mountains.

Gouyave, where the revolution commenced at midnight on March 2, 1795, and where Governor Home was captured the following morning, was back in the hands of the British and would remain British until Grenada was granted its independence on February 7, 1974.

Despite the British defeat of the French and some of Fédon's forces on June 9-10, 1796, the most wanted man in the British Empire, Julien Fédon, escaped capture. The French surrendered. Julien Fédon and his revolutionaries did not. Instead, they continued to control their bases in Grenada's interior.

THIRTY–SIX

Where's Julien Fédon?

Whatever Julien Fédon's flaws, he was dauntless and never missing in action. His energy appeared to increase along with the difficulties of the situation. It would have been out of character for him not to participate in the defense of Gouyave and its vicinity on June 9, 1796, when Nicolls landed at Palmiste Bay and then marched to Morne Granby and Morne Nesbit. It is widely believed Fédon was at Dougaldston Estate at the time, advising the French commander about how their combined troops could defeat the invading British forces—as he did at Belvedere in March and April of 1795.

Fédon went back to Belvedere's mountains with his estimated 300 troops only after Jossey de Tournecy, the French commander headquartered at Dougaldston, disappointed him with a decision to surrender. Dispirited as Fédon may have been, he had two choices: 1) surrender and be executed, or 2) continue his war against the British without any help from Victor Hugues. Fédon refused to surrender.

Everybody wanted a piece of Fédon's flesh: Nicolls and Colonel Campbell, for their humiliating defeats; Abercromby, for Fédon's audacity of fomenting insurrection against Britain; the politicians and authorities in St. George's, for the monstrous headaches that Fédon caused; and British planters and aristocrats, for ruining their estates.

There is no archival evidence that Fédon was at Dougaldston on June 9-10. Based on the topography and accessibility of Douglaston, however, it is likely that Fédon was there and, with his troops, escaped via the Dougaldston forest when he saw that capture was imminent. It would have been foolhardy to fight the British in Gouyave rather than at Dougaldston. In Gouyave, they would have been too exposed, making capture too easy. And if forced to retreat, it was too perilous to use known routes between Gouyave and Belvedere. The isolated Dougaldston Estate provided a safe haven, where Fédon could assist the French commander as well as escape—a strategy would allow Fédon to fight another day.

As Belvedere laborers of the 1950s were fond of saying, "Belvedere is in the back of Dougaldston," meaning behind the impenetrable mountain ranges and valleys that separate the two estates. As a youth, I hiked to Fédon's Camp with Father Bernard Kadlec, a Roman Catholic priest, from Dougaldston, Grand Roi, Concord, Grand Étang, and other points.[1]

I once hiked to Dougaldston, too, from an area near my home in Belvedere called "River Turning." River Turning was cultivated with nutmeg, cocoa, coffee, banana and ground provision. As a youngster, I often wondered what lay beyond the mountains farther south. I knew that the mountain ranges extended to Fédon's Camp in the east and to other areas in the parish of Saint John to the west. One morning in the dry season, I left with Rex, my dog, to scale the mountain. As we left River Turning and ascended, the view was stunning. I could see my home and other houses in Belvedere, Chadeau, and Clozier. The water in ravines looked clear and cool and ready to drink, and the crayfish were undisturbed. Rex and I went up hills and down dales, as we left the cultivated areas of River Turning. The view became more and more fascinating. Soon we could see the deep blue sea in the east and in the west, along with villages in the parishes of Saint John and Saint Andrew where galvanized roofs glittered in the sunshine.[2]

My spirits were soon dampened by a midday downpour that left me soaking wet, the sun hiding behind the clouds, and the deep hunger that made my belly rumble. Every step became more and more arduous, as Rex and I struggled along the slippery path through valleys and steep hills. By midafternoon, the sunshine returned. We were on a ridge, and I saw cultivated lands in the distance directly ahead.

By late afternoon, I heard voices. Rex and I moved as fast as we could in the thick woods, and the voices became louder. I started calling out and encouraged Rex to bark. The voices responded, as we came upon lands cultivated with cocoa, bananas, and nutmegs. We had come upon Dougaldston Estate.

The laborers we encountered said that we were lucky, because they were about to leave the field for the boucan. Returning to Belvedere via the mountains was not an option, as we would surely get lost in the forest as the sun set and it became dark.

Rex and I got a lift to Gouyave and a second lift back home to Belvedere. I couldn't wait to leave Gouyave, because I didn't want my schoolmates there to see me in my old waterproof boots with toes protruding, other parts too, wearing old and dirty clothes, and with my cutlass in hand!

The route Rex and I traveled over the mountain was the same isolated area between Belvedere and Dougaldston that runaways, enslaved people, and revolutionaries all used. And on June 9th or 10th, 1796, Julien Fédon mostly used that route from Dougaldston's great house, through the forest, past rivulets and streams, and over the mountains to escape to Morne Qua Qua.

⎯⎯∞⎯⎯

Over the ensuing centuries, Julien Fédon has been revered as a freedom fighter by many and recognized for his bravery and, interestingly, for his refusal to surrender. The truth is, though, that Fédon did offer to surrender in exchange for safe passage to Guadeloupe. He was a British subject of Grenada, after all, and a criminal wanted for high treason. When safe passage to Guadeloupe was declined, he had no choice but to keep on fighting.

That put the British in an awkward position. True, they neutralized the French and repossessed Gouyave; they captured French soldiers, officers, and many of Fédon's revolutionaries; but the rebellion continued. Julien Fédon was alive and continued the revolt, no doubt to the mortification of Abercromby—who badly wanted Fédon's head.

Like former Council President Kenneth Francis Mackenzie, who in March 1795 offered 20 Johannes (the Portuguese coins then used in Grenada), or approximately three British pounds, to anyone who captured Fédon dead or alive, Sir Ralph Abercromby in June 1796 was willing to pay £500 sterling for Fédon's head. That was an enormous amount of money to resist.

Whether Abercromby was disgusted with General Nicolls for not capturing Fédon during the recapture of Gouyave is unknown. When the two generals met in Carriacou in early June, Abercromby had outlined two courses of action for Nicolls: 1) end the rebellion, and 2) capture Fédon, dead or alive. Abercromby gave Nicolls soldiers and weapons, but Nicolls merely coaxed the French to surrender. Did Abercromby and Nicolls actually plan to first defeat the French?

Abercromby was anxious to quickly stabilize Grenada, however, because he wanted to focus on other troubled areas in the West Indies. He wanted to put an end to Spanish and French piracies, and he wanted to conquer Spanish Puerto Rico and Spanish Trinidad. Perhaps a visit to Grenada would motivate the troops and the British Grenadians to capture Julien Fédon once and for all.

Meanwhile, where was Julien Fédon's family?

THIRTY–SEVEN

Where's Julien Fédon's Family?

Although the Fédon family was close-knit, there is no evidence that any immediate family member was with Julien Fédon at Dougaldston or Gouyave on June 9-10, 1796. The family did not abandon him, however, and he did not forsake them. For their own security, it was likely too dangerous for this large family to remain together, considering that some were being sought for crimes committed against the King of England and his representatives in Grenada.

Six Fédons, including Julien, were on the list of "Attained Traitors" wanted for high treason. They included Bartholomew Bernard Fédon, Jean Baptiste Bernard Fédon, Jean Fédon, Julien Fédon, Louis Bernard Fédon, and Pierre Bernard Fédon. Michaud Christophe, Julien's half-brother, was also on the list. If any of those individuals had surrendered or were apprehended, they would have been tried in the Court of Oyer and Terminer, for rebelling against the monarchy. Apparently, no Fédon was caught or surrendered, because no records indicate that they were tried in that court.[1]

The whereabouts of the Fédon clan remains unexplained. The surnames of many revolutionaries—such as Ventour, Philip, De Coteau, Besson, Roy, and Dragon—are still carried by families in 21st-century Grenada, but nobody carries the name Fédon.

⸙

It was remarkable that Pierre Fédon, a poor Frenchman, and Brigitte, his Martiniquan wife, brought forth eight children and many grandchildren.

Most of the Fédons were born, baptized, and married in the parishes of Saint Mark and Saint John. Pierre and Brigitte's children rallied around their mother after the death of their father and gave her Pierre's eight-acre property that they inherited rather than dividing it among themselves. The siblings also supported their brother, Julien, whose leadership and love they appreciated. After the rebellion, however, all of the Fédons vanished from Grenada. And during the past 227+ years, no one has traced them or claimed to be a descendant.

THE OUTBREAK OF COVID 19 in 2020 prevented this writer from visiting Trinidad & Tobago to examine 18ᵗʰ and 19ᵗʰ centuries documents written in Spanish, French and English where he has a hunch information on the Fédon family may be found.

ONE CAN ONLY SPECULATE ABOUT how Julien and Marie Rose Fédon, along with their two girls, dealt with the ordeals they faced. Based on the scanty information available, it appears that it was painful for the family when Julien sacrificed everything to pursue the rights of French mulattos.

Julien Fédon and his wife were partners in every sense. Marie Rose cosigned most of their business transactions, including the purchase of Belvedere Estate and the sale of Lancer. And on the first morning of the revolution, Marie Rose prepared meals for both the revolutionaries and the prisoners at Belvedere. Prisoner Dr. John Hay, for example, wrote about how he attempted to purchase coffee:

> A negro boy was disposing of coffee to the prisoners; I requested he would bring me a cup; he desired I would give him the money first, which I did; the coffee was sent with a bit of bread by Fédon's wife, and the money returned.[2]

That response by Marie Rose was a small expression of gratitude to Dr. Hay for his past good deeds toward herself and her family, such as declaring that she was never a slave when the discriminatory government of Grenada accused her of such. Relationships were fostered between the two families, since Dr. Hay and the Fédons lived and worked in the same parishes.

WITH THE PENDING ATTACK AGAINST the revolutionaries on April 8, 1795, Marie Rose, her daughters, and the wives and children of revolutionaries spent the night of April 7th at Fedon's military headquarters rather than in the Belvedere flatlands where British soldiers were about to invade. Weeks before, as early as March 17th, the family had abandoned their home, Belvedere House, where proclamations had been drafted during the early days of the rebellion. Belvedere House was close to Mount Saint John, making it an easy target for the British to capture—which they did several times.

April 8, 1795, was the last time that Marie Rose Cavelan Fédon and her daughters were reportedly seen. On that morning, they were at Morne Qua Qua, or Morne Vauclain, when Governor Home and other prisoners were executed; there was no other safe place for them to be. They couldn't descend the mountain in the heat of battle, since they could have been killed in the crossfire. Fédon shielded his teenage daughters and comforted them in the tense moment when British forces appeared to be coming closer and the musket balls dropping nearer. The writings of Dr. Hay and Rev. M'Mahon recorded this last sighting of Fédon, his wife, and daughters together. "He began the bloody massacre in presence of his wife and daughters unfeeling spectators of his horrid barbarity."[3]

Dr. Hay and Rev. M'Mahon also provided information regarding the last time two other Fédons were seen. In the late afternoon of April 8, 1795, Hay, M'Mahon, and Kerr—whom Fédon had exonerated—descended from the Morne Qua Qua (Camp of Death) to Fédon's military headquarters (First Camp, Camp Equality). After leaving Camp Equality descending east towards Madame Peschier Estate, the three men noticed Jean Pierre Fédon's body and his tearful wife, Marguerite. "His wife, observing that I had lost most of my clothes, pressed me to accept a shirt and a pair of stockings, which I did," wrote Dr. Hay. This act of compassion by Marguerite Fédon in the midst of here despair further illustrates the kindness of Fédon women.[4]

Since that day, April 8, 1795, the whereabouts of any of the women in the Fédon family has remained unknown. Long before the rebellion was conceived, Marie, one of Julien Fédon's four sisters, was residing at Carenage, Spanish Trinidad, with her husband Michel Beleran. It seems logical that women and children of the Fédon family would have joined family members in Trinidad after the massacre in April 1795—and perhaps changed their names—but we have no evidence of either of those likelihoods.

Less than a year after the end of Fédon's Revolution in June 1796, Sir Ralph Abercromby captured Spanish Trinidad in April 1797. For decades, the colony had been harboring French creoles and their slaves, mixed-race people, runaways from Grenada and Saint Vincent, and American and French privateers. With Trinidad becoming British, some of Julien Fédon's family may have fled to French islands or the nearby Spanish Main (Venezuela) to avoid detection. It will be interesting to see whether documents accounting for the plight of the Fédon family one day surface in the Trinidadian, Spanish, or British archives—perhaps under the names Cavelan, Beleran, or Forgérie.

⸺❧⸺

History has accounted for one member of the Fédon family: Charles Nogues, husband of Marie Louise Fédon, Julien's sister. Nogues, a tailor in La Baye, was Fédon's aide-de-camp and partially responsible for victories in the Pilot Hill and Grenville Bay areas during the early months of the rebellion.

The relationship of Nogues and Fédon was once very amicable; for example, in 1790, Nogues and Marie Louise Nogues sold a piece of land in Gouyave to Julien and Marie Rose Fédon. Whether Nogues was captured in Saint Lucia by the British, where he went to work for Victor Hugues, and brought back to Grenada as a prisoner—or whether he returned to

Grenada to see his wife and son after the British recaptured Saint Lucia—is unknown. What is certain, however, is that Nogues was executed in the St. George's Market Place on August 11, 1796, for high treason. While awaiting execution, he wrote a message to his wife and son. The fact that his message exists in the British archives indicates that it was never delivered to Marie Louise:

> A la Gaol a 10 aout 1796, l'essois le derniere moment de ma vie pour te faire me adieu je l'embrasse toi et mon fils ne te chagrine pas preud Bon courage Soit tranquelle Les anglaise ne te fernot Bien parseque il ne fait pas a guerre au femme ny au enfant et salut et fraternite je meure.[5]

Translated: "At the Gaol on August 10, 1796, try the last moment of my life to make you farewell. I kiss you and my son. Do not grieve you preud. Good courage. Be calm. English won't do you harm because it does not war against women and children. Salvation and fraternity. I die."[5]

By then, Marie Louise Fédon Nogues may have joined her sister Marie in Trinidad. Or if she were still in Grenada, she might have been expelled to British Honduras (Belize) along with other wives of revolutionaries.

***

DESPITE THE BRITISH FORCING THE French to surrender and subsequently, on June 9-10, capturing Gouyave, General Nicolls and his commanders still couldn't report to Abercromby that Julien Fédon was either killed or captured—or that Fédon's battalions had even surrendered. For Abercromby, success meant apprehending Fédon and ending the rebellion. At that point, Abercromby left Saint Vincent and returned to Grenada to lay the ground for defeating Julien Fédon—once and for all.

THIRTY–EIGHT

General Abercromby on Belvedere's Border

Sir Ralph Abercromby, one of the greatest military leaders in British history, once visited the far-off areas of Madame Chadeau, Mount Saint John, and Belvedere.

Many Grenadians have little knowledge of those areas. That's not surprising, because the once-renowned coffee estates in that remote part of Grenada no longer exist. The nearest village is Clozier. Today, the area consists of small lots of farmlands where few people live but from there, one can get a panoramic view of Fédon's Camp Mountain range in the south especially during sunny days and moonlights.

In Saint Vincent, General Abercromby personally led the attack in the interior of that island against the Caribs, who sided with the French. It was after his victory in Saint Vincent that Abercromby came ashore in Grenada.

> On the 16th General Sir Ralph Abercromby arrived at Gouyave in his Majesty's Ship of War, *Anethusa*, and was shortly after escorted to Mount Saint John and Madame Chadeau by the St. George's light cavalry.[1]

General Abercromby may have been informed that the area provided the best view of Morne Vauclain or Morne Qua Qua and that he would be stepping foot on Fédon's Belvedere Estate, in boundary with Chadeau and Mount Saint John. Or he may have been anxious to see for himself why British officers continually used Mount Saint John to attack Fédon—and each time failed. If Abercromby had stood on any hill in that area, he may have seen the roof of Belvedere House about half-mile away.

Abercromby's visit to Mount Saint John, Chadeau, and Belvedere motivated British soldiers belonging to local regiments:

> He took an opportunity of thanking Captain McBurnie for his spirited conduct at Post Royal, and on many other occasions, and requested that Captain McBurnie would in his name express his thanks to all the gentlemen of his Corps for their spirited exertions on every occasion, and in particular, that of Post Royal, which Captain did immediately.[2]

Before leaving Mount Saint John, Abercromby "strictly forbade any negotiating whatsoever with Fédon" and offered a reward of £500 sterling "for that Monster Dead or Alive." That was a lot of money at the time and would allow someone to buy many acres of land or allow a slave to pay his or his family's way out of slavery. Historian, Curtis Jacobs wrote in his doctoral thesis: "The payment for Fédon's capture dead or alive rose from five pounds local currency in 1795 to 500 pounds sterling in 1796."[3]

General Abercromby provided General Nicolls with his reason for feeling no mercy toward Fédon. "The Atrocity of his Character and the Cruelties of which he has been guilty render it impossible to treat with him upon any other terms." Abercromby apparently forgot that the British were performing similar barbarities on revolutionaries and slaves who supported Fédon. Moreover, Abercromby determined that Fédon was guilty without benefit of a trial.[4]

As a British aristocrat, chances are that some of General Abercromby's wealthy friends had invested in sugar estates in Grenada only to learn that their investments were now worthless due to Julien Fédon's destruction of properties. Perhaps that's why Abercromby did not extend the same civility toward Fédon and other revolutionaries that he bestowed on French soldiers from Guadeloupe. Actually, Abercromby ambition, his overall purpose for being in the West Indies at all, was to recapture former British colonies and capture other Spanish and French territories.

Abercromby may have spent a cold night in Mount Saint John or returned to Gouyave and slept on his ship, *Arethusa*, as the next day he sailed to Saint George's and shortly after sailed again.

Having gone to Fédon's backyard, where he had a vivid view of Belvedere, Morne Qua Qua, and the surrounding mountain range, Abercromby ordered a new plan of attack for Nicolls to capture Julien Fédon—but, this time, not from Belvedere.

THE FOLLOWING YEAR, 1797, ABERCROMBY captured Trinidad by forcing Governor Don José Maria Chacón to surrender. That may have caused Chacón to bitterly regret supporting the British in March 1795, when he helped them suppress Fédon's Rebellion by sending three battle ships and 40 soldiers. It was also Chacón who caused the British to capture and hang Pierre Alexandre and the seize letters between Fédon and Victor Hugues. Less than two years after that, Abercromby seized Chacón and his island.

The Spanish king was not pleased with the surrender of Trinidad by Chacón, who lost favor and died in exile. If Fédon knew about that turn of events, he surely would have been pleased over the humiliation of Chacón. The outcome of Fédon's Rebellion may have been quite different without Chacón's early interference.

THERE IS A CONFLICTING TIMELINE as to when Sir Ralph Abercromby actually set foot on Grenada's soil. The Grenada Handbook, written in the late 19th century, states that Abercromby led the battle against French forces when he landed at Palmiste Bay on June 9th, 1796, and sailed for Saint Vincent on June 10th (or the following day) after capturing Gouyave, Morne Nesbit, and Morne Granby.[5]

Some 20th-century scholars imply that Abercromby may have remained in Grenada longer in order to plan the attack of Morne Qua Qua on June 19th and then sailed to Saint Vincent. However, the eyewitness account of Henry Thornhill, a lawyer who lived in Grenada, and the information that William Dyott, as noted in his diary, both specifically indicate that it was Nicolls who captured Gouyave and its environs on June 9-10, 1796—and that Nicolls had implemented plans given to him by Abercromby a few days before on Carriacou.

The undisputed facts are: "On the 16th, the Commander-in-chief, Sir Ralph, arrived at Chadeaus" where he briefed the commanders stationed there about his plans to attack Fédon at Morne Qua Qua and he ordered all regiments in the area be removed. What is factual is Abercromby ended rebellions in Saint Lucia, Saint Vincent, and Grenada—and indirectly in Dominica—within a four- to six-week period: April 26-June 19, 1796.[6]

THIRTY—NINE

Fédon Is Encircled

At the end of March 1796, after the British had defeated Fédon at Post Royal, Madame Hook's, and other nearby bases in Saint Andrew, British troops remained in the vicinity. For additional security, they created a base on the cliffs of Soubise, overlooking the sea and the barren rocks of the Marquis and Soubise islets. Throughout April and May, General Nicolls awaited General Abercromby's thousands of troops, who would end the rebellion by routing Fèdon from the mountains of Belvedere—especially Morne Qua Qua.

William Dyott continued recording daily activities in his diary. He revealed that the revolutionaries remained aggressive and courageous, occasionally waging guerilla attacks on British troops. Nothing was too insignificant for Dyott to note:

> Three villains (Dutchmen) deserted from the 25th Regiment to the enemy. One of them was afterwards taken at Gouyave, and we had him hung up on the highest tree we could find ... Nine soldiers that were straying rather too far from the camp was taken by the enemy.[1]

Dyott also documented his living conditions:

> My tent, I believe, infested with every species of reptile the island produces: a scorpion, lizard, tarantula, land crab, and centipede had been caught by my black boy, and the mice were innumerable.[2]

He slept at the base on Soubise Estate, one of the first estates created by early French planters:

> Having nothing to dread from any attack from the enemy after it was light … rode on the beach between *Soubise* and La Baye … and then rode to headquarters at Post Royal Hill.[3]

FINALLY ON JUNE 9, THE bored troops camped in La Baye area received orders to move. At 7 P.M., most of the British soldiers began the arduous journey from Post Royal, "Morne Soubige" and La Baye to recapture Chadeau and Mount Saint John. Dyott noted that it was a dangerous march for the regiments:

> Our march for the last three miles was literally up and down precipices, half-way up the leg in clay, and through a wood where I believe no human foot had ever been stepped. A party of the enemy had attacked our advanced guard … they annoyed us with their bush fighting from the woods.[4]

Since the areas (today La Force and Windsor) were maroon strongholds, Dyott may have referred to runaway slaves loyal to Fèdon. He continued:

> After marching twenty-one hours without scarce a halt through thick woods, deep rivers, etc. took post on some rising ground about three o'clock in the afternoon of the next day with the intention of attacking a hill in our front called Madame Chadeau.[5]

IT IS A PITY THAT Dyott did not witness the invasion of Gouyave and Morne Nesbit. What a vivid description he would have given! While thousands of British troops were invading French-controlled Gouyave, and with Fèdon's and French forces at Dougaldston on June 9-10, Dyott and his regiments were struggling to get to Chadeau, where they would endure sporadic attacks by the revolutionaries, as documented by Dyott in his diary.

General Nicolls, victorious in Gouyave, Morne Granby, Morne Nesbit and Dougaldston, visited Chadeau on June 12th. He informed the troops that he ordered a brigade stationed in Gouyave to join them. The brigade included several regiments, Löwenstein Jägers (German and Dutch mercenaries), and 200 Loyal Black Rangers. Did Nicolls intend to spring another attack from Mount Saint John against Fédon, who had by then retreated to Morne Vauclain?

ON JUNE 13TH, JULIEN FÈDON sent emissaries, with a flag of truce, to the British commanders in Chadeau. He realized that he did not have sufficient ammunition or enough forces to defeat the powerful British army, as he had in March and April of 1795. In a sense, the French had already disappointed him by surrendering. So Fédon proposed a surrender at Morne Qua Qua, providing that "he and his associates were to be sent unmolested to Guadaloupe." That proposal was flatly rejected.[6]

When General Sir Ralph Abercromby, Commander-in-Chief of all British forces in the West Indies, appeared at Chadeau on June 16th, protocol dictated that General Nicolls accompany his commander; but he did not. It is apparent that Abercromby was not pleased with how Nicolls was directing the war. Although Nicolls had saturated Chadeau and Mount Saint John with troops, Abercromby suspended the strategy of attacking Fèdon at Morne Qua Qua from that locale.

The fall of Post Royal, Pilot Hill, Battle Hill, Morne Nesbit, Dougladson, Gouyave and other bases did not leave Fèdon with just his principal base at Morne Vauclain/Morne Qua Qua. Always clever and one step ahead, Fédon had three other bases in virtually inaccessible mountain peaks and treacherous valleys. Mitchel near Mount Saint Margaret in Saint Andrew and Madame Ache's and in the interior of Beausejour in Saint George were all crucial for him. The three bases were within proximity of the Grand Étang forest and Morne Qua Qua. Throughout 1795, Acting Governor Kenneth Francis Mackenzie and several British officers had tried unsuccessfully to capture the strategically located Mitchel and Madame Ache's bases.

Although Abercromby sailed from Grenada on June 17th or 18th, he had left General Nicolls with 6,000 to 8,000 soldiers—including the dreaded Löwenstein Jägers, commanded by Graf von Heillimer—to mount a simultaneous, four-pronged attack on Fèdon's four bases. If this tactic were successful, Julien Fèdon and his revolutionaries would have no more major bases in which to hide or launch attacks.

⸘⸘⸘

MEANWHILE, THE BRITISH REGIMENTS IN Chadeau were anxious to leave. While encamped in La Baye, Soubise and Post Royal, they had complained about the heat, scorching sun, and lack of rain. In Chadeau, the grumbles were about days and nights of cold, misty weather. Dyott noted:

> It rained almost incessantly … Our encampment was a ploughed field … We were all just as wet as if we had lain in a river, and both under the tents and all around them was half-way up the leg in mud.[7]

⸘⸘⸘

THE DAY AFTER ABERCROMBY'S VISIT to Chadeau, the restless soldiers were relieved when ordered to depart Chadeau at 3 a.m. on June 17th and capture Fèdon's bases at Mitchel and Madame Ache's on June 18-19, which was about the same time that the Löwenstein Jägers would attack Fèdon at Morne Qua Qua. Due to a shortage of food supplies, the forces at Chadeau left late—at 7 a.m. on June 18th—under the command of General Campbell.

⸘⸘⸘

THE PLAN DRAWN UP BY General Sir Ralph Abercromby and his commanders was fairly simple, but implementing it was not. Nevertheless, Abercromby had confidence in his officers and troops, many of whom had fought in similar mountainous environments in Saint Lucia between late March and May of 1796. Even before French General Goyrand surrendered Saint Lucia on May 26, Abercromby had started sending his key aides, such as Brigadier General John Hope and commanders of his foreign mercenaries, to analyze the situation. It was the valiant German and Dutch commandos who principally defeated Saint Lucia's revolutionaries for Abercromby. He was confident that they would do the same for him in Grenada.

The British forces from Chadeau or Mount Saint John were to travel in a southeast direction to capture two Fèdon bases, Mitchel and Madame Ache's. Leaving Gouyave at about the same time, Graf von Heillimer and the best men of his Lowenstein Jägers, along with the elite regiment of Royal Estrangers, and the 57th Regiment would approach Morne Qua Qua from the southwest (modern-day Grand Roi, Concord, or Woodford) or from other locations on the western coast.

The Jägers, upon reaching the Grand Étang area, would move slightly east to climb the peaks of Morne Qua Qua from the south.

On the Belvedere side of Morne Qua Qua, the few troops left in Mount Saint John would move closer to Fèdon's military headquarters, in the hills of Belvedere, to capture revolutionaries fleeing north.

Fèdon's base in Beausejour mountain, leading to Morne Qua Qua, was less crucial for the British than the other bases but still had to be captured to prevent the revolutionaries from absconding and taking refuge in Fédon's three other bases. Although impassable mountain peaks, deeps valleys, and thickly wooded forests separated Fédon's four bases, Abercromby's plan was to encircle and capture Fèdon's main base, Morne Qua Qua.

Count Graf von Heillimer's Jägers were given the task of taking the base at Morne Qua Qua and, hopefully, capturing Julien Fèdon—dead or alive. Fresh from his success and experience in Saint Lucia, Graf von Heillimer was ready to beat Fédon at his own game: preparation, shrewdness, and aggressiveness.

The strategy of Count von Heillimer and his elite mercenaries worked perfectly. In the still of the night on June 18, von Heillimer and his battalions left lit torches and campfires in their camps, while they stealthily moved to Morne Qua Qua and hid near the top of hills until the crack of dawn.

As the sun rose over La Baye and the revolutionaries were fast asleep at Morne Qua Qua, the attack commenced. The revolutionaries were shocked, some were killed, and others escaped—but not before killing 20 prisoners.

After 16 long months of frustration and embarrassment, the British had finally captured the mountain peak known by various names: Morne Vauclain, Morne Qua Qua, Camp of Death, Fédon's Camp, and Second Camp. Fédon's forces had been removed from their citadel.

Unfortunately, von Heillmer left no account of his dramatic seizure of Morne Qua Qua on June 19, 1796, although he did depend on the knowledge of Loyal Black Rangers to guide him through the forest as he climbed up to Fédon's Camp. Most accounts, whether real or exaggerated, quote the Grenada Handbook, 1897-1945. The accuracy of the information in the handbook is questioned by some; moreover, the human element is missing.

⸻ ∞ ⸻

Fortunately, William Dyott, who commanded three regiments for Brigadier General Campbell, provided some idea of the hardships experienced by European soldiers marching into the mountains of Grenada—from Chadeau in Mount Saint John to Mitchel and then to Madame Ache's:

> The first three miles I had to take my brigade was through a thick wood with a negro for my guide ... the line continued its march through a country of wood, (except two or three rivers, deep, rapid, and full of rocks) till about five o'clock, when the enemy appeared in front of their post called Mitchel's Camp.[8]

General Campbell divided the force into two brigades, one led by Dyott and the other by Lieutenant Colonel Gilman, who had seen action in Saint

Lucia. After leaving Chadeau, the brigades moved in two columns fairly close to each other.

—⚭—

BASED ON MY KNOWLEDGE, HAVING grown up in the area, and stories of laborers in the 1950s living or working in Belvedere and Chadeau who used almost the same routes when going to and from different places in Saint Andrew, these are the likely routes that the soldiers must have taken from Chadeau to Mitchel and then to Madame Ache's:

After moving through the cultivated areas and forests of Chadeau, they would descend into a deep valley into Belvedere and enter Fraze Estate, which bordered Belvedere, and cross the noisy river flowing down from Belvedere. Since it rained consistently, the soldiers, mules, and horses would have had difficulties climbing the steep hills of Fraze into Ferme Peschier.

The soldiers would then have descended into a forest in what today is the Village of Morne Longue. After crossing the Morne Longue River and a number of ravines, they would have marched through several coffee estates—Beauregard, Nianganfoix, and Adelphi—and other properties owned by French mulattos.

Led by slaves who were faithful to their British masters and the Loyal Black Rangers, the British soldiers would have descended into various valleys, climbed more steep and slippery hills, and crossed more rivers and streams until they came upon a popular path that today is Grand Étang Main Road. The revolutionaries, blocked a part of the Grand Étang Main Road by "having trees felled across it in all directions," but the British brigades got around it and worked their way into today's Adelphi and other points south.[9]

Along the route, the British brigades endured sniper attacks from revolutionaries. Dyott documented an incident:

> There was a curious circumstance happened on the march, which shows what determined soldiers by trade Germans are ... We saw a negro hut about 100 yards below us, and a poor black devil ran

out of it … The Captain of the Jägers … immediately levelled at him, dodging him through the trees and killed the wretch.[10]

Upon reaching Fèdon's base at Mitchel, the soldiers were confronted by more revolutionaries. For the first time since the beginning of the revolution, however, there was no French assistance—no French consultants, no French troops, and no additional weapons from Guadeloupe. Julien Fèdon and those loyal to him had to defend themselves.

FORTY

Battles For Mitchel and Madame Ache's

The capture of Mitchel, a crucial Fédon's base, President Mackenzie attempted numerous times to seize in 1795, was about to happen. The battle lasted almost two hours resulting in victory for the British. The combined British regiments and German Yougers were too much for the revolutionaries. "We took possession of their camps (which consisted of about 50 wretched huts) … and the two brigades halted for the night," Dyott recalled. He mentioned that Fèdon's forces did not give up easily:

> After we got into our huts at Mitchel's, several shots were fired from the woods, one of which struck an officer of the 9th Regiment … one of the privates was wounded in the thigh by a shot from one of these rascals in the woods, and bled to death in five minutes.[1]

Dyott also summarized the journey from Chadeau to Mitchel:

> We had a very fatiguing march from Chadeau to Mitchel. The day was very hot, and from the excessive rains up to our ankles in mud. A great number of men lost their shoes.[2]

MEANWHILE, AS THE BRITISH PENETRATED the valleys, mountains, and forest and got nearer to Morne Qua Qua, the foreign regiments led by Graf von Heillimer and Lieutenant Colonel Gledstanes were enduring the wrath of Fèdon's forces on the southwestern side of Grenada. Like General Campbell's battalions from Chadeau, the British brigades depended on Loyal Black Rangers to show them the trails.

—∞—

Early the next morning, Sunday, June 19, and having left a regiment to protect Mitchel, General Augustus Campbell and his troops resumed their march—this time going west. They were on their way to capture Madame Ache's in Saint George.

Dyott's description was perfect:

> We passed what is called the Grand Étang. This is a circular lake…surrounded by high mountains covered with woods from the very edge of the lake to their summit.[3]

On Dyott's right, in the distance, were the peaks of Morne Qua Qua, one of them the Camp of Death or Fédon's Camp. (During our early teens, my friends and I sometimes raced from Fédon's Camp to Grand Étang to see who could reach the lake and jump in first.)

By 9 a.m., the battle for Julien Fèdon's last stronghold, Madame Ache's, had begun. The battle was really nasty and lasted for three hours. Dyott and General Campbell allowed the Germans to attack Fédon forces:

> The Yougers and light infantry companies attacked the enemy… Asche's Camp…The enemy was strongly posted at this place…We entered a thick wood without track or path; half-way up the leg in clay, and to pass up and down two or three mountains almost perpendicular in order to gain possession of a very high ridge.[4]

Fèdon's revolutionaries fought hard. To capture Madame Ache's, the British soldiers and mercenaries climbed a narrow ridge "literally in the form of a pig's back"—but Fèdon's forces, hidden behind the trees, "picked off several of the Yougers and killed and wounded some men of the 8th Light Infantry that were in front," according to Dyott. The battle for Madame Ache's was one of the fiercest in the 16-month long war:

I was with General Campbell at the end of the ridge, having
come up from the rear to see what was going on, and I believe,
as far as I can judge, that no men ever showed more the zeal or
intrepidity than the light companies in the attack.[5]

Dyott also acknowledged the dexterity of Fèdon's men:

It is astonishing with what incredible alacrity the
negroes got through the woods, and how nimbly
they scrambled up and down the hills.[6]

General Campbell and his two commanders, Dyott and Gilman, had
fulfilled their mission of capturing Mitchel on June 18th and Madame Ache's
the next day. The sound of guns and cannons echoing in the valleys of Saint
George attracted civilians. Dyott and other soldiers were disappointed,
though. Why? No rum! He explained:

After two days' severe, harassing marches, at the end
of each a sharp action, and notwithstanding this post at
Ache's that we had just taken was only four miles from
St. George's, and that many people came out during the
engagement, there was not a drop of rum to give the
men as a reward for their exertions.[7]

General Augustus Campbell's regiments received no news about the
whereabouts of Count von Heillimer's and Gledstanes' troops that had
departed Gouyave on June 18th:

On the 20th, the day after we took Ache's, the
General got a letter from the Governor at St. George's
to say that the enemy camp at Mount Quoca had been
taken on the 19th.[8]

Abercromby's plans were executed with precision by von Heillimer,
Gledstanes, and Campbell:

- **June 18:** Campbell, Gilman, Dyott, and troops left Chadeau in Mount Saint John.
- **June 18:** Campbell, Gilman, Dyott, and troops captured Mitchel; slept there.
- **June 19:** Campbell, Gilman, Dyott, and troops captured Madame Ache's.
- **June 18:** von Heillimer, Gledstanes and troops left Gouyave.
- **June 18:** von Heillimer, Gledstanes and troops camped near Morne Qua Qua.
- **June 19:** von Heillimer, Gledstanes and troops captured Morne Qua Qua.

THE BRITISH BASKED IN their victory. June 19, 1796, is recognized as the day Fédon's Rebellion ended. In an essay in 1894, British historian Sir John William Fortescue described Fédon's Revolution and the Haitian Revolution as "Massacre, plunder, and ruin, of war not only between the French and the English, of the subject against the dominant race, of the black man against the white."[9]

British Grenadians were now enjoying the thrill of victory. The agony of many defeats at the hands of Fédon had evaporated. Campbell, the lieutenant colonel who led the ill-fated assault on Fédon's military headquarters when Governor Home and 47 others were murdered, was now a hero. So was Count von Heillimer.

British Grenadians "subscribed for a Sword or Sabre of £100 sterling to be presented to von Heillimer as a grateful mark of the very essential Service that Officer had rendered the Colony by the capture of the main Camp of the Rebels."[10]

As for Brigadier General Oliver Nicolls, he remained in Gouyave during the capture of Morne Qua Qua and the other three bases on June 18-19.

The British neglected, however, to thank a group of people who kept Grenada in British hands during most of the 16-month conflict. They were the Loyal Black Rangers—freed Africans and slaves who sided with their British masters and formed the majority of the military when England had few soldiers in the colony.

Unlike Abercromby, who had thousands of soldiers at his disposal when he arrived in Grenada in 1796, Colonel Colin Lindsay arrived from Saint Lucia on March 12, 1795, with a small force of 150 men. General Nicolls arrived on April 13th of that year with only his assistants. He was a visionary who understood the African population, whether enslaved or freed, was essential in order to defeat Fédon. Nicolls recruited loyal slaves and organized them into regiments that formed the front line when the British attacked Fédon across the colony. They were the first to die for the British cause.

As Nicolls received battalions sailing on British fleets during 1796, he was faced with a deteriorating health situation. Within days of landing, soldiers died like flies from yellow fever or dengue fever. Nicolls contracted dengue but survived. It was felt that "the plague" or "bulam fever," as it was also called, came to the West Indies from Africa on slave ships and then transmitted to North America and Europe. Dengue fever was attributed by some to be the cause of Colonel Colin Lindsay's suicide at Mount Saint John on March 22, 1795. As the epidemic peaked in 1796, Nicolls relied heavily on the Loyal Black Rangers.

In battles, the Loyal Black Rangers were commanded to lead attacks, hunt for revolutionaries in the mountains, and destroy food crops—especially the plantain fields upon which the revolutionaries depended. The trained, disciplined, and knowledgeable Loyal Black Rangers knew the terrain, which helped defeat Julien Fédon, but they were not invited to the celebration table. It is unknown whether they were ever rewarded with freedom.

The mixed-race Captain Louis de la Grenade made sure he got recognition, though.

Yet, there was still one missing link in the British defeat of Fédon at Morne Qua Qua on June 19, 1796. No one had brought the head or body of Fédon to St. George's. Where was Julien Fédon?

FORTY–ONE

Hunting for Fédon

For General Oliver Nicolls, there was nothing but disenchantment. He had been enthusiastically welcomed back to Grenada on April 13, 1795. Yet, Sir Ralph Abercromby placed more confidence in the commanders who brought him victory in Saint Lucia than in Oliver Nicolls, who had been stationed in Grenada during an earlier time in his military career.

Abercromby was mainly responsible for the French surrender at Gouyave. General Nicolls merely implemented Abercromby's strategies—and wasn't able to find Julien Fédon, dead or alive. Nobody wanted the head of Fédon more than Abercromby, so he must have been annoyed with Nicolls for not capturing Fédon. Perhaps a reason why Nicolls did not accompany his commander-in-chief to Mount Saint John.

Nicolls, who continued as commander of British forces in Grenada, did not give up the search for Fédon. Weeks went by, and no one captured Fédon to claim Abercromby's £500 sterling reward. British Grenadians, such as writer and lawyer Henry Thornhill, presented lofty excuses for that failure. Thornhill wrote:

> By these last very important successes, the stubborn heart
> of this Monster of Rebellion was entirely broken, the rebels
> having lost all their Posts and Artillery, and obliged to fly to
> the woods and mountains for shelter … excepting that the Arch
> Traitor Fédon with a few of his Associates who, there is every
> reason to conclude, made their escape in a canoe.[1]

In a letter to Major General Thomas Graham, dated August 11, 1796, Nicolls wrote, "Fédon himself has very narrowly escaped twice or thrice being taken, the last time was by throwing himself down a place where no one of our soldiers, white or black, dare venture after him."[2]

Although Nicolls did not inform Graham as to where and when Fédon "narrowly escaped twice or thrice," perhaps the first was on June 19 when von Heillimer scaled Morne Qua Qua.

IN THE 1950S, EXCITED LABORERS on Belvedere Estate related to me one of Fédon's survival episodes. They claimed to know the cliff where Fédon allegedly threw himself over. My papa, Frederick Adams, had a garden in the mountains of Belvedere, and he showed me the precipice from which Fédon allegedly jumped.[3]

During slavery, slave masters allowed the enslaved to create gardens in the woods near cultivated fields. More than 227 years later, the descendants of slaves still own gardens in Belvedere. But Frederick Adams and other laborers also had gardens in the remotest areas of Belvedere, such as the Morne Qua Qua Mountain range. They visited those areas a few times a year, mainly in the dry season, to search for yams and also to hunt. As a youth, looking at the precipice from our garden in Morne Golette was scary.[4]

Listening to my papa's colorful description of what happened on June 19, you'd think he had been an eyewitness: "Rather den surrendering, Fédon jumped from de precipice between First Camp and Second Camp—but de coward British, finding de bottom of de precipice too dangerous, were afraid to go down dere to find Fédon body or capture him. Fédon was a real man!"[5]

IN 2003, I VISITED FÉDON'S Camp for the first time in 36 years. What an ordeal! I went alone and used the path from the former prison boucan in the flatlands of Belvedere to Fédon's Camp, as outlined in Dr. Hay's and Rev. M'Mahon's books. Apart from getting lost, I passed close to the precipice where my papa and other laborers said Fédon jumped on June 19, 1795. I was cautious, because a single slip would land me in the deep valley below. I sat about 100 yards away and had a good view of Morne Golette, other peaks, valleys, and ravines.

WHEN NICOLLS BRIEFED MAJOR GENERAL Thomas Graham in August 1796 that Fédon may have escaped on July 27, 1796, he may have been referencing Mount Sinai—which was closer to the Saint Andrew and Saint David coasts than Morne Qua Qua. Nicolls surmised that Fédon's "object, and that of the few remaining out in the Woods, is to get off in a Canoe; we have by good intelligence, destroyed several that were preparing in the woods for that purpose, and I trust that this, their last hope, will fail them."[6]

By then, word that Julien Fédon had drowned on his way to Spanish Trinidad was spreading across the colony and beyond. Evidently, Nicolls did not wholly accept that rumor, so his search for Fédon continued. On July 26, word came that Fédon was seen at Mount Sinai—probably from Loyal Black Rangers, whom General Nicolls was using to hunt revolutionaries suspected of hiding in the mountains. Mount Sinai, east of Grand Étang Lake and Morne Qua Qua, is clearly visible from Morne Qua Qua (Fédon's Camp). Julien Fédon was apparently moving to the coast a few miles away.

To learn that Fédon was in the colony must have been exciting news for Nicolls. The rebellion had ended five weeks before, and the British had made the St. George's Market Place a killing field. Revolutionaries who were caught or surrendered—including French whites, mixed-race people, and slaves and their children loyal to the French—were tried, hanged or shot. Some bodies were chopped into sections and drawn around the town. Meanwhile, in Grenada's southeastern mountains, revolutionaries had split into small, independent groups, making it difficult for anyone to capture them.

Grenada's maroons traditionally survived as small groups, avoiding slave catchers such as Louis de La Grenade. Julien Fédon and other revolutionaries likely used the same strategy. Maroons may also have protected and guided Fédon as he inched his way toward the island's east coast, where there were hidden bays and offshore islands. While Fédon thoroughly knew his way from Morne Vauclain, Belvedere, and Mount Saint John to the western coast of Gouyave and Victoria, the west coast has fewer hidden bays and no offshore islands; therefore, escaping via the east was more logical. It is unlikely, though, that Fédon knew the terrains from Morne Qua Qua, Mount Sinai and Mount Lebanon to the southeastern coast of Saint Andrew and Saint David, so someone must have helped him get there.

Early on the morning of July 27, General Oliver Nicolls dispatched the best of his troops and Loyal Black Rangers to Mount Sinai. They reported a glimpse of Fédon near his hut, "situated on the brink of a precipice," but did they believe that he would jump into the seemingly bottomless chasm, where no soldier dared to go?[7]

That was the last time Fédon was said to have been seen on Grenada's soil. All reports of the whereabouts of Julien Fédon after July 27, 1796, are mere speculation. The only certainty: Julien Fédon was never caught.

⊸⊸⊸

WITHIN THE RUGGED FORESTS OF Morne Vauclain, Mount Saint Margaret, Mount Saint Lebanon, and Mount Sinai were several caves—perhaps used centuries before by the indigenous people when hunting in the interior—which the enslaved and the self-emancipated used as hiding places. In 2013, I went to Fédon's Camp with a retired hunter who had hunted in the vicinity for decades. He confirmed the existence of caves, although they were almost impossible to discover in the thick forest. While scouting Belvedere and the mountains of Belvedere as a youth, however, I saw very large holes that appeared to be entrances to caves; the adults always said those holes were dug by hunters searching for tatou (armadillo)! The jungle did not only provide escape routes for revolutionaries but places to live. It was in the vicinity Jacques Chadeau was caught.

⊸⊸⊸

Julien Fédon emerged on the political scene rather suddenly on March 2-3, 1795. His early success was mainly due to Africans who supported him and the French weapons and soldiers provided by Victor Hugues on Guadeloupe.

Julien Fédon vanished even more suddenly—and without a trace—in July 1796.

FORTY-TWO

Julien Fédon – Fact and Fiction

Julien Fédon's saga ended on July 27, 1796. But fictionalizing and mystifying him began in 1838 with Edward Lanza Joseph's novel, *Warner Arundell: The Adventures of a Creole.* This fascination with Fédon has continued through the 20th century and into the 21st century. In addition, theatrical productions about Julien Fédon, including "A Day in West Indian History" (written by this writer and staged at the St. John's Christian Secondary School in Grenada in 1966) and Chris DeRiggs's 2022 historical drama, "Julien Fédon" have added to the Fédon mystique.

Hollis Liverpool, author and renowned calypsonian, known as "Chalkdust"—who earned his Ph.D. in history and ethnomusicology from the University of Michigan—once wrote a calypso addressing "Misconceptions." The witty calypso landed him the titles of National Calypso Monarch of Trinidad & Tobago in 1993 and *EVERYBODY'S* Magazine World Calypso Monarch in 1994. One wonders if the next time Chalkdust is rendering "Misconceptions," he would add a new line: "Another misconception is Julien Fédon started a slave rebellion in Grenada…No! No! No!"

Julien Fédon would probably be flattered to know that writers have credited him for instigating a slave rebellion. Rather, his first and foremost reason for the uprising focused on landowning mixed-race people seeking civil liberties. And it was that segment of Grenada's population that rose up against the local British administration.

Misunderstanding the history of Fédon's Revolution is, unfortunately, common. In Thomas Turner Wise's comprehensive account of the first two months of the rebellion, written in St. George's in May 1795, not once did he imply that slaves orchestrated it—but he did acknowledge the misconceptions of others. He wrote:

> A Great many Misconceptions having been entertained, and a great many Misrepresentations having been made, which have happened in Grenada, since the Commencement of the Insurrection...I have humbly to crave your Indulgence, in permitting me to lay before you an Historical Review of those Events.[1]

As they awoke on Tuesday, March 3, 1795, British and French Grenadians and their slaves in St. George's were alarmed when a sailor on "his way to Grenville" informed them "that the French had landed there...and that they were on their march to Saint George's." A letter from Lieutenant-Governor Ninian Home dispatched from his Paraclete Estate near Grenville confirmed the tragic news. A few hours later, another letter from Home, written at Lafortune Estate in Saint Patrick, revealed, "No French have landed at La Baye; but the free people have risen against the whites."[2]

The latter information was accurate. "Free people" had, indeed, "risen against the whites," but the message in Home's letter was misleading. He meant that free people had risen up against white Britishers, because the white French population bravely supported Fédon. Planned by free mixed-race persons of French ancestry, the rebellion was led by a wealthy, French-speaking mulatto, Julien Fédon.

Both Dr. John Hay and Rev. Francis M'Mahon were apprehended by their friends and neighbors during the very first hour of the rebellion, but they did not accuse the slaves of inciting the rebellion in their respective narratives. Dr. Hay said:

> I was awakened by a violent rapping in my back gallery and my chamber door... I perceived a number of armed men ... I knew by sight, but only recollect the names of Joseph Le Blanc, Pierre

Labat, whites; Etienne Ventour, Pillage, Antoine Roy, Medgar Chantimel, and Sylvain Dragon, coloured people.[3]

On March 28, 1795, as acting governor, Kenneth Francis Mackenzie dispatched his first formal report about the rebellion to William Bentinck, 3rd Duke of Portland and British Home Secretary responsible for colonial affairs. Not a single word about a slave rebellion, revolt, or uprising was mentioned in Mackenzie's five-point report. He noted:

> General insurrection of French Free Coloured people on 2nd March, massacre of White English inhabitants at Grenville, capture of White English inhabitants at Charlotte Town, including Lieutenant Governor (Ninian) Home who was on his way back to St. George's by sea, and others from several estates in the Country.[4]

No documents have ever substantiated the claim that any slave or former slave planted the seeds of rebellion. That is the fantasy of some modern scholars. In summarizing Fédon's Revolution, they often describe the event as the most protracted slave rebellion in the British West Indies. Yet the 16-month event was not, in fact, a slave revolt.

Although by his actions on March 3 or 4, 1795, Julien Fédon may have unwittingly abolished slavery, not every slave joined his cause.

The looting of estates was perpetrated by revolutionaries. Slaves later participated or were forced to participate. "Numbers of negroes, and parties were sent out in all directions to collect cattle, horse, and provisions of every kind; in short, a general plunder took place of all English estates," observed Dr. Hay.[5]

The enslaved were, indeed, caught in the middle of a mulatto uprising. "My father's negroes proved all faithful. Four of the best men were murdered by the French for refusing to join them," wrote Samuel Cary, Jr. to his father in Massachusetts. That said, all correspondences between members of the Cary family did describe Fédon's Revolution as "a slave revolt."[6]

Professor Susan Clair Imbarrato who wrote about the Cary family, owners of Mount Pleasant Estate in Saint Mark, legitimized the assertion of the rebellion being "a slave uprising." This assertion is recorded in her 2018 book, in *Sarah Gray Cary from Boston to Grenada: Shifting Fortunes of an American Family, 1764-1826*, published in 2018 in which she wrote:

> The Cary family of Chelsea, Massachusetts, prospered as plantation owners and managers for nearly two decades in the West Indies before the Grenada slave revolts of 1795–1796 upended the sugar trade.[7]

That misinformation, branding Fédon's Rebellion or Revolution as a slave revolt, is presented too frequently in libraries and research institutions as factual thus validating erroneous information as scholarly work thereby propagating a chain reaction.

THE BRITISH WERE WILLING TO exact revenge on anyone who supported Julien Fédon, and the slaves were easy targets. The first person that the British executed for aiding Fédon was a slave. Two slaves argued, and one told the British that the other had abetted the revolutionaries. Without proof or interrogation, the British immediately killed the slave. This malicious act of cruelty caused a planter, in his report to London, to ask: "Besides, supposing the poor negro-man had followed his master Bontems to the rebel-camp, was it not probable that he obeyed his master's orders in doing so? And was not this understood to be the first duty of a slave?" Bontems, evidently a white French planter and a revolutionary, was executed by the British in July 1796.[8]

Both sides used slaves to their advantage. Fédon placed his confidence in many slaves; without them, his rebellion would not have lasted 16 months. They remained loyal to him even after the rebellion ended. Many Loyal Black Rangers, as the British called its armed slaves, lost their lives for the British cause. Some quit to join Julien Fédon. Without the Loyal Black Rangers, though, it would have taken longer for the British to crush the rebellion.

The rebellion generally referred to as "Fédon's Revolution" caused the decline of the French-speaking population and the French influence in Grenada and forever changed the island's socioeconomic landscape. The person most responsible for that profound shift was the unsung hero, Julien Fédon.

Some things simply don't change. Whether Julien Fédon was loved or hated in 1795-1796, today's Grenadians likewise consider him either a beloved historical figure or a hated one.

Did he drown on the high sea allegedly on his way to Trinidad or did he escape to the Spanish Main (Venezuela), Haiti, or Cuba? This question has been raised in the court of public opinion for centuries and 21st century Grenadians are also divided on the answer.

Acknowledgments

Although they departed this life a long time ago, I still want to recognize the laborers of Belvedere Estate, the descendants of slaves and East Indian indentured servants; many were born on the estate. They revered Julien Fédon. Since I was the only youngster born on the estate and attending secondary school, many laborers, such as Mr. Layman Brown, challenged me to write about Julien Fédon when I grew up. I even started a Fédon book while attending the Grenada Boys' Secondary School, which amounted to about two or three pages. My conscience is finally cleared, knowing I obeyed the laborers by writing this book. Without the mandate of those mostly illiterate laborers and the impact of Father Raymund Devas and Father Kadlec Bernard, this book would not have materialized.

While *Julien Fédon – Revolutionary, Patriot and Insurrectionist: The Untold Story of a Mulatto Leader* was just about completed, I elected to first release *Belvidere Estate – Fédon's House: Voices from the Past* before publishing this one. Readers who enjoyed that first book frequently asked, "When would you make the other Fédon book available?" This encouragement led me to fine tune *Julien Fédon – Revolutionary, Patriot* and bolster it with additional research.

Mrs. Maudlyn Ogiste of Saint Mark was very helpful as I tried pinpointing the areas of what was Julien Fedon's Lancer property and Samuel Cary's Mount Pleasant Estate in Saint Mark Parish. Unfortunately, I am unable to locate Pierre Fédon's 8.5-acre property.

Numerous times Norris Marshall, born in Ferme Peschier, and I—armed with Dr. John Hay's and Rev. Francis M'Mahon books—visited and verified all the sites, in Chadeau, Belvedere, and Ferme Peschier, that Hay and M'Mahon mentioned in their respective narratives. We examined the ruins of Lacrofiade, Belvedere, and Ferme Peschier great houses and the prison boucan where the revolutionaries initially held the elite prisoners.

In November 2017, while climbing Fédon's Camp to ascertain the proximity of revolutionaries and British troops and the routes that the revolutionaries, prisoners, and British forces took, John Wells (Brother John) and his son Kenrick Harper (my cousin) were very patient with me. I struggled in the torrential rain, high wind, and poor visibility to keep up with them and complete the trek.

Brother John also accompanied me in January 2020 to visit Pilot Hill, Battle Hill, Soubise, and Post Royal — sites of major battles between Fédon's revolutionaries and Britishers.

And, I thank my contemporaries Henry Duncan, Ann Marshall, Elton Sylvester, Jacqueline Scoon, and Enoch Ragbarsingh for confirming sites and names in Belvedere and Fédon's Camp we absorbed when growing up among Belvedere's laborers.

I am grateful to the staff of the Grenada Supreme Court Registry's office for helping me locate documents. While chatting with Mrs. Xiomara Cherbin-Forsyth, Registrar, on a visit, I realized that she is the granddaughter of a schoolmate, Evelyn 'Bratt' Bullen. He was executed with Prime Minister Maurice Bishop and other dear friends by their colleagues which ended the Grenada Revolution of 1979-1983. Therefore, I hope Mrs. Cherbin-Forsyth uses her managerial position to ensure the 1979-1983 Revolution documents are catalogued and digitized.

Glenroy Andrews is exceptional. He takes pride in helping Grenadian and foreign researchers in their quest to research the nation's history. With great alacrity, Mr. Andrews assisted me to find deeds and indentures decaying in the poorly lit area. The government must make him "curator" of the 17th- and 18th-century documents. Fortunately, the documents were moved to a different building in 2020, but Covid-19 prevented me from visiting the new location.

I owe a wealth of gratitude to Winthrop Holder, a "Trini to the bone" and retired New York City schoolteacher, for reading and critiquing various chapters over the years.

Accolades to Eugene Sawney, a schoolmate, and his wife Lisda. Sawney preferred to read various drafts of the manuscript in print. Therefore, the task fell on Lisda to download the chapters, print hundreds of pages and then hand them to Eugene. In addition, she scanned his corrections and emailed them to me.

My sincere thanks to Nolan Paterson for reproducing numerous drafts and to Vally Sharpe of United Writers Press for her design of this book and preparing it for digital publishing.

Although I kept changing different cover concepts, sometimes telling him it is completed only to suggest changes later, Lennox Robinson—Saint Vincent-born and Trinidad-raised—kept his cool. Much praise to him for his illustration.

To Jane Zarem, who also edited *Belvidere Estate-Fedon's House*, you deserve a gold medal. Jane not only edited the manuscript of *Julien Fédon: Revolutionary, Patriot and Insurrectionist* but became fascinated about individuals and events such as "The Carys of Massachusetts," "Louis La Grenade," "Philippe-Rose Roume" and the naval battle off St. George's during the American Revolution. She went beyond editing responsibilities to verify facts. And she read the manuscript twice to make sure the writing flowed well in order to appeal to a wide public and consumer market.

Interchange of
Names & Spelling

To make this book as authentic as possible, people names and places are spelled how they were recorded in documents.

Belvedere and Belvidere Estate, Saint John – The same estate.

Belvedere House – Home of Marie and Julien Fédon and their two girls.

Belvedere Great House – Belvedere House or Julien Fedon's House, home of estate managers until the 1960s.

Chadeau or Madame Chadeau – The same estate in Mount Saint John; Chadeau is in the Parish of Saint John and boundary with Saint Andrew.

Fédon's Camp – This writer continues the tradition of Belvedere's laborers by calling Fédon's Military Headquarters overlooking Belvedere, 1st Camp and the highest peak of Morne Qua Qua, 2nd Camp. The laborers called the two camps or mountain peaks Fédon's Camp. However, 2nd Camp, Morne Vauclain, Camp of Death is officially named Fédon's Camp where a monument is erected.

Fedon's House – Also called Belvedere House.

Fedon's Military Headquarters, Camp Equality or 1st Camp – Cliffs over Belvedere where there were many huts occupied by Julien Fédon and close aides during the early months of the revolution. Valuables from British owned estates were brought there such as the rugs from Revolutionary Hall Great House.

Ferme Peschier and Madame Peschier – The same estate below 1st Camp on the Saint Andrew side.

Gouyave, Goyave, Charlotte Town, de'Lance, Gouyane - Same place.

Grand Pauvre – The town and Parish of Grand Pauvre; the town was renamed by the British, Victoria and the parish, Saint Mark.

La Baye – The original town of Grenville located in Soubise-Marquis area where the Revolution commenced.

Lacrofiade – An estate in Mount Saint John owned by Jean Fédon.

Morne Vauclain, Morne Qua Qua, Camp of Death, Fédon's Camp, 2nd Camp – Different names for the same place - the second highest mountain peak in Grenada.

Morne Qua Qua - A mountain range south of Belvedere with various peaks running east to west, from Saint Andrew to Saint John, and in boundary with Belvedere. Its highest peak is also called Morne Qua Qua or Fédon's Camp.

Morne Qua Qua (2) – It is not the Morne Qua Qua referred to in this book and during Fédon times although it is nearby. This Morne Qua Qua has two humongous volcanic rocks.

Mount Saint John – In boundary with Belvedere and north of Belvedere. In boundary with Saint Andrew. It consisted of various estates; the most popular ones were Madame Chadeau or Chadeau estate and Lacrofiade both the revolutionaries and British used as bases.

Madam Hook or Madame Hooks – The same estate.

Michel and Mitchel – A Fedon base east of Grand Etang lake located on the property of a mulatto.

Morne Jaloux – An estate in Mount Saint John once owned by Louis de La Grenade

Mulatto, people of color, mixed race – referring to the same people.

Notes

In my attempt to make this book enjoyable and informal while simultaneously presenting the formality of "Notes/Footnotes/Endnotes" for researchers and academic institutions, I did not provide "small numbers" or "note identifiers" for each quotation and reference within a paragraph. Instead, I provide a number at the end of the paragraph for quotations and references in that paragraph.

Introduction

1. *"a life of Marie Antoinette of France": Marie Antoinette* by Joan Haslip.

   "But I was told,": Ibid.

   "Hoping that in every generation": Ibid.

2. *"Hoping that this could be a small":* Dr. Edward L. Cox autographing, *Free Coloreds in the Slave Societies of St. Kitts and Grenada, 1763-1833* for Herman G. Hall, February, 1990.

3. *"Belvedere":* Meaning beautiful view coined by French and Italians centuries ago.

   "Belvidere": How the British spelled it in most documents.

   "rum talking": When Caribbean people are socializing and sipping rum.

4. *The West Indian:* Established by C.F.P.Renwick and T.A. Marryshow in 1915.

   "statehood": Conferring self-government by Great Britain to its Eastern Caribbean colonies in the 1960s; final constitutional change before the granting of independence during the 1970s-1980s.

5. *"History is written by winners":* Philippe Girard, *Toussaint Louverture: A Revolutionary Life*, p.3.

6. *"Until the lions have their own historians":* Chinua Achebe, Nigerian Author during 1994 interview with the *Paris Review.*

   "to listen at night for the sound of Fédon's white stallion": Oral stories by Grenadians and by Beverley A. Steele, *Grenada: A History of its People*, p.146.

7. *"While none of the British islands": Scotland, the Caribbean and the Atlantic World, 1750-1820* by Douglas J. Hamilton, p.38.

8. *"Emancipate yourself from mental slavery":* Marcus Garvey at public meeting, St. George's, Grenada, 1935 from M.Z. Mark, *The Struggle to Construct and Disseminate A Philosophy of Life.*

9. Jacques Chadeau capture: *Minutes of the Council, 28 May, 1808.* Grenada Registrar

   "a detachment of the Loyal Black Rangers": Grenada Handbook and Directory, 1897 and later editions.

   Point St. Eloi also called Cherry Hill.

10. Joachim Philip was betrayed on Petite Martinique: *The Registry, Grenada Supreme Court: Legislative Minutes, 1801-1817.* Also letter from Acting Governor Rev. Samuel Dent to Lord Robert Hobart, Secretary of State for War and the Colonies. British Colonial Office archive.

11. Also, see George Brizan's *Grenada: Island of Conflict.* p.80.

12. "65 estates @ £6,000 each": Francis M'Mahon, *A Narrative of the Insurrection in the Island of Grenada, in the year 1795.* p.128.

13. *"Monsters or rather devils in human shapes":* Henry Thornhill, *A Narrative of the Insurrection and Rebellion in the Island of Grenada from the Commencement to the Conclusion.* p.2.

14. Selwyn R. Cudjoe: *Beyond Boundaries: The Intellectual Tradition of Trinidad & Tobago in the Nineteenth Century.*

   Edward Lanza Joseph: *The Adventures of a Creole.* London: Saunders and Otley, M.DCCC.XXXVIII, 1838; edited in 2001 by Bridget Brereton, Rhonda Cobham, Mary Rimmer and Lise Winer Dunstan. UWI Press.

15. Dunbar Campbell: *Blood of Belvidere: A Grenada Novel.* 2013.

16. *"Times have changed, the circumstances are different":* Press conference at UN Plaza hotel, summer 1983.

Chapter 1: Pierre Fédon Departs France

1. *"FÉDON Pierre"* from Archives Nationales dossier f/b/39. On Pierre Fedon, see Curtis Jacobs, *The Fédons of Grenada, 1763-1814.*

2. *"Isle de La Grenade"* – The French name for Grenada.

3. Versailles – Home of French Monarchs.

4. West Indies – The original name for islands in the Caribbean Sea given by Christopher Columbus. West Indian - People born in the West Indies.

5. New World – The Americas and Caribbean referred to by 15th century explorers and after.

Chapter 2: Pierre & Brigitte Fédon in Grenada

1. Robert Melvill served in the Seven Years' War; governor of captured islands; Acting Governor of Grenada in 1764 and 1770-1771.

2. *"horned cattle…horses…sheep…mules:"* Oaths of Allegiance, Grand Pauvre, MS 166, Collection, Hamilton Beinecke College, NY, in the 1763 tax roll for Grand Pauvre; National Archives, Colonial Office archives, 101/1, p.26.

3. *"New or Adopted Subjects."* – How England described French nationals born or residing on its captured islands. See *Grenada Handbook and Directory,* 1897 and later editions.

4. French estate owners fled: The progenies of the fleeing rich French planters constituted the powerful French-Creole class for more than a century in Trinidad.

George Scott – Grenada's first British governor (1762-1764) when the conquered island was under military rule.

Spanish Trinidad – When Spain owned Trinidad until 1797 when the British conquered it.

5. "Pariosse of Grand Pauvre": British named it, Parish of Saint Mark.

6. deeded the property to their mother: *Registry - Grenada Supreme Court, French Deeds, 1787-1789.*

Chapter 3: Julien Fédon, Son of Grenada

1. *"Acte de marriage": The Registry, Grenada Supreme Court, Register for the Parish of Grand Pauvre, 1779-1783, p.2.*

2. *"Revalidé le marriage": Gouyave Register of Baptisms, marriages and burials.*

3. *"avons Realisé le marriage:": The Registry, Grenada Supreme Court, Register for the Parish of Grand Pauvre, 1779-1783.*

4. *"A mulatto of French"*: Edward Cox, *Free Coloreds in the Slave Societies of St. Kitts and Grenada, 1763-1833.* p.87. University of Tennessee Press, 1984.

   "With the exception of": Ibid., p.87.

5. *"A Certificate of Freedom"* issued to Marie Rose: Curtis Jacobs, *The Fédons of Grenada, 1763-1814.*

   "two of His Majesty's Justices": Ibid.

6. *"By John Hay and Walter Carew"*: Ibid.

7. *"I thought I had"*: Francis M'Mahon, *A Narrative of the Insurrection in the Island of Grenada, in the year 1795.* p.12.

8. *"beads from the mountains:"* As late as the 1960s, the trees flourished in Belvedere woodlands.

9. *"Fédon directed some…"*: Ibid., p.22.

Chapter 4: The Fédon Siblings

1. *"Mr. M'Mahon, Mr. Kerr"*: John Hay, *A Narrative of the Insurrection in the Island of Grenada: Which Took Place in 1795.* p.79.

2. *"24 juillet 1780": The Registry, Grenada Supreme Court, Register for the Parish of Grand Pauvre, 1779-1783, p.2.*

3. *"Mariage de jean Pierre Fédon"*: Ibid.

4. "Feydon": Ibid.

   "Foedon": Ibid.

5. *"Contract de Mariage de Jean feydon"*: *The Registry, Grenada Supreme Court, French records.*

6. *"le nommé Jean foedon"*: *The Registry, Grenada Supreme Court, Register for the Parish of Grand Pauvre*, p.4.

7. *"Ce jourd'hui vingt"*: Ibid.

8. *"Bapteme de margueritte Rose Anne foedon mestive"*: Ibid.

9. Kalinago -The people of Grenada who European colonizers met and annihilated. Europeans called them Caribs, Siboney and Arawak.

10. *"revalidé le mariage"*: Endangered Archives Project [EAP] 295/2/3/1 *Gouyave Register of Baptisms, marriages and burials.*

11. *"Nous soussigné Miss. Apost."*: Ibid.

12. *"agê aux environs"*: *The Registry, Grenada Supreme Court, Register for the Parish of Grand Pauvre, 1779-1783*, p.3.

13. For more about the Fedon-Cavelan marriages and baptisms, see Curtis Jacobs, *The Fédons of Grenada* and Tessa Murphy, *A Reassertion of Rights: Fedon's Rebellion, Grenada, 1795-96.*

Chapter 5: Battle off St. George's

1. Battle off St. George's - see *Grenada Handbook of 1897* or later editions thru 1945.

2 July 2, 1779: Ibid.

3. July 6, 1779: Ibid. Also see Richard Hiscocks, *American Revolutionary War 1776-1783.*

4. *"We have various reports here of fleets"*: *The Cary Papers Collection*, Massachusetts Historical Society, Boston. For further reading - *Sarah Gray Cary from Boston to Grenada: Shifting Fortunes of an American Family, 1764-1826* by Susan Clair Imbarrato.

5. *"The French war brought inconveniences"*: Ibid.

6. Returning to France, d'Estaing found himself embroiled in the French Revolution and guillotined by the Republicans for supporting Queen Marie-Antoinette. See Richard Hiscocks, *American Revolutionary War 1776-1783.*

7. Henri Christophe: Books about the Haitian Revolution provide Christophe' contributions.

Chapter 6: Fedon Family Manumits Slaves

1. Isaac Marseile, a 21-month-old baby: *The Registry, Grenada Supreme Court, Deed Book R1*, p.170-71.

2. *"Persons manumitting slaves"*: *The Laws of the British Colonies, in the West Indies and Other Parts of America, Concerning Real and Personal Property, and Manumission of Slaves: With a View of the Constitution of Each Colony* by John Henry Howard, 1827. National Library of Australia, p.60.

3. *"Guardians of Slaves"*: *The Registry, Grenada Supreme Court, Deed Book B2*, pp.109-111.

4. *"I, Louis Petit Monlauban"*: *The Registry, Grenada Supreme Court. Deed book*. p.29.

5. *"Negro Woman Slave…about thirty years old"*: Ibid., p.29.

6. *"all the privileges and advantages of a free-born subject of Great Britain"*: Ibid., p.29.

7. Julien and Marie Rose manumitted their slave, Louis: *The Registry, Grenada Supreme Court, Deed Book A2*. The couple manumitted eight slaves that day.

8. That same day, Julien's mother Brigitte: Ibid.

9. Julien Fédon also granted freedom to Guillaume: *The Registry, Grenada Supreme Court, Deed Book B2*, p.181-183.

   "not likely to become burdensome to the Public": Ibid.

10. And on July 10, 1791, Julien and Marie Rose: *The Registry, Grenada Supreme Court, Deed Book B2*, pp.109-111.

11. Eighty slaves were included: *The Registry, Grenada Supreme Court, Deed Book C4*.

12. Sold their Lancer property for £3,150: *The Registry, Grenada Supreme Court, Deed, Lancer Deed*. p.291.

   "those ten negroes and other slaves": *The Registry, Grenada Supreme Court, Deed, Lancer Deed Book C4*.

   In January 2020, the Lancer Deed was in fairly good condition at *The Registry, Grenada Supreme Court*. The deed begins on p.283 and a duplicate on p.180 in another deed book.

Chapter 7: Julien & Marie Rose Purchase Belvedere

1. that a copy never got to Lushington & Law: The deed remained in Grenada and was not sent to England. *The Registry, Grenada Supreme Court: Abstract of sundry Transactions to and by William Lushington and James Law Esqrs. and Lists of the Deeds in their possession*.

2. Court of Common Pleas: A British judicial system introduced in its colonies. After the 13 North colonies won their independence, the former colonies continued the system for civil and criminal cases.

3. Bosanquet & Fatio: A London based mortgage company.

   French planter Andrew Philippe, on April 13, 1773: See Donald Polson, *The Tolerated, the Indulged and the Contented: Ethnic Alliances and Rivalries in Grenadian Plantation Society 1763-1800*. A Thesis Submitted for the Degree of PhD at the University of Warwick. University of Warwick, 2011.

4. Madam Jacques: Ibid.

5. *"partly on Saint Dominique Street"*: https://discovery.nationalarchives.gov.uk.

6. *"Memorandum of Agreement"*: *The Registry, Grenada Supreme Court, Deed Book*. Up to January 2020, the documents were readable but decaying.

   "Julien Fédon of the Parish of Saint Mark": Ibid., *Deed Book C4*, p.252.

7. *"with the buildings thereon"*: Ibid., *Deed Book C4*, p.253.

8. *"And also all those other twenty negro and other slaves"*: Ibid., *Deed Book C4*, p.260.

   "female cattle": Ibid.

9. *"Dwelling houses and all outhouses, kitchens":* Ibid., *Deed Book C4*, p.286.

10. *"He, the said Julien Fedon":* Ibid., *Deed Book C4*, p.252.

11. *"The frenal sum of three thousand":* Ibid., *Deed Book C4*, p.254.

12. *"One thousand two":* Ibid., *Deed Book C4*, p.258, 267.

13. *"Received the day":* Ibid., *Deed Book C4*, p.282.

14. *"personally":* Ibid., *Deed Book C4.*

15. *"Towards the north with":* Ibid., *Deed Book* C4.

16. On ownership of Belvedere, see Curtis Jacobs, *The Fédons of Grenada, 1763-1814.*

Chapter 8: From Lancer to Belvedere

1. Fraze Estate: Like Belvedere, Fraze in the 21st century consists of small farming lots. It is the steep hill after leaving Belvedere going to Grenville or the long precipitous hill after leaving Chantilly going to Gouyave. The former great house was located on the plateau.
2. Lancer deed of the sale: The deed is detailed. It lists name and number of slaves, tools and buildings. *The Registry, Grenada Supreme Court, Deed Book C4*, p.283.
   "Twelve Quarries or thirty-eight acres": Ibid.
3. *"bounded ... towards the North by Tufton Hall Estate":* Ibid.
4. *"the west by lands of the Honourable William Smith Esquire":* Ibid.
5. *To Sarah Dean now living...":* 'William Smith of Grenada', *Legacies of British Slave-ownership database.*
6. *"the sum of five shillings of current money":* The Registry, Grenada Supreme Court, Deed Book C4, p.283.

Chapter 9: Exploiting the Fédons

1. not the deed for Belvedere: *The Registry, Grenada Supreme Court: Abstract of sundry. Transactions to and by William Lushington and James Law Esqrs. and Lists of the Deeds in their possession*, p.25. Many Lushington and Law transactions are in Deed Book, C4.

2. *"loan of £3,000 sterling to James Campbell Esquire":* Ibid.

3. *"fifty thousand pounds sterling money of Great Britain":* The Registry, Grenada Supreme Court, p.33.

3. Michael Scott: A member of the Grenada's Assembly owned lands near Belvedere.

4. *"Lushington and Law have no Title Deeds":* The Registry, Grenada Supreme Court: Abstract of sundry Transactions to and by William Lushington and James Law Esqrs. and Lists of the Deeds in their possession, p.25.

5. Essie Campbell and some siblings: Not the descendants of the Campbells of the 18th century.

6. *"Duncan Town":* Oral history.

   "Some people name Duncan": Oral history from Belvedere laborers and my mama, Lucy Adams, of the 1950s.

7. *"The shambolic handling"*: *Home of Wedderburn Manuscripts, National Archives of Scotland.* See also Douglas J. Hamilton, *Scotland, the Caribbean and the Atlantic World, 1750-1820.* p.68.

"fatal incorrectness." Ibid., p.68.

Chapter 10: Julien & Marie Rose Liable to Pinel Family

1. Copies of Monsieur Pinel's 1763 and Paterson's 1780 maps are in the Library of Congress and other archives.

2. The original 1780 map is in the John Carter Brown Library at Brown University, Providence, RI. The Centre for the Study of the Legacies of British Slavery, UCL, London, has made estates, lots and landmarks in Paterson's map easier to identify.

3. His estate totaled 249 acres: The various owners of Belvedere,1763-1792 especially the Mount Saint Clair section (Lot 31) is recorded in each deed created in 1792 between the Pinel children, James Campbell and Julian Fédon.

4. He sold the estate in 1775: Centre for the Study of the Legacies of British Slavery. https://discovery.nationalarchives.gov.uk

   Jean-Pierre Saulger: *A mulatto of French extraction.*

5. *"four hundred and fifty six acres"*: Included in 1792 deed - https://www.ucl.ac.uk.

6. *"five hundred pounds local currency"*: Ibid.

   "The said coffee and cocoa plantation": Ibid.

   "plantation slaves, stock and premises.": Ibid

7. By 1792, they were adults living in French Martinique and Tobago: Ibid.

8. *"legions of lawyers from some top Am Law 100 firms"*: law.com and *Wall St. Journal* 4/26/18.

9. *"This Indenture Tripartite made the Sixth Day of June"*: Centre for the Study of the Legacies of British Slavery, UCL, London: https://discovery.nationalarchives.gov.uk.

10. Grenada Court of Chancery in 1770: Ibid.

11. "The Honorable William Smith": Ibid.

Chapter 11: Scots In Control

1.*"By 1795, Grenada was divided"*: George Brizan, *Grenada: Island of Conflict, P 57.*

2. in 1766, 13 of the 21 seats in Grenada's: See, Douglas J. Hamilton, *Scotland, the Caribbean and the Atlantic World, 1750-1820.*

3. By 1795, almost every governor: Ibid., p.74.

4. Only four years later: Ibid., p.74-75.

5. Other British nobles who purchased: Ibid., p.66-67.

6. In 1722, Simon de Gannes: Gerard A. Besson, *The Cult of the Will*, p.34.

French Quebec: When France and England had colonies in what is now Canada.

7. Rosa de Gannes, a daughter of Simon de Gannes: See, Gerard A. Besson, *The Cult of the Will*, p.34.

married another French Creole: Ibid., p.35.

8. Rosa allowed her eldest son, 22-year-old Philippe-Rose Roume: Ibid., p.35.

9. Meanwhile, with the help of Francois Besson: Ibid., p.35.

10. See books on Roume's involvement in the Haitian Revolution.

11. *"I had the pleasure of"*: Douglas J. Hamilton, *Scotland, the Caribbean and the Atlantic World, 1750-1820*. p.174. Also, https://discovery.nationalarchives.gov.uk.

12. Dundas discussed Ninian Home: Ibid., p.174.

Chapter 12: White French Roman Catholics

1. Grenada's white French population: Edward L. Cox, *Free Coloreds in the Slave Societies of St. Kitts and Grenada - 1763-1833.* Cox provides census data of white French, French speaking mixed race and the enslaved population in Grenada.

2. free mulattos and free Africans owned about 8 percent: Ibid.

3. to exclude French Catholics from the legislature: Colonial Office and The Beinecke Lesser Antilles Collection at Hamilton College, NY.

4. In 1791, Saint Domingue's free mulattos: See C.L.R. James, *The Black Jacobins: Toussaint L'Ouverture and the San Domingo Revolution*. Also, Philippe Girard, *Toussaint Louverture: A Revolutionary Life* and other books about the Haitian Revolution.

5. warning to Britain about Saint Domingue came from Grenada: *British Colonial Office 101/32, Governor Mathews to Henry Dundas, Dec. 8, 1791.*

Chapter 13: People of Color

1. Free mulattos of French descent: Edward L. Cox, *Free Coloreds in the Slave Societies of St. Kitts and Grenada - 1763-1833.*

2. all afraid of the maroons: John Angus Martin, *Island Carib and French Settlers in Grenada*. A Grenada National Museum Book, 2013.

3. A 1763 survey revealed 455: Edward L. Cox, *Free Coloreds in the Slave Societies of St. Kitts and Grenada - 1763-1833*. p.14. Also, see British Colonial Office archives.

4. In 1763, there were 711 white British males: Ibid., p.24.

5. By 1777, Grenada's white male population was 1,034: Ibid., p.24.

6. In 1783, Grenada had 940 free French-speaking people of color: Ibid., p.81.

only 185 free English-speaking people of color: Ibid., p.81.

7. *quarteroon* in St. Domingue and a *quadroon* in Grenada: See, Philippe Girard, Edward L. Cox, Donald Polson, C.L.R. James and other researchers. They defined the percentage of European and African blood in people of color in their respective books.

8. In 1772, for example, free Africans owned: British Colonial Office files. Also, Edward L. Cox, *Free Coloreds in the Slave Societies of St. Kitts and Grenada - 1763-1833* and Donald Polson, *The Tolerated, the Indulged and the Contented: Alliances and Rivalries in Grenadian Plantation Society 1763-1800.*

9. "*Symbolic reward and signals*": Donald Polson, *The Tolerated, the Indulged and the Contented: Ethnic Alliances and Rivalries in Grenadian Plantation Society 1763-1800.* p.163.

10. "*This man was educated in England*": Dr. John Hay, *A Narrative of the Insurrection in the Island of Grenada: Which Took Place in 1795.* p.14.

11. "*the mulatto army established:*" C.L.R. James, *The Black Jacobins: Toussaint L'Ouverture and the San Domingo Revolution.* p.129.

12. In 1783, slaves owned by British planters totaled 16,240: Edward L. Cox, *Free Coloreds in the Slave Societies of St. Kitts and Grenada - 1763-1833*, p.81.

13. Carib leader Joseph Chatoyer: He led the revolt in St. Vincent during the Fédon's Revolution; Sir Ralph Abercromby crushed both revolts. See books about St. Vincent's history. Chatoyer is a national hero of St. Vincent and the Grenadines.

Chapter 14: Julien Fédon and the Americans

1. Bermuda sent a delegate, Henry Tucker: *National Historical Publications and Records Commission.*

2. such as Samuel Cary and Mather Byles of Massachusetts: *Samuel Cary Papers,* Massachusetts Historical Society, Boston. For further reading - *Sarah Gray Cary from Boston to Grenada: Shifting Fortunes of An American Family, 1764-1826* by Susan Clair Imbarrato.

3. send him to England as a traitor: *Samuel Cary Papers,* Massachusetts Historical Society, Boston.

Chapter 15: The Carys of Boston

1. *Cary Family Papers,* Massachusetts Historical Society, Boston.

2. About the Cary family, see Susan Clair Imbarrato *Sarah Gray Cary from Boston to Grenada, Shifting Fortunes of An American Family, 1764-1826.* Johns Hopkins University Press. 2018.

3. "*I give my House and Land in Boston … to my son Samuel Cary and his heirs for ever.*": Ibid. "*£2200 Stl £1000 in money the other in House and land.*" Ibid., p.45.

4. *"In January 1774, Sarah Gray Cary":* Ibid., p.1.

5. *"The negroes are more in awe":* Ibid., p.14.

6. *"The negroes came running to us":* Ibid., p.115.

7. *"My father's negroes proved all faithful:"* Samuel Cary Jr. *letters.* Massachusetts Historical Society, Boston.

8. *Cary, Jr.'s life is in jeopardy:* A member of the St. George's Regiment, Cary, Jr. was part of Captain Gurdon's troops that seized Gouyave during the first days of the rebellion.

   Promoted to a lieutenant. See Henry Thornhill, Esq., *A Narrative of the Insurrection and Rebellion in the Island of Grenada from the   Commencement to the Conclusion.* p.12.

   Also, Thomas Turner Wise, *A Review*, p.16.

   "I went up the other day with McCarthy": Shifting Fortunes of An American Family by Susan Clair Imbarrato, p.115.

9. *"If we are taken and have our slaves": Cary Family Papers*, Massachusetts Historical Society, Boston.

10. *"There was very little society":* Ibid., also see *Shifting Fortunes of An American Family* by Susan Clair Imbarrato, p.71.

11. *"on June 1, 1791, with seven of their children":* Ibid p.81.

12. *"a negro insurrection.": Cary Family Papers*, Massachusetts Historical Society, Boston.

Chapter 16: The Fédon Revolution Begins

1. Britishers on Front Street: Where the present police station, post office and court house are located.

2. *"uncommonly quiet, and many of their doors are shut":* John Hay, *A Narrative of the Insurrection in the Island of Grenada: Which Took Place in 1795.* p.21.

3. *La Baye:* The British called the town, Grenville Town. It was later moved to its present location.

4. *"Out of fifteen English inhabitants":* Gordon Turnbull, *A Narrative of the Revolt and Insurrection of the French Inhabitants in the Island of Grenada.* p.19.

5. Pierre Lavallée—*"a strong, active, good looking young man":* Francis M'Mahon, *A Narrative of the Insurrection in the Island of Grenada, in the year 1795.* p.13.

6. *"at the side of a precipice":* John Hay, *A Narrative of the Insurrection in the Island of Grenada: Which Took Place in 1795.* p.28.

7. *"only thirty-two":* Ibid., p.22.

   "thirteen commissioned officers": Ibid.

   "forty-six adopted subjects": Ibid.

Chapter 17: Fédon's First Steps and British Missteps

1. *"Vive la république:" (Long Live the Republic!)* John Hay, *A Narrative of the Insurrection in the Island of Grenada: Which Took Place in 1795.* p.44.

2. *"Julien Fédon, General:"* Communique from Fédon and Besson to the British administration in St. George's, March 4, 1795. Henry Thornhill, Esq., *A Narrative of the Insurrection and Rebellion in the Island of Grenada from the Commencement to the Conclusion.* Appendix II.

   "Besson, Officer of:" Ibid.

3. *"Joseph Le Blanc and Pierre Labat, whites":* John Hay, *A Narrative of the Insurrection in the Island of Grenada: Which Took Place in 1795.* p.23.

   "Etienne Ventour, Pillage, Antoine Roy": Ibid. p.23.

   "Mr. Olivier, a French gentleman": Francis M'Mahon, *A Narrative of the Insurrection in the Island of Grenada, in the year 1795.* p.12.

4. *"distressing scenes of murder:"* Henry Thornhill, Esq., *A Narrative of the Insurrection and Rebellion in the Island of Grenada from the Commencement to the Conclusion.* p.6.

5. *"Fédon was not:"* George Brizan, *Grenada: Island of Conflict.* p.80. Macmillan, 1998.

6. "Old House": A cultivated field growing nutmeg, coffee, cocoa, ground provision and bananas in the 20th century. The foundation of the coffee boucan where Governor Home and other prisoners were initially held and ruins of slave huts were still there.

7. *"to dress the wound":* John Hay, *A Narrative of the Insurrection in the Island of Grenada: Which Took Place in 1795.* p.31.

   "dangerously wounded": Ibid., p.31.

8. "set out in all directions": Ibid., p.35

9. "Royal Proclamation:" Henry Thornhill, Esq., *A Narrative of the Insurrection and Rebellion in the Island of Grenada from the Commencement to the Conclusion.* Appendix I.

10. Mackenzie dispatched to Belvedere, via Gouyave: Ibid. and in Gordon Turnbull, *A Narrative of the Revolt and Insurrection of the French Inhabitants in the Island of Grenada.* pp.43-44.

11 *"about 4 o'clock, p.M."* Ibid. p.44.

   "of rum, wine, and porter.": Ibid.

11. *"The negroes brought rum to the men from every house or hut that he passed":* A Brief Enquiry into the cause of, and conduct pursued by, the Colonial Government, for quelling the insurrection in Grenada. From its Commencement on the Night of 2nd of March, to the Arrival of General Nichols the 14th of April 1795. In a letter from a Grenada planter to a merchant in London. p.41.

   "the enemy … carried with them": Gordon Turnbull, *A Narrative of the Revolt and Insurrection of the French Inhabitants in the Island of Grenada.* p.44.

12. Jean Pierre Lavallee: Francis M'Mahon, *A Narrative of the Insurrection in the Island of Grenada, in the year 1795.* pp.25-28.

13. *"The Old Cemetery."* During the 1950s, Belvedere's laborers and their children including the author never ate fruits and harvested ground provisions from the Old Cemetery.

14. *"Marseillois Hymn and burning some English flags."* Francis M'Mahon, *A Narrative of The Insurrection in the Island of Grenada, in the year 1795.* p.29.

" feasting, dancing and singing.": John Hay, *A Narrative of the Insurrection in the Island of Grenada: Which Took Place in 1795.* p.47.

Africans give thanks to African deities: For the impact of African religions on Julien Fédon see Curtis Jacobs', *The Fédons of Grenada, 1763-1814.* Ph.D. thesis, UWI, 2002.

15. *"Seeing the state of the militia":* Letter from Captain Philip B. Gurdon to President K. F. Mackenzie. Gordon Turnbull, *A Narrative of the Revolt and Insurrection of the French Inhabitants in the Island of Grenada.* pp.45-46.

Chapter 18: Fédon Destroys Lindsay

1. *"He cannot rest in peace":* Stories by Belvedere' laborers of the 1950s including Abraham Simon.

2. *"[After Lindsay's] initial success:"* Colonial Office, London, letters from Kenneth Francis Mackenzie.

3. *"Exposing himself to, and going through":* Henry Thornhill, Esq., *A Narrative of the Insurrection and Rebellion in the Island of Grenada from the Commencement to the Conclusion.* p.16.

4 *"The General once had a fall from his horse":* Ibid.

5. *"a madman":* National Archives of Scotland: The Home Papers.

6. *manchineel:* Stories by Belvedere laborers of the 1950s.

"to drive him crazy": Ibid.

7. *"I confess":* Thomas Turner Wise, Esq. *A Review of the events, which have happened in Grenada, from the Commencement of the Insurrection to the 1st of May.* p.32.

8. *"Supreme Governor:"* Ibid.

9. *"From the first Moment":* Ibid., p.33.

10. *"The Mules, every one":* Ibid., p.37.

11. *"one hundred working Negroes":* Ibid., p.39.

"more Negroes and Mules": Ibid., p.39.

12. *"thought it proper to rest the troops":* Gordon Turnbull, *A Narrative of the Revolt and Insurrection of the French Inhabitants in the Island of Grenada.* p.72.

"This delay of only two hours": Ibid., p.72

13. *"We were marched along the pasture":* John Hay, *A Narrative of the Insurrection in the Island of Grenada: Which Took Place in 1795.* p.54.

14. *"I take it upon myself to spare your lives":* Ibid p.55.

15. *"Post at Fédon's House":* Gordon Turnbull, *A Narrative of the Revolt and Insurrection of the French Inhabitants in the Island of Grenada.* p.74.

"Post Before Belvidere House": Ibid., p.76.

16. *"Sir, upwards of one-half"*: Francis M'Mahon, *A Narrative of the Insurrection in the Island of Grenada, in the year 1795.* p.114.

    "I must request": Ibid.

17. *"He came out"*: Gordon Turnbull, *A Narrative of the Revolt and Insurrection of the French Inhabitants in the Island of Grenada.* p.78.

Chapter 19: No Time For Celebrating

1. *"We were then marched up a steep hill"*: John Hay, *A Narrative of the Insurrection in the Island of Grenada: Which Took Place in 1795.* p.56.

2. *"excessively cold and rainy"*: Ibid., p.57.

3. *"Fortune de la guerre"*: Ibid., p.57.

4. *"two or three glasses of Madeira"*: Ibid., p.57.

    "coloured people": Ibid., p.57.

5. *"two armed Spanish Brigs"*: Henry Thornhill, Esq., *A Narrative of the Insurrection and Rebellion in the Island of Grenada from the Commencement to the Conclusion.* p.12.

6. *"We began our march"*: John Hay, *A Narrative of the Insurrection in the Island of Grenada: Which Took Place in 1795.* p.61.

    "stand or sleep": Ibid., p.61.

7. *"their Commissary of war"*: Thomas Turner Wise, Esq., *A Review of the events, which have happened in Grenada, from the Commencement of the Insurrection to the 1st of May.* p.51.

8. *"on the 18th of March"*: *A Brief Enquiry into the Causes of, and Conduct pursued by the Colonial Government for quelling the Insurrection in Grenada…In a Letter from a Grenada Planter.* p.97.

9. *"Alexandre was tried by a Court Martial."*: Thomas Turner Wise, Esq., *A Review of the events.* p.55.

Chapter 20: British Blunders – Fédon's Ingenuity

1. *"a post is immediately"*: Gordon Turnbull, *A Narrative of the Revolt and Insurrection of the French Inhabitants in the Island of Grenada.* p.88, 84, 85.

2. "about 6,000 Negroes": Thomas Turner Wise, Esq., *A Review of the events.* p.54.

3. *"The critical situation of this island"*: Gordon Turnbull, *A Narrative of the Revolt and Insurrection of the French Inhabitants in the Island of Grenada.* p.88.

4. *"under the command"*: Ibid., p.87.

5. *"along with a"*: Ibid., p.87.

6. *"nine-pounder."* A cannon used in 18th century wars.

7. *"about one hundred men."* Gordon Turnbull, *A Narrative of the Revolt and Insurrection.* Ibid., p.88.

    "under the cover of a hill": Ibid., p.88.

8. *"hill called Telescope House"*: Ibid., p.89.

   "had two pieces of cannon": Ibid., p.88.

9. *"appeared so strong"*: Ibid., p.88.

   "They [the insurgents] evidently": Ibid., p.91.

10. *"took the fleet to Charlotte Town"*: p.93.

11. *"about two miles"*: Ibid., p.94.

12. *"with proper guides"*: Ibid., p.93.

13. *"with eight hundred"*: Ibid., p.96.

    "the camp before Belvedere": Ibid., p.96.

14. *"making war in the woods"*: John Hay, *A Narrative of the Insurrection.* p.46

15. *"Michel's does not lie"*: A Brief Enquiry into the cause of, and conduct pursued by, the Colonial Government, for quelling the insurrection in Grenada. From its Commencement on the Night of 2nd of March, to the Arrival of General Nichols, on the 14th of April 1795. In a letter from a Grenada planter to a merchant in London. p.164.

16. *"They were attacked"*: Ibid., p.161.

17. *"attacked by a negro"*: Ibid., p.162.

    "fell victim to the contagious fever": Gordon Turnbull, *A Narrative of the Revolt and Insurrection of the French Inhabitants in the Island of Grenada.* p.95.

18. *The night proving rainy"*: Ibid., p.142-145.

19. *"about two hundred yards from Grand* Étang *house"*: Ibid., p.151.

    Upon the whole": Henry Thornhill, *A Narrative of the Insurrection and Rebellion in the Island of Grenada from the Commencement to the Conclusion.* p.25.

    "not thinking it safe to proceed": Ibid., p.25.

20. *"had no fewer than four roads"*: A Brief Enquiry into the cause of, and conduct pursued by, the Colonial Government, for quelling the insurrection in Grenada. From its Commencement on the 2nd of March, to the Arrival of General Nichols, on the 14th of April 1795. In a letter from a planter to a merchant in London. p.164.

    "Grand Bras River": Ibid., p.164 and Gordon Turnbull, *A Narrative.* p.94.

21. *"great hardships, losing"*: Ibid., p.164 and Gordon Turnbull, *A Narrative.* p.95.

22. *"future operations"*: Ibid Gordon Turnbull, *A Narrative.* p.97.

    "an immediate attack upon": Henry Thornhill, *A Narrative of the Insurrection and Rebellion in the Island of Grenada from the Commencement to the Conclusion.* p.26 and *A Brief Enquiry into the cause. Letter from a Grenada planter to a merchant in London. p.178-180.*

23. *"the attack proposed might"*: Ibid.

24. *"From the best authority"*: Ibid.

    "very few fireworks": Ibid.

25. *"the best authority possible"*: Ibid.

26. *"the most favorable opportunity"*: Ibid.

    "Success seems now": Ibid.

Chapter 21: Night of April 7, 1795

1. *"From the strict guard"*: Francis M'Mahon, *A Narrative of the Insurrection in the Island of Grenada, in the year 1795.* p.35.

2. *"making war in the woods."* John Hay, *A Narrative of the Insurrection in the Island of Grenada.* p.46.

3. *"1st That the prison"*: Ibid., p.67.

4. *"The General, his Secretary"*: Ibid., p.72.

5. *"Ollivier brought some canes"* Ibid., p.72.

   "but must gradually extend to every corner of the globe" Ibid., p.73.

6. *"the tyrannical government of Home"*: Ibid., p.74.

7. *"the health of all the ladies at Good Chance"*: Ibid., p.72. Located near 21st century Ferme Peschier and Morne Longue.

8. *"a mattress was allotted"*: Ibid., p.73.

9. *"Fédon was first in bed"*: Ibid., p.73.

10. *"Fédon slept in his clothes, with his pistols"*: Ibid., p.72.

11. *"A guard was provided"*: Ibid., p.74.

12. *"I could well perceive that"*: Francis M'Mahon, *A Narrative of the Insurrection in the Island of Grenada, in the year 1795.* p.34.

    "I was ordered from my hut": Ibid., p.35.

13. *"On the afternoon of the 7th of April"*: John Hay, *A Narrative of the Insurrection in the Island of Grenada: Which Took Place in 1795.* p.75.

    "the truth of the report": Ibid., p.75.

14. *"Neither was the door"*: Francis M'Mahon, *A Narrative of the Insurrection in the Island of Grenada, in the year 1795.* p.35-36.

15. *"The prisoners passed"*: Ibid., p.36.

16. *"They had cut down the face of the Hill"*: Ibid., p.34.

Chapter 22: Massacre

1. *"Captain Joseph, the General orders"*: Francis M'Mahon, *A Narrative of the Insurrection in the Island of Grenada, in the year 1795.* p.36.

2. *"Monster of Monsters"*: Thomas Turner Wise, Esq. *A Review of the events, which have happened in Grenada, from the Commencement of the Insurrection to the 1st of May.* p.85.

3. *"Julien Fédon and his nefarious"*: Ibid., p.100.

4. *"The mind is struck"*: Gordon Turnbull, *A Narrative of the Revolt and Insurrection of the French Inhabitants in the Island of Grenada.*

5. *"composed of the corps of seamen"*: Henry Thornhill, *A Narrative of the Insurrection and Rebellion in the Island of Grenada from the Commencement to the Conclusion.* p.26 and *A Brief Enquiry into the cause.* p.27-28.

6. *"two Grenadier Companies":* Ibid., p.28 and in report from General Campbell to General Vaughan in Martinique.

7. *"got within 20 yards of the gun, when he fell"* Ibid., p.28.

8. *"rolled large stones upon our men":* report from Campbell to General Sir John Vaughan. *"The troops now being exposed":* Ibid.

9. *"Camp of Death," "Camp of Equality"* and *"Camp of Liberty":* John Hay, *A Narrative of the Insurrection in the Island of Grenada: Which Took Place in 1795.* p.78.

10. *"I counted ten men killed":* Ibid. p.80.

11. *"The failure of the enterprise":* Gordon Turnbull, *A Narrative of the Revolt and Insurrection of the French Inhabitants in the Island of Grenada.* p.100.

12. *"were raw and undisciplined young men":* Ibid., p.100.

13. *"Soldiers … threw down":* John Hay, *A Narrative of the Insurrection in the Island of Grenada Which Took Place in 1795.* p.79.

14. *"He [Fédon] observed to me":* Ibid., p.78.

15. uprooted trees, shrubs, and boulders: Curtis Jacobs in *The Fedons of Grenada* believes Fédon followed tactics used in African wars.

16. *"impatient":* Thomas Turner Wise, Esq. *A Review of the events, which have happened in Grenada, from the Commencement of the Insurrection to the 1st of May.* p.88.

    "General Campbell says": Henry Thornhill, *A Narrative of the Insurrection and Rebellion in the Island of Grenada from the Commencement to the Conclusion.* P .29.

17. *"The President, having":* Report from Lt. Col. Campbell to General Vaughan in Martinique.

18. *"At one time, the firing":* Francis M'Mahon, *A Narrative of the Insurrection in the Island of Grenada, in the year 1795.* p.36.

    "Captain Joseph, the General orders you": Ibid., p.36.

19. *"the firing appeared nearer to us":* Ibid., p.36.

20. *"The Fall of Fédon's brother":* Thomas Turner Wise, Esq. *A Review of the events, which have happened in Grenada, from the Commencement of the Insurrection to the 1st of May.* p.93.

21. *"to have mercy on the innocent":* John Hay, *A Narrative of the Insurrection in the Island of Grenada: Which Took Place in 1795.* p.76.

    "They have none on our people below": Ibid.

22. *"but his [Fédon's] principal motive":* Gordon Turnbull, *A Narrative of the Revolt and Insurrection of the French Inhabitants in the Island of Grenada.* p.103.

23. *"Fédon began the bloody":* John Hay, *A Narrative of the Insurrection in the Island of Grenada: Which Took Place in 1795.* p.76.

24. except for Wilson Ravine: Oral history from Belvedere laborers of the 1950s and before. (The ravine separates Belvedere from Fraze. On Belvedere's Main Road on reaching Wilson Ravine, one continues to Fraze leading to Birchgrove and Grenville; or, one can follow the road to the right leading to Ferme Peschier, Morne Longue and Fédon's Camp.)

Chapter 23: Pilot Hill

1. *"where the others were"*: *A Brief Enquiry into the cause of, and conduct pursued by, the Colonial Government, for quelling the insurrection in Grenada. From its Commencement on the Night of 2ⁿᵈ of March, to the Arrival of General Nichols, on the 14ᵗʰ of April 1795. In a letter from a Grenada planter to a merchant in London.* p.177.

2. *"In every instance"*: Gordon Turnbull, *A Narrative of the Revolt and Insurrection of the French Inhabitants in the Island of Grenada.* p.111.

3. *"a general officer, vested"*: Ibid.

4. *"None could be more pleased"*: Ibid., p.112.

   "He was, by the arrival": Ibid.

5. *"the enemy from Pilot Hill"*: Ibid., p.113.

6. *"ordered a detachment"*: Ibid.

7. *"three hundred faithfuls and trusty"*: Henry Thornhill, *A Narrative of the Insurrection and Rebellion in the Island of Grenada from the Commencement to the Conclusion.* p.32.

8. *"Two gun-boats, each"*: Gordon Turnbull, *A Narrative of the Revolt and Insurrection of the French Inhabitants in the Island of Grenada.* p.115-116.

   "with about nine hundred troops": Ibid.

Chapter 24: Fédon Takes Back Gouyave

1. *"at the first cock-crow"*: John Hay, *A Narrative of the Insurrection in the Island of Grenada: Which Took Place in 1795.* p.132.

2. *"My return astonished"*: Ibid., p.127.

3. *"I proceeded to Guyave by water"*: Ibid.

4. *"rat-hole."* Ibid., p.138.

   "Whereas, from the lenity": Ibid.

5. *"the cry of Vive la République"*: Ibid., p.135.

   "at the first cock crow": Ibid., p.132.

6. *"and negroes…savage to a degree"*: Ibid., p.137.

7. *"Monster of all Monsters"*: Turner Wise, P87.

   "the men from Guadaloupe": John Hay, *A Narrative of the Insurrection.*, p.137.

8. *"although the hill above Gouyane House"*: *The Cary Papers*, Massachusetts Historical Society.

9. *"the loss of the important port of Gouyave"*: Henry Thornhill, *A Narrative of the Insurrection.*, p.40.

Chapter 25: The Enigmatic Julien Fédon

1. partly the result of fiction writers: Novels by Edward Lanza Joseph, David Franklyn, Dunbar Campbell and others.

2. Europe to Australia, have cited Fédon's Revolution: Kit Candlin, Michael Duffy, Douglas Hamilton, George Brizan, Beverley A. Steele, Curtis Jacobs, Tessa Murphy and others.

Chapter 26: Governor Ninian Home

1. *"Here you, Home Tyrant of the French"*: Francis M'Mahon, *A Narrative of the Insurrection.*

   makeshift prison, a two-floor boucan: The ruins of the prison, a coffee boucan, were there in 2020.

2. *"to surrender, and to offer honourable terms"*: John Hay, *A Narrative of the Insurrection in the Island of Grenada: Which Took Place in 1795.* p.34.

   "Being their prisoner": Ibid.

3. *"to put all the prisoners to death"*: Ibid., p.37; also, in the letter from prisoners to Mackenzie dated Camp at Belvidere, Friday, March 6, 1795.

4. "at so late an hour": Ibid., p.46.

5. *"The island was theirs by right"*: Ibid., p.46-47.

6. "one of the thirteen Scots": Douglas J. Hamilton, *Scotland, the Caribbean and the Atlantic World, 1750-1820* p.173-174. Also, *Home of Wedderburn Manuscripts, National Archives of Scotland.*

7. *"White people are much wanted in this island"*: *Home of Wedderburn Manuscripts,* National Archives of Scotland.

   "For many of the French": Ibid.

8. French Royalists: French citizens loyal to the French monarch.

9. A 1764 deed is the first evidence: In January 2021, the deed was still at *The Registry, Grenada Supreme Court.*

10. *"indenture of three parts between John Reubin"*: Ibid.

11. *"the Names of the Negroes"*: Ibid.

12. *"from the sands of the sea"*: Ibid.

13. *"11 quarries of land"*: Ibid.

    "10 quarries, 32 acres": Ibid.

14. *"between the Honorable Ninian Home of the said island of Grenada, Esq"*: Ibid., Deed book, H1, p.247.

15. *"the island is to be saved"*: Gordon Turnbull, *A Narrative of the Revolt and Insurrection of the French Inhabitants in the Island of Grenada.* p.59.

    "united exertions": Ibid.

16. *"the instant an attack is made"*: Francis M'Mahon, *A Narrative of the Insurrection in the Island of Grenada, in the year 1795.* p.124.

17. "St. George's, 6th March 1795": Gordon Turnbull, *A Narrative of the Revolt and Insurrection of the French Inhabitants in the Island of Grenada.* p.59.

    "The island is to be saved by your": Ibid

18. *"I have the mortification":* Letter From a Grenadian Planter in: *A Brief Enquiry into the causes of, and conduct pursued by, the Colonial Government for Quelling the Insurrection in Grenada: From the Night of the 2nd of March, to the Arrival of General Nichols on the 14th of April 1795.*

19. It was Oronoko, a house slave: Francis M'Mahon, *A Narrative of the Insurrection in the Island of Grenada, in the year 1795.* p.18.

20. "De people in Town": Stories told to the author by his Papa, Frederick Adams, and other laborers.

Chapter 27: Victor Hugues

1. *"from which it is evident":* John Hay, *A Narrative of the Insurrection in the Island of Grenada: Which Took Place in 1795.* p.53.

2. *"50 Negroes with cutlasses":* Thomas Turner Wise, Esq. *A Review of the events, which have happened in Grenada, from the Commencement of the Insurrection to the 1st of May.* p.78.

3. *"swords and pistols":* John Hay, *A Narrative of the Insurrection in the Island of Grenada.* p.43.

4. *"We summon you, and all the Inhabitants":* Henry Thornhill, *A Narrative of the Insurrection and Rebellion in the Island of Grenada from the Commencement to the Conclusion.* Appendix II.p.2.

5. *"Declaration":* Ibid, p.3.

6. *"la Déclaration ci-jointe":* Thomas Turner Wise, Esq. *A Review of the events.* p.9.

7. *"It was probably owing to the success":* Gordon Turnbull, *A Narrative of the Revolt and Insurrection of the French Inhabitants in the Island of Grenada.* p.15.

8. *"probably":* Ibid.

9. *"All men living in the colonies":* The entire declaration is in the French and other archives.

10. *"We are pained to see how divided you are":* Archives Nationales, Paris. p.246. John Debrett, *A Collection of State Papers Relative to the War Against France* (J. Debrett, 1796), v.3, 2: 170172; Fr.

    Fr. Raymund Devas, *A History of the Island of Grenada, 1498-1796.*

11. *"We reiterate that as long as your":* Ibid.

Chapter 28: Philippe-Rose Roume

1. a guest at his wedding to Marie-Anne Elisabeth Rochard: Philippe Girard, *Toussaint Louverture,* p.180.

2. *This Indenture made the Sixteenth Day of February": In January 2021, the deed was still at The Registry, Grenada Supreme Court.* p.257 in a deed book.

3. *"Roume was not even a Frenchman":* C.L.R. James, *The Black Jacobins Toussaint L'Ouverture and the San Domingo Revolution.* p.273.

4. *"Proclamation au nom de la République"*: Proclamation in the name of the Republic, the law and the King, *"by Philbert-François Rouxel de Blanchelande and Philippe Rose Roume, February 11, 1791: p.53-56.*

Chapter 29: Toussaint Louverture

1. *"Louverture alone left behind"*: Philippe Girard, *Toussaint Louverture,* p.3.

2. On Louverture's family, see Philippe Girard, *Toussaint Louverture.* Basic Book, NY. 2016.

3. Dutty Boukman was a self-emancipated African from nearby British Jamaica.

4. "Haiti": The name the indigenous Taíno called their island.

5. *"chose some of the bravest slaves"*: C.L.R. James, *The Black Jacobins: Toussaint L'Ouverture and the San Domingo Revolution.* p.129

Chapter 30: Louis La Grenade

1. *"I am glad you are safe"*: Francis M'Mahon, *A Narrative of the Insurrection in the Island of Grenada, in the year 1795.* p.38.

   "not blame La Grenade": Ibid.

   "they had always": Ibid.

2. *"Louis La Grenade"*: A candid evaluation of La Grenade can be found in Edward L. Cox, *Free Coloreds in the Slave Societies of St. Kitts and Grenada, 1763-1833.*

3. *"I have had some conversation"*: *Colonial Office Archives,* London.

4. *"He never conspired"*: Herman Hall, *Belvedere Estate, Fedon's House.* p.143.

5. He once invoiced the government for £935. 5s: *Colonial Office Archives,* London.

6. *"from the best authority possible"*: Henry Thornhill, *A Narrative of the Insurrection.* p.26.

7. *"the Colored People ought"*: Gordon Turnbull, *A Narrative of the Revolt and Insurrection of the French Inhabitants in the Island of Grenada.* p.32.

8. *"Provision for myself and family"*: Edward L. Cox, *Free Coloreds in the Slave Societies of St. Kitts and Grenada, 1763-1833.* p.149.

   "enjoy every Privilege as a free white person.": Letter from Louis La Grenade to Assembly, July 6, 1776. Colonial Office archives, London.

   "pair of pistols valued at fifty guineas and a sword": Edward L. Cox, *Free Coloreds in the Slave Societies of St. Kitts and Grenada, 1763-1833.* p.149.

9. *"From Louis Lagrenade et al"*: http://founders.archives.gov/documents/Washington/05-07-02-0151, Univerity Press of Virginia. pp.274-277.

10. *"We The free Coloured Individuals"*: Ibid.

11. *"the very unexpected address"*: GW to Jefferson, 15 June 1791., Ibid.

   "are parties in a domestic quarrel": See *The Papers of Thomas Jefferson,* Princeton University Press.

Chapter 31: Self-Emancipated Africans

1. *"as free as he was"*: John Hay, *A Narrative of the Insurrection in the Island of Grenada: Which Took Place in 1795.* p.28.

2. *"armed with pikes, some mounted with iron"*: Ibid, p.42.

   "Upon my entering the gate": Ibid. p.52.

3. *"two slaves named L'autriment and Vincent"*: British Colonial Office Archives. *Better Treatment of Slaves and for the More Speedy and Effectual Suppression of Runaway Slaves,* 10 December 1766. Also, see, Edward L. Cox, *Free Coloreds in the Slave Societies of St. Kitts and Grenada, 1763-1833,* p.34 and Donald Polson, *The Tolerated, the Indulged and the Contented:* University of Warwick, 2011.

   "Pompey, the chief of runaway Negroes": Edward L. Cox, *Free Coloreds in the Slave Societies* p.34.

4. *"perfectly acquainted with the mode"*: John Hay, *A Narrative of the Insurrection in the Island of Grenada.* p.46.

5. *St. George's Chronicle* and *New Grenada Gazette* issues of 19 August 1790: Beverley A. Steele, *Grenada: A History of its People,* p.72.

6. Samuel Cary, Jr.: *The Cary Papers Collection,* Massachusetts Historical Society, Boston.

Chapter 32: 1796 - A Turning Point

1. *"making war in the woods"*: John Hay, *A Narrative of the Insurrection* p.46.

2. La Sagesse, La Tante, Spitze des Fort Jeudi, Petit Bacaye and Isles Caliveny. See maps of French Grenada.

Chapter 33: Divided Purposes

1. *"Citizen Goyrand one of"*: Letter from Sugue to General Nicolls, Henry Thornhill, *A Narrative of the Insurrection and Rebellion in the Island of Grenada.* Appendix p.11.

2. *"concern that many black citizens"*: Ibid., p.13.

3. *"have been hanged"*: Ibid.

4. *"To Citizen FEYDON"*: *Archives Nationales,* Paris; and Fr. Raymund Devas, *A History of the Island of Grenada, 1498-1796.*

5. *"I come to take the chief command"*: John Hay, *A Narrative of the Insurrection in the Island of Grenada: Which Took Place in 1795.* p.81.

6. *As soon as it was light": William Dyott's Diary 1781-1845,* p.90.

7. Joseph Chatoyer, the Carib leader in Saint Vincent: He battled the British in 1795-96.

Chapter 34: The Battle for Post Royal

1. *"A strong Party of Regulars and Militia:"* Henry Thornhill, *A Narrative of the Insurrection and Rebellion in the Island of Grenada from the Commencement to the Conclusion.* p.43.

2. *"a captain, 50 British soldiers":* William Dyott's Diary 1781-1845, p.97.

   "The party marched at four o'clock": Ibid., p.98.

3. *"We marched all night and":* Ibid., p.99.

4. *"A few shots fired by the black corps":* Ibid.

5. *"I was ordered on to their support":* Ibid.

6. *"He was determined to move":* Ibid.

   "We had proceeded about half a mile": Ibid.

7. *"The next day":* Ibid., p.100.

   "During the night of the 24ᵗʰ and": Ibid.

8. *"intensely hot.":* Ibid., p.104.

   "The flames from the huts": Ibid., p.102.

9. *"The consequence was the light infantry": Ibid., p.103.*

10. *"valiant defence of Post Royal."* Ibid.

    "about eight hundred men": Henry Thornhill, *A Narrative of the Insurrection and Rebellion in the Island of Grenada from the Commencement to the Conclusion.* p.45.

11. *"March 26ᵗʰ - Employed in burying the dead":* William Dyott's Diary 1781-1845, p.104.

12. *"The negroes and people of colour":* Ibid.

Chapter 35: Gouyave Falls

1. Adjutant General John Hope from Saint Lucia: He arrived in Grenada on May 28, 1796. Henry Thornhill, *A Narrative of the Insurrection and Rebellion* p.46.

2. *"between three and four thousand men":* Ibid.

   "his orders and instructions": Ibid.

3. *"the reinforcement that had arrived from":* Ibid.

4. *"That the English troops employed":* John Hay, *A Narrative of the Insurrection in the Island of Grenada.* p.78.

5. *"with his troops from Carriacou":* Henry Thornhill, *A Narrative of the Insurrection.* p.46.

6. "Charlotte Town": Named after Queen Charlotte, wife of King George III.

Chapter 36: Where's Julien Fédon?

1. *"Belvedere is in the back of Dougaldston":* Heard by the author growing up in Belvedere.

2. *River Turning.":* A cultivated field consisting of nutmeg, banana, coffee and cocoa during the 1960s and before.

Chapter 37: Where's Julien Fédon Family?

1. "Attained Traitors": The British compiled a list of revolutionaries to arrest and execute them.

    Court of Oyer and Terminer: To try and execute revolutionaries.

2. *"A negro boy was disposing of coffee"*: John Hay, *A Narrative of the Insurrection in the Island of Grenada: Which Took Place in 1795.* p.29.

3. *"He began the bloody massacre"*: Ibid., p.76.

4. *"His wife, observing"*: Ibid., p.80.

5. *"A la Gaol a 10 aout 1796…"* (At the jail August 10, 1796): *National Archives, London.*

Chapter 38: General Abercromby on Belvedere's Border

1. *"On the 16ᵗʰ General Sir Ralph Abercromby"*: Henry Thornhill, *A Narrative of the Insurrection*, p.47, and in *William Dyott's Diary 1781-1845*, p.115.

2. *"He took an opportunity of thanking"*: Ibid., p.47. Henry Thornhill, *A Narrative.*

3. "strictly forbade any negotiating": Ibid.

4. *"The Atrocity of his Character and the Cruelties."* *William Dyott's Diary 1781-1845.*

5. *Grenada Handbook of 1946* and before. p.34.

6. *"On the 16ᵗʰ"*: *William Dyott's Diary 1781-1845.* p.115 and Henry Thornhill, *A Narrative* p.47.

Chapter 39: Fédon is Encircled

1. *"Three villains (Dutchmen)"*: *William Dyott's Diary 1781-1845*, p.108.

2. *"My tent, I believe"*: Ibid., p.109.

3. *"Having nothing to dread"*: Ibid., p.107.

4. *"Our march for the last three miles"*: Ibid., p.111.

5. *"After marching twenty-one hours"*: Ibid., p.110.

6. *"he and his associates were to be sent"*: Ibid., p.114.

7. *"It rained almost incessantly"*: Ibid., p.113.

8. *"The first three miles I had"*: Ibid., p.116.

9. *"having trees felled across it"*: Ibid.

10. *"There was a curious circumstance"*: Ibid., p.117.

Chapter 40: Battles for Mitchel and Madame Ache's

1. *"We took possession of their camps"*: Ibid., p.117.

   "After we got into our huts": Ibid., p.117.

2. *"We had a very fatiguing march"*: Ibid., p.118.

3. *"We passed what is called the Grand Étang"*: Ibid.

4. *"The Yougers and light infantry"*: Ibid.

5. *"literally in the form of a pig's back"*: Ibid.

   "picked off several of the Yougers": Ibid., p.119.

   "I was with General Campbell": Ibid.

6. *"It is astonishing"*: Ibid.

7. *"After two days' severe harassing marches"*: Ibid.

8. *"On the 20th, the day after"*: Ibid., p.120.

9. *"Massacre, plunder"*: Sir John William Fortescue: *MacMillan's Magazine*, October, 1894.

10. *"subscribed for a Sword"*: Henry Thornhill, *A Narrative of the Insurrection*. p.48.

Chapter 41: Hunting for Fédon

1. *"By these last very important successes"*: Henry Thornhill, *A Narrative of the Insurrection*. p.48.

2. *Fédon himself"*: Major General Thomas Graham Papers*. National Archives of Scotland; also see Curtis Jacobs, *"Flight into legend: the last sighting of Julien Fédon in Grenada."*

3. My papa, Frederick Adams: Adopted father of author. Additional information: Herman Hall's *Belvidere Estate-Fédon's House*.

4. Morne Golette: An area in Morne Qua Qua Mountain range west of 1st Camp.

5. *"Rather den surrendering"*: Oral account by Frederick Adams and other laborers.

6. *"object, and that of the few remaining"*: Letter to Major General Thomas Graham*. National Archives of Scotland.

7. *"situated on the brink of a precipice"*: Father Raymund Devas, *Up Hill and Down Dale in Grenada* (St. George's, Grenada, and London: Sands and Co., 1926), p.14. National Archives of Scotland.

Chapter 42: Julien Fédon: Fact & Fiction

1. *"A Great many Misconceptions having been entertained":* Thomas Turner Wise, Esq. *A Review of the events, which have happened in Grenada from the Commencement of the Insurrection to the 1st of May.*

2. *"that the French had landed":* Henry Thornhill, *A Narrative of the Insurrection and Rebellion.* p.3.

   "No French have landed at La Baye": Gordon Turnbull, *A Narrative of the Revolt.* Letter from Governor Ninian Home to his Secretary. p.32.

3. *"I was awakened by a violent":* John Hay, *A Narrative of the Insurrection.* p.23.

4. *"General insurrection of French Free Coloured people:* Colonial Office Archives, London.

5. *"Numbers of negroes and parties":* John Hay, *A Narrative of the Insurrection.*

6. *"My father's negroes proved all faithful":* Cary Family Papers, Massachusetts Historical Society.

   "a slave revolt": Ibid.

7. *"before the Grenada slave revolts of 1795–1796":* Susan Clair Imbarrato, *Sarah Gray Cary from Boston to Grenada.* Johns Hopkins University Press, 2018. Ch. 4.

8. *"Besides, supposing the poor negro-man":* A Brief Enquiry Into The Causes Of: In a Letter from a Grenada Planter. London, 1796. p.51.

Bibliography

Archival sources about the early life of Julien Fédon do not exist or are still to be found. There is no formal collection one can refer to as, "The Julien Fédon Papers" or "The Fédon's Rebellion/Revolution Papers." Documents written during 1795-1796 and years later about Julien Fédon, the Fédon's Rebellion or Revolution are housed in institutions such as the Massachusetts Historical Society, Syracuse University, archives in the United Kingdom, France and the U.S.

The principal archival source is the Registrar's Office in Grenada where one can find the deeds of Julien and Marie Rose Fédon estate transactions and marriage and birth certificates of some Fédon family members. The documents are not cataloged. They are scattered and bundled with other documents. The papers are brittle and disintegrate when one touches them. I understand the Mormons a few years back photographed the documents. Professor Curtis Jacobs also photographed some of the decaying documents for educational institutions in the UK to digitize. Those institutions such as Center for the study of Legacies of British Slavery administered by the University of London (UCL) and University of Manchester are releasing them. The Grenada Plantation Records dating from 1737-1845 are held in the repository of the custodians Schomburg Center for Research in Black Culture, Manuscripts, Archives and Rare Books Division.

In describing the battle sites, this writer used his thorough knowledge of the landscape and areas where they occurred and oral stories of Belvedere Estate laborers of the 1930s-1960s.

Manuscript and Archival Sources

- Boston Public Library, Ma.
- Center for the Study of the Legacies of British Slavery, London
- Massachusetts Historical Society, Ma.
- Registrar's Office, The Registry of the Supreme Court, St. George's, Grenada.
- The Schomburg Center for Research in Black Culture, NY
- The Papers of Thomas Jefferson – Princeton University, NJ

Books

Anonymous - Wise, Thomas Turner. *A Review of the events, which have happened in Grenada, from the Commencement of the Insurrection to the 1ˢᵗ of May.* St. George's, Grenada, 1795.

Benjamin, John. *Short History of Grenada.* St. George's, Grenada, 1991.

Brizan, George. *Grenada: Island of Conflict.* Oxford: Macmillan Caribbean, 1998.

Cox, Edward. *Free Coloreds in the Slave Societies of St. Kitts and Grenada 1763–1833.* University of Tennessee Press, Knoxville, 1984.

Cudjoe, Selwyn R. *Beyond Boundaries, The Intellectual Tradition of Trinidad & Tobago in the Nineteenth Century.* University of Massachusetts Press, 2003.

Devas, Raymund. *Up Hill and Down Dale in Grenada.* Sands, London, Edinburgh and Glasgow, 1926.

Devas, Raymund. *Conception Island or The Troubled History of the Roman Catholic Church in Grenada.* (London: Sands & Co., 1932),

Devas, Raymund. *A History of the Island of Grenada, 1498-1796.* St. George's, Grenada, 1964.

Drayton, Edward. Compiler and Colonial Secretary. *The Grenada Handbook, Directory and Almanac for the year 1897.* Sampson Low, Marston & Co., London, 1897.

Duffy, Michael. *Soldiers, Sugar, and Seapower: The British expeditions to the West Indies and the War against Revolutionary France.* New York, Oxford University Press, 1987

Girard, Philippe. *Toussaint Louverture: A Revolutionary Life*. Basic Books, NY, 2016.

Hall, Herman G. *Fedon's House–Belvidere Estate: Voices from the Past*. HH Digital, 2016.

Hamilton, Douglas, J. *Scotland, the Caribbean and the Atlantic World, 1750-1820*. Manchester University Press, 2005.

Haslip, Joan. *Marie Antoinette*. New York, 1987

Hay, John. *A Narrative of the Insurrection in the Island of Grenada Which Took Place in 1795*. London: J. Ridgeway, 1823.

Hiscocks, Richard. *American Revolutionary War 1776-1783*.

Imbarrato, Susan Clair. *Sarah Gray Cary: From Boston to Grenada - Shifting Fortunes of an American Family - 1764-1826*. Johns Hopkins University Press. 2018.

James, C.L.R. *The Black Jacobins Toussaint L'Ouverture and the San Domingo Revolution*. New York: Vintage Books, 1963.

Jeffrey, Reginald. *W. J. Dyott's Diary 1781-1845: A selection from the journal of William Dyott*. London: Archibald, Constable and Company, 1907.

Joseph, Edward Lanza. *Warner Arundell. The Adventures of a Creole. Sauders & Otley, London, 1838*.

M'Mahon, Francis. *A Narrative of the Insurrection in the Island of Grenada in the Year 1795*. Printed by John Spahn, 1823.

Philp, Mark, ed. *The French Revolution and British Popular Politics*. Cambridge University Press, 1990.

Steele, Beverley A. *Grenada: A History of its People*. Oxford, Macmillan Education, 2003.

Thornhill, Henry. *A Narrative of the Insurrection and Rebellion in the Island of Grenada*. Gilbert Ripnel, 1798. Barbados.

Turnbull, Gordon. *A Narrative of the Revolt and Insurrection in the Island of the French Inhabitants in the Island of Grenada*. Edinburgh, Scotland, 1795.

Williams, Eric. *From Columbus to Castro: The History of the Caribbean 1492-1969*. Andre Deutsch, 1970.

Dissertations

Cornelius, Mary. *"Becoming Catholic: religion and society in colonial Grenada, 1763-1838."* PhD diss., University of Glasgow, 2020.

Jacobs, Curtis. "The Jacobins of Mt. Qua-Qua: Fedon's rebellion in Grenada, 1762-1796." PhD diss., University of the West Indies, 2002.

Murphy, Tessa. "A Reassertion of Rights: Fedon's Rebellion, Grenada, 1795-96." PhD diss., Syracuse University, 2018.

Polson, Donald. "The Tolerated, the Indulged and the Contented: Ethnic Alliances and Rivalries in Grenadian Plantation Society 1763-1800." PhD diss., University of Warwick, 2011.

Articles

Commentary. "The Belvidere Estate. The most extensive nutmeg cultivation in St. John's Parish." *The Federalist* newspaper, Wed., September 29, 1897.

Fortesque, J.W. *The West Indian Rebellion.* Macmillan's magazine, October, 1894.

Hall, Herman. "Grenada: From the Fédon's Rebellion to Statehood." *The West Indian* newspaper. Fri., March 3, 1967, Grenada.

Hall, Herman. "The Caribbean in the making of 1776." *200 Years of West Indian-American Contributions.* July, 1976, NY.

Jacobs, Curtis. "The last the last sighting of Julien Fédon in Grenada, July 27, 1796." *(Private Collection.)*

Reports

A Brief Enquiry into the cause of, and conduct pursued by, the Colonial Government, for quelling the insurrection in Grenada; From its Commencement on the Night of 2nd of March, to the Arrival of General Nichols, on the 14th of April 1795. In a letter from a Grenada planter to a merchant in London. London 1796.

Oral History

From the laborers of Belvedere estate, 1900-1960, as overheard by the author as a child and adult. Adults such as Beatrice McDowell, Frederick Adams, Charles Adams, Brisbane Calliste, Layman Brown, Edora Buckmire and Sylvester Millette.

And, from contemporaries such as Norris Marshall, Ann Marshall, Henry Duncan, Elton Sylvester, Winston Benjamin, Lloyd Mirah and Enoch Ragbarsingh who remembered similar stories told to them by adults about Julien Fédon when we were growing up.

After more than 60 years of hiking to Fédon's Camp, November 20, 2017, may have been the author's last but it was his first in an all-day storm—torrential rain, thick mist, ferocious wind, and slippery mud. *(Photo by Kenrick Harper.)*

L to R: Kenrick Harper, cousin of the author and son of John Wells, author Herman G. Hall, and Brother John Wells, in the vicinity where Governor Ninian Home and 47 other Britishers were massacred on April 8, 1795. Selfie taken on a stormy day, November 20, 2017.

On November 20, 2017, the author may have stood at the summit of Fédon's Camp/2nd Camp/Morne Qua Qua for the last time. Governor Ninian Home and other Britishers were executed there and buried in a shallow ditch on April 8, 1795, by the orders of Julien Fédon. *(Photo by Kenrick Harper.)*

**To Schedule Speaking Engagements
or to Contact Herman G. Hall:**

Please send an email to:

editor@everybodysmag.com

Made in the USA
Middletown, DE
24 February 2022

61678991R10210